Bahrain

Bahrain

Political Development in a Modernizing Society

Emile Nakhleh

LEXINGTON BOOKS
Lanham • Boulder • New York • Toronto • Plymouth, UK

Published by Lexington Books
A wholly owned subsidiary of The Rowman & Littlefield Publishing Group, Inc.
4501 Forbes Boulevard, Suite 200, Lanham, Maryland 20706
http://www.lexingtonbooks.com

Estover Road, Plymouth PL6 7PY, United Kingdom

Copyright © 2011 by Lexington Books
Originally published in 1976 by D.C. Heath and Company

All rights reserved. No part of this book may be reproduced in any form or by any electronic or mechanical means, including information storage and retrieval systems, without written permission from the publisher, except by a reviewer who may quote passages in a review.

British Library Cataloguing in Publication Information Available

Library of Congress Cataloging-in-Publication Data

The hardback edition of this book was previously cataloged by the Library of Congress as follows:

Nakhleh, Emile A. 1938–
 Bahrain: political development in a modernizing society.

 Biography: p.
Includes index.
 1. Bahrain—Politics and government.
DS247.B28N34   301.5′92′095365   75-37274
ISBN 978-0-7391-6858-5

Printed in the United States of America

To the people of Bahrain

Contents

	List of Tables	ix
	Preface	xi
	Preface to the 2011 Edition	xiii
Chapter 1	Introduction	1
Chapter 2	Education and Bahrain's Political Development	13
Chapter 3	Communication and Political Socialization: The Role of the Clubs and the Press	39
Chapter 4	Labor and Political Development	75
Chapter 5	Foreign Policy and Political Development	95
Chapter 6	Toward a Democratic Structure: The Constitutional Assembly	117
Chapter 7	The First National Election and the Formation of the Constitutional Assembly	133
Chapter 8	Conclusion: Toward a Functional Model of Urban Tribalism	165
	Epilogue	169
	Notes	171
	Bibliography	179
	Index	189
	About the Author	193

List of Tables

2-1	Population by Five-Year Age Groups and Nationality, 1971	17
2-2	Population Increase in Bahrain, 1941-71	17
2-3	Percentage of Illiterate Population by Age Groups and Sex, 1971	19
2-4	Percentage of Illiterate Population in Urban and Rural Areas by Age Groups, 1971	19
2-5	Population of Major Civil Divisions by Urban-Rural Residents	20
2-6	Attending School Population 5 to 24 Years of Age by Single Years of Age and Nationality (Bahraini and Non-Bahraini), 1971	21
2-7	Nonschool Attending Population 5 to 24 Years of Age by Single Years of Age and Sex (Bahraini Nationals), 1971	22
2-8	Student Enrollment from 1940-41 to 1960-61 in Elementary and Secondary Schools	23
2-9	Student Enrollment on All Levels, 1961-62 to 1972-73	24
2-10	Bahraini College Graduates and Their Fields of Specialization, 1950-72	26
2-11	Distribution of First-Year Bahraini College Students in Middle Eastern Universities, 1972-73	28
2-12	Ministry of Education Budget Compared to the National Budget, 1965-73	28
2-13	Enrollment Increase by Sex, 1961-62 to 1971-72	29
2-14	Schools by Type, Level, and Availability of Laboratories, Workshops, and Libraries, 1971-72	30
2-15	Primary School Curriculum in Bahrain, 1972	33
2-16	Administrative and Teaching Staff of Primary, Intermediate, and General and Commercial Secondary Schools by Qualification and Sex, 1971-72	35
3-1	Bahrain Clubs and Associations by Type, 1967-71	43
3-2	A Sample of the Clubs and Societies in Bahrain	44
3-3	Distribution of Personal Income for Major Items by Income Levels	59

3-4	Population by Five-Year Age Groups and Sex (Bahraini Only)	60
3-5	Illiterate Population Ten Years of Age and Over by Age and Sex (Bahraini Only)	61
3-6	Bahraini Privately Owned Newspapers/Magazines	67
3-7	Bahraini Government-owned Newspapers/Magazines	67
3-8	Non-Bahraini Newspapers/Magazines Read Regularly in Bahrain	69
4-1	Actual and Expected Bahraini Population, 1941-86	86
4-2	Economically Active Population by Industry and Nationality, 1971	87
4-3	Economically Active Population by Occupation and Nationality, 1971	89
4-4	Economically Active Population Classified by Level of Education (Males and Females), 1971	91
4-5	Occupational Distribution of Those with a Secondary Education in Bahrain, 1971	92
6-1	Constitutional Assembly Election Districts	127
7-1	Official List of Constitutional Assembly Candidates	157
7-2	Elected Constitutional Assembly Members and Their Districts	159
7-3	Demographic Analysis of the Electorate	162
7-4	Membership of the Constitutional Assembly	163

Preface

This book is based on three years of field research in Bahrain, originally started as a Fulbright Senior Research Fellowship. It is inevitable, in the course of such a study, that the author will incur several obligations of gratitude to the many who directly or indirectly assisted along the way. It is also inevitable, in the nature of things researched, people contacted, documents obtained, and manuscripts reviewed, that problems will develop and snags will appear. To acknowledge the debt of gratitude is a simple task gladly performed; to sort out the problems, to manage in spite of them, and to state them rationally is often a difficult task requiring scholarship, discretion, and diplomacy. A successful blend to these ingredients is sometimes known as *intellectual hunchmanship*.

I must first thank Dr. John J. Dillon, Jr., president of Mount St. Mary's College in Emmitsburg, Maryland, for the encouragement and support he gave me throughout my research. I must also acknowledge the encouragement that William Sands, editor of *The Middle East Journal*, also gave throughout this research. The Department of State's Bureau of Educational and Cultural Affairs is usually responsible for translating the Fulbright Fellowship into reality; consequently, I gratefully acknowledge the unfailing cooperation of Arthur B. Allen, director of the Near Eastern and South Asian Programs, and his staff, particularly Miss Mary E. McDonough, former senior academic program officer.

While in Bahrain, the assistance I received from many directions was often essential to the success of my research. I would like to thank the staff of the United States Embassy in Manama, Bahrain, in particular the former second secretary, William A. Kirby. As deputy principal officer at the Embassy, as a specialist in Middle Eastern and Gulf affairs, and as a seasoned diplomat, he made my stay in Bahrain truly meaningful. In spite of all the trials and tribulations inherent in establishing the new American Embassy in Bahrain, he constantly saw to it that, as the first U.S. senior research endeavor in Bahrain, my project proceeded with maximum ease. My family and I were spared innumerable inconveniences due to his help. I would also like to thank the Naval Control of Shipping Office for kindly permitting us to use their facilities during our stay in Bahrain.

On the Bahraini government side, I would like to acknowledge gratefully the cooperation I regularly received from several high officials in various ministries. In the Ministry of Foreign Affairs and in the Ministry of Information, sincere thanks go to Shaikh Muhammad bin Mubarak al-Khalifa, minister of foreign affairs, and to his staff in both ministries, especially Shaikh 'Isa bin Muhammad al-Khalifa, director of information,

Ahmad Kamal, director of publications, Husayn Sabbagh, director of radio programming, and Salman Taqi, former editor of *al-Bahrain al-Yom*.

My persistent search for laws, decrees, and other legal documents was always made fruitful by the constant cooperation of Salah al-Madani, former head of the Legal Department. In the Ministry of Education, I gratefully acknowledge the assistance of the minister of education, Shaikh 'Abd al-'Aziz al-Khalifa, and particularly Hamad Salyti, the Ministry's director of planning. At the Ministry of Labor and Social Affairs, the former ministers, Jawad al-'Urayyid (presently minister of state for cabinet affairs), and Ibrahim Hmidan (formerly the public prosecutor), the Ministry's director-general, 'Abd al-Rahman Darwish, and the Ministry's labor consultant, W.B. Berry, were very helpful, especially in my attempt to wade through the mass of information relating to manpower needs and prospects in Bahrain. The staff at the Statistical Bureau of the Ministry of Development and Engineering Services spared no effort in providing me with all available statistical reports and abstracts. I am also grateful to Rashid Hasan al-Dubayb of the Petroleum Bureau in the Ministry of Finance and National Economy for providing the annual reports concerning crude oil production in Bahrain.

Although the Arabic press in Bahrain is limited in size and output, the editors and writers of the two major newspapers provided valuable information. My gratitude goes to the editor of *al-Adwa'*, Mahmud al-Mardi, the editor of *Sada al-'Usbu'*, 'Ali Sayyar, and their cadre of journalists: Muhammad Qasim al-Shirawi, Ibrahim Bashmi, 'Ali Salih, and 'Aqil Swar. Many other people contributed indirectly to the success of my research, and their acquaintance made my stay in Bahrain all the more pleasant. I will always cherish the friendship of Mr. and Mrs. Jasim Murad, Mr. and Mrs. 'Ali Murad, Mr. and Mrs. Mahmud al-Mardi, Mr. and Mrs. 'Ali al-Amin, Mr. Wafiq Sa'di, Mr. and Mrs. William Kirby, Mr. and Mrs. Per Sjogren, and Dr. and Mrs. Frithjof Wannebo.

There is no doubt that this book would not have been borne were it not for the efforts and encouragement of my wife. She simultaneously performed several tasks admirably: mother, housewife, sounding board, executive secretary, tireless debator, proofreader, and, of course, coffee maker and typist.

It is understood that none of the above-mentioned people bears any responsibility for the shortcomings or deficiencies present in this book; I alone am responsible.

Preface to the 2011 Edition

The bloody confrontations in Bahrain's Pearl Square (Duwwar al-Lulu) between the opposition and the ruling family, which started in February 2011, and the growing demands for genuine political reform in that country underscore the importance of this book. The persistent demands of the opposition to resurrect the old constitution and allow for free elections give added credibility to the issues I researched in Bahrain in the early 1970s and wrote about in the 1976 book, *Bahrain: Political Development in a Modernizing Society*. The book is being reprinted in order to highlight the constitutional process that unfolded in 1972–1973 and the hopes it raised among the Bahraini people. The ruling Amir, Shaykh Isa Bin Salman Al Khalifa, promulgated a constitution, which allowed for the election of a National Assembly. Those hopes were dashed less than two years later, however, when the ruling family turned its back on that process. Following a heated dispute in 1974–1975 between the ruling family and the opposition in the National Assembly over the government's decision to impose a security law that would allow for detaining critics of the government without charges, the ruler dissolved the National Assembly, suspended the constitution, asked his brother the prime minister to form a new government, and proceeded to rule by decree.

Now almost forty years later the protesters are demanding the ruling family return to the constitution. Although political conditions in Bahrain have changed in the past four decades, many of the grievances raised then have remained the same. The relatively wealthy Sunni minority Al Khalifa family continues to rule Bahrain, a small island country in which the large Shia majority is generally excluded from power and influence. Many Shia live in villages and poorer sections of the capital Manama. They tend to be poor, underemployed, and disenfranchised. A few prominent Shia families have cooperated with Al Khalifa and have been amply rewarded with access to wealth and high government positions, including ministerial positions.

The February 2011 protests were not controlled or driven by the Shia religious leadership. Because the Shia community constitutes a majority of the population, most of the protesters are Shia. Like their counterparts in Tunisia, Egypt, Yemen, Libya, Jordan, and elsewhere, Bahraini protesters are as diverse—economically, politically, and religiously—as their own society. They are villagers, city dwellers, laborers, farmers, professionals, teachers, health providers, and government employees. They seek dignity, justice, respect, and the opportunity to live as free citizens. For the most part, they tend to be inclusive, tolerant, peaceful, and pragmatic. They use Facebook and Twitter, not weapons or suicide belts, to spread their message and to communicate with the outside world. They basically want the regime to draw up a new social contract, which would allow the citizenry to have a say in public policy and to manage their lives freely and without coercion by the government and its security services. Although different in ideology and social status, the opposition movement in the early 1970s raised similar demands for participation in decision making, honest and transparent government, a just distribution of the oil wealth, freedoms of expression, assembly, and press, and an independent judiciary. Several of the prominent opposition figures in the early 1970s were Sunni liberal nationalists whose rhetoric reflected anti-colonial, Pan-Arab nationalist tendencies. Today, many of the demonstrators focus on issues of social justice, human dignity, and employment.

The Al Khalifa ruling family is as entrenched today as it was in the early 1970s when the book was written. King Hamad, who changed his title from Amir (prince) to king as part of the "National Charter" package of reforms in 1991–1992, was the crown prince forty years ago. His uncle, Shaykh Khalifa, has held the position of prime minister throughout this period, and the key cabinet posts—for example, defense, foreign relations, and internal security—continue to be held by members of the ruling family. Politically and economically, Bahrain remains a "Family, Inc." The opposition demanded then and insists now that the system of economic and political autocracy must end. When the previous ruler began to state publicly that he supported the idea of a modern constitution, there was dissention within the family between the liberal wing headed by the foreign minister and other younger members and the conservative wing headed by the prime minister and other senior family members. The ruler prevailed, at least initially.

As the 2011 demonstrations gathered steam and as the ruling family offered to negotiate with the opposition all issues of contention, media reports again indicate a split within the ruling family on reform. According to these reports, the crown prince and the king's son Shaykh Salman and the foreign minister are said to lead the pro-reform, liberal wing of the family. The prime minister and other older family members in the conservative bloc oppose granting meaningful concessions to the opposition. They believed then and seem to believe now that such concessions would weaken the ruling family's grip on the country and would bring about internal instability and Sunni-Shia sectarianism. Opposition to reforms inside the conservative faction of the family was deep and visceral and led the prime minister to lash out against anyone who in the prime minister's view advocated reform or even encouraged a reform agenda. During my stay as the first Senior Fulbright Research Scholar in Bahrain in 1972–1973, I interviewed most political candidates and attended all public political rallies on the eve of the elections, which not surprisingly angered the prime minister. A week before the December 1973 elections, the prime minister informed the U.S. ambassador in Kuwait, who was responsible for the lower Gulf emirates, that my field investigation of domestic politics could endanger my stay and if I did not desist, he would declare me *persona non grata* and order me expelled. I did lay low until the elections were over and stayed till the end of my Fulbright academic year.

Chapter 7 of the book discusses at length the ideological divisions within the family regarding political reform and the transformation of the country from a tribal fiefdom to a modern state. It is clear forty years have not erased these ideological cleavages within the family about how to reconcile family rule with the demands of their people for justice, dignity, and equal access to economic opportunity. In the 1970s, the opposition called for a constitution and a government accountable to its people; this year, the opposition demands a constitution and a transparent government. Some opposition groups are calling for replacing the prime minister with the crown prince; others are demanding an end to monarchy. It is equally clear the so-called reforms of the early 1990s have failed to create a genuine constitutional monarchy as was promised at the time. The king remains the key decision maker in the country and the primary source of legislation. The king gerrymandered electoral districts in order to elect a pliable lower house with no legislative powers, and continues to appoint members of the upper house. Under the original constitution, a unicameral National Assembly was elected freely, but without women voters or candidates. The Shia electorate showed then as it has shown in the last two elections that it is a diverse community, does not have a single political or social ideology, and rarely votes as a bloc.

The feverish debate of the civil rights issues on the eve of the elections to the National Assembly in 1973 and its dissolution in 1975—as is amply demonstrated in this book—is as relevant today as it was four decades ago. Despite the passage of time and the dramatic changes that have occurred in Bahrain since then, these issues remain as volatile today. In the early 1990s, the Bahraini government under the new ruler initiated a series of political reforms that were longer on promise than reality. The February 2002 political "reforms" included the institution of monarchy under which Amir Hamad would become King Hamad. Much euphoria characterized the country during that period, and citizens and civil society institutions responded favorably to the reform initiatives of the ruler. A year later the popular mood, however, soured and opposition to the "reform" package and perceived restrictions on freedoms of speech and assembly grew dramatically. Over 90 percent voted for the reform package under the National Action Charter, but only 54 percent participated in the national election in October 2002. Confrontations between human rights advocates, including liberal Sunnis and Shias, and the government erupted, and tensions became more acute. Several opposition activists were arrested. Clubs and societies, including women's organizations, became more energized in their opposition to the "reform" initiative and demanded that genuine reform can only occur through a restoration of the 1973 constitution. According to academic analysis by Bahraini activists who were involved in the reform efforts of that period, the general view was that the reforms were a sham and were intended to keep the ruling family in full control of the country.[1]

Similar to his father's experience in 1973, the new king was caught between those who opposed reform—inside and outside the ruling family—and popular organizations that advocated even more accelerated society-based reforms. The opposition no longer accepts reforms as a gift from the ruler; the people have a right to these reforms. The king reached out to different segments of society and used his royal position to distribute wealth and property to those who needed it through *"makrama"* or royal benevolence. He also promised the lower house would have legislative powers, which almost two decades later has not materialized. It is interesting to note that when the protests erupted in February 2011, the king responded, among other things, by giving every Bahraini family a gift of 1,000 Bahraini Dinars.

The discussion of the democratic process in chapters five and six in the 1976 book and the comprehensive survey of the views of different segments in society regarding that process shed ample light on the protest movement's demands for reform and the Al Khalifa's resistance to become more inclusive. The ruling family would do well to review the history of those formative years. It is not clear whether the ruling Al Khalifa family will have the luxury of time it had in the 1970s and 1990s to address the growing demands for genuine political reform. The Bahraini people, as we have seen in Tunisia, Egypt, Libya, Yemen, Iraq, and elsewhere are getting impatient with their autocratic rulers. The regime narrative of "either us or chaos" is no longer persuasive. It is becoming clearer by the day that the old Middle East is giving way to a new one driven mostly by young people who want a life of dignity and hope, which ossified autocracies are finding it difficult to comprehend. The young generation feel empowered to catch up with the globalized world of the twenty-first century, whereas the decades old authoritarian kleptocracies remain stuck in the past, erroneously believing that coercion would keep them in power and their people quiescent. Bahrain is no exception.

Finally, the photo on the cover depicts a scene from Bahrain in 1972 on the eve of the elections to the first ever National Assembly. The Bahraini artist, Muhammad Bosta, wanted to show how the entire Bahraini society supported the impending constitution and had such high hopes for such a document. The three representatives in the painting holding up the constitution above their heads are a woman, a farmer, and a factory worker. Women were denied the right to vote, and workers were denied the right to collective bargaining or to unionize. Farmers, mostly Shia, remain mired in poverty. At an art exhibit where this painting was on display for sale, which the author attended, the prime minister walked by it and whispered derisively, "The people don't dictate the constitution; it's given to them by His Majesty the Amir." The youth of Pearl Square in February 2011 seemed to have another opinion!

Emile Nakhleh
March 2011

Note

1. Ali Qasim Rabi'a, *Committee of the Popular Petition: On the Path of National Struggle in Bahrain* [Arabic] (Beirut, Lebanon: Dar al-Kunuz al-Adabiyya, 2007).

Bahrain

1 Introduction

Notes on Research: Scope and Approach

This is a case study of political development in Bahrain.[a] It is the first effort of its kind that treats the newly independent states of the Gulf as a subject of study rather than as an object of policy in some other state's long-term plans for that region. A clear relationship does exist, however, between the processes of nation building, and all of the forces that influence these processes, and the role that the Gulf states play, actively or passively, in world politics. That is, American policy makers cannot be expected to draw long-range policy contingencies via-à-vis the Gulf states without an understanding of the traditional, cultural, economic, and political conditions presently prevailing in the region.

This book is designed to serve a multiplicity of readerships: Gulf governments, leaders and other elites; international business leaders, especially since Bahrain is striving to become the "front office" of the Gulf; and American policy makers. Political scientists and students of the developing countries, including the Gulf, constitute another obvious group to which this book is directed. This study is primarily based on original sources and field research. Most of the original material is still in Arabic, which means it has not been made available to American readers. Moreover, some of the material has never been published anywhere else. The paucity of information available in this country concerning any aspect of the Gulf, coupled with interest in Gulf affairs due to the energy crisis, will render this book a significant addition to the discipline of political science.

The research treated the entire process of nation building in Bahrain as that of a newly independent developing country, especially as this process related to the following:

1. The nature and properties of the political system as a method of government
2. The educational system as it relates to political socialization and leadership training

---

[a] Very limited research has been conducted by American scholars on the region, save for oil-related research. The paucity of information available in America on the Gulf region is evidenced by the fact that in the period 1883-1968 only one Ph.D. dissertation in universities across the United States even referred to Bahrain. Library of Congress, *American Doctoral Dissertations in the Arab World, 1883-1968* (Washington, D.C.: U.S. Government Printing Office, 1970).

3. The citizens and their ability, legally and extralegally, to influence the process of decision making
4. Economic development and its relationship to political development, both domestic and foreign
5. The making, attributes, and goals of foreign policy as a reflection of domestic inputs
6. Bahrain's recent venture into democracy—the move from a system of traditional tribalism into an urban system in which new elements are invited to create certain inputs into the political system

As can be seen, the research focused on five well-known crises of nation building: identity, integration, penetration, participation, and distribution.[1]

This study of political development and modernization in the context of the nation building process has three purposes: It provides a testing ground for new concepts in comparative politics; it allows the researcher to assess the validity and applicability of the systems approach as an effective functional tool; and it sheds some light on the evolution of a developmental dialectic in a specific environment, in this case Bahrain, from a purely empirical perspective.

The question that must finally be asked is whether one, in light of the unique conditions of a Gulf state such as Bahrain and considering the direct influence of those conditions on the decision-making process in the context of the Gulf, can talk convincingly about a universal social science model by which the functionalism of the polity can be observed and assessed? As shown later, the facts reviewed in this work have suggested the possibility of yet another new model, which might best be applied to the Gulf amirates (Shaykhdoms). Beyond the realm of theorizing, there remains another, very practical inquiry: what has the country under study done in its attempt to neutralize and overcome the crises of nation building? This activity usually encompasses the area of governmental structure, delineating the channels of authority, popular participation in governing, and the general social, economic, and educational development of a new citizenry.

In the last two decades political scientists have shown significant interest in the whole process of nation building in the newly independent countries of Asia and Africa, and these scientists have advanced several conclusions, models, and generalizations. In *The Politics of the Developing Areas*,[2] Professors Gabriel A. Almond and James S. Coleman attempted to show that the political system model can be usefully employed in the study of political development in the new countries. In his introduction Professor Almond advocated the establishment of a functional approach to politics in terms of the articulation and aggregation of interests, political socialization, and recruitment of leadership.[3] The basic theoretical defense for the system approach put forward by Professor Almond is that societies have similar characteristics, such as structure and functions. In order to further the application of these conceptual tools, the Committee on Comparative Politics[b] of the Social Science Research Council sponsored in the early sixties a series of research projects, which examined and tested the applicability of modern comparative politics approaches to the study of development and modernization in the newly independent countries. Several volumes have so far resulted from this endeavor as a part of a series known as "Studies in Political Development," which has spanned more than a decade.[c] Through the study of modernization and political development the political scientists involved have attempted to work within the framework of the five crises of nation building.

The primary goal of these works has been to develop a functional approach to comparative politics[d] and to experiment with the new concepts in the new context of developing political systems.[4] However, by the time the seventh volume of "Studies in Political Development" was being discussed, the Committee on Comparative Politics had concluded that political development could be viewed in terms of equality, capacity, and differentiation.[5]

In the context of the development syndrome, *differentiation* refers to role separation and specialization in modernizing societies.[6] To be used as an indicator of political development, *equality* must be viewed in terms of its reference to citizens and citizenship.[7] The third concept, *capacity*, refers to the political system's ability to create, to respond, to survive, and to adapt.

Case studies by definition are focused on a thorough analysis of a particular situation according to a postulated universal hypothesis. The results and conclusions of the case study, in turn, determine the validity of the previously stated hypothesis. In the case of Bahrain, the first observation that a researcher takes cognizance of is the startling difference be-

---

[b] Members of the committee at that time were: Lucian W. Pye (chairman); Gabriel A. Almond; Leonard Binder; R. Taylor Cole; James S. Coleman; Herbert Hyman; Joseph LaPalombara; Sidney Verba; Robert E. Ward; and Myron Weiner.

[c] These books were all published by Princeton University Press, Princeton, New Jersey, and they follow the following sequence: Lucian W. Pye, ed., *Communication and Political Development* (1963); Joseph LaPalombara, ed., *Bureaucracy and Political Development* (1963); Robert E. Ward and Dankwart A. Rustow, eds., *Political Modernization in Japan and Turkey* (1964); James S. Coleman, ed., *Education and Political Development* (1965); Lucian W. Pye and Sidney Verba, eds., *Political Culture and Political Development* (1965); Joseph LaPalombara and Myron Weiner, eds., *Political Parties and Political Development* (1966); and Leonard Binder et al., eds., *Crises and Sequences in Political Development* (1971).

[d] It is interesting to note that Professor Almond had entitled his introduction to Almond and James S. Coleman, eds., *The Politics of the Developing Areas*, as follows: "A Functional Approach to Comparative Politics" (p. 3). (Princeton, N.J.: Princeton University Press, 1960).

tween theorizing on nation building and the realities of developmental politics. The sections on education, communication, and popular participation in this book attempt to illustrate and clarify this point.

Several factors have influenced the selection of Bahrain for extensive field research. As a newly independent and developing country of the Asian-African bloc, Bahrain clearly falls within what Professor Irving Louis Horowitz calls the Third World.[e] Professor Horowitz describes the First World as encompassing Europe and North America and the Second World as being the Soviet Union and its satellites. Concerning the Third World, Professor Horowitz defines the term as appropriate to the nation-states of Africa, Asia, and Latin America.

A second factor, which must be considered, is that as a Gulf Arab amirate, Bahrain exhibits certain characteristics in its social fabric, economic structure, and body politic that are basically unique to the Gulf region, that is, a modernizing form of tribalism, a limited population, and a limited educational level. Still a third factor is that because of Bahrain's small territory and population,[f] it is possible to study the entire country as a total entity, a task that is impossible in countries such as India or even Egypt. This smallness in size and population usually contributes to the development and perpetuation of a personal form of government on virtually all levels—nationally and locally. This phenomenon, which has also been abetted by the ruler's adherence to the Islamic principles of *shura* and his open communication with his people, leaves little room for policy patterns that would transcend the policy maker himself. Whatever public administration exists in the country has, for the most part, been an extension of the top decision makers and not of the institution itself.[g]

Fourth, as a relatively oil-poor country, Bahrain has been forced to develop an entrepôt, services-oriented economy. In addition, it has been the conscious policy of the government to encourage major international industries, businesses, and banking firms that have direct economic ties to the oil-rich Gulf countries to home port in Bahrain. To do this, the government of Bahrain has taken a liberal attitude and a practical posture concerning the presence of foreigners on the island. Also, to facilitate the establishment of head offices for major international companies in Bahrain, the government has offered such inducements as tax relief, an excellent communications network, and housing and other social amenities, which a

---

[e] For a thorough analysis of the relationship of the Third World to the two other worlds, see Irving Louis Horowitz, *Three Worlds of Development: The Theory and Practice of International Stratification*, 2nd ed. (New York: Oxford University Press, 1972).

[f] Two hundred and fifty-six square miles and 216,000 people. See State of Bahrain, Ministry of Finance and National Economy, *Statistical Abstract*, 1972, pp. 1 and 6.

[g] The establishment of new deputy ministerial positions in 1972 and 1973 in the Ministries of Development and Finance reflected a desire on the part of the government to institutionalize decision making through the appointment of qualified high-level bureaucrats.

European or American businessman might find enticing.[h] What is of interest here is the fact that propensities toward pragmatism and liberalism in the economic sphere usually spill over into the realm of politics as well. In this regard a persistent problem of the government has been the necessity to distinguish functionally between its policy of encouraging private enterprise and its responsibility toward and protection of the nonmerchandising class.

To study political development in the context of the above characteristics, it was necessary to examine all facets of the social and political activities in which the country has engaged, either by way of the public sectors or the private sector. More specifically, this work includes an examination of Bahrain's educational tradition and the present system of education as being the country's principal agent of political socialization. As in most developing countries, the newly independent state of Bahrain has yet to analyze the role of the school in the modern polity. That one-fourth of the entire population attended school (primary through high school) in 1971 is substantive evidence of the strains and stresses under which the educational system functions. On very practical terms, unless there is a correlation between the inputs and outputs of the educational system and unless the country's needs will be served by its high school and college graduates, whose numbers are increasing at an alarming annual rate, the country's political system will, in the next five to ten years, definitely hear the rumblings of an unemployed intelligentsia. The situation is compounded by the fact that in 1971 60 percent of the population was under 20 years of age and that the population is expected to double in less than a generation's time.

Two other agents of political socialization are also examined in this work: the clubs, which in this context are viewed as a substitute for political parties; and the Arabic-language press, especially the two local weeklies, *al-Adwa'* and *Sada al-'Usbu'*. In spite of the restrictive conditions under which the Bahraini political press has operated since 1965, the year in which the Press Law was enacted, the press has often responded to national issues and has frequently contributed to the formation of a national political opinion.

Obviously the country's move toward popular participation, albeit on a very limited basis, constitutes an integral part of this study. The idea of the constitution, the ruler's consultations with the country's leading elites, the national election to the Constitutional Assembly and the composition of the Assembly itself are essential to the attempt to democratize the governance of the country. Since this development did not occur in a vacuum, the

---

[h] Through their long tradition of commercialism and centuries-old contacts with other civilizations and cultures, the people of Bahrain have nurtured the virtues of tolerance, pragmatism, and reason. Bahraini officials usually do not like to admit the fact that the government's liberal policy on liquor has attracted many businessmen, foreign and Arab alike, to locate in Bahrain.

political atmosphere of the country on the eve of the election, which was held 1 December 1972, is also examined. The election analysis, especially since the Constitutional Assembly so correctly reflected the social makeup of the country, is central to this section of the study.

The Constitutional Assembly, which was officially convened by the ruler on 16 December 1972, began its constitutional debates on 2 January 1973. By late May 1973 the Assembly had concluded its debates on the draft constitution, originally prepared by the Council of Ministers, and had recommended that the ruler ratify it. These constitutional debates, the political trends that emerged in the Assembly, and the major issues that underlay the debates are an extremely important link in the political development of contemporary Bahrain. However, due to their significance, the constitutional debates should be treated in a separate study, and although reference is occasionally made in this work to the constitutional debates, they are excluded from this book.

As a major public policy output, the foreign policy of the state of Bahrain is a rational reflection of the complex domestic politics and the factors influencing the body politic. Foreign policy of such a ministate as Bahrain has recently assumed worldwide proportions, primarily because of the Gulf's oil, the energy crisis, and the United States' imminent need for Gulf oil, at least for the foreseeable future. The presence of the United States Navy, as part of the Middle East force, in Bahrain, adds yet another dimension to Bahrain's international relations. Therefore, it is imperative that the support, setting, and making of foreign policy be included in this study.

To complete these notes on the scope, method, and mechanics of the research itself, three other points should be made: The first is that the analysis made throughout this work is not based on any regional standards of comparison. That is, a criticism of the educational system in Bahrain, for instance, does not necessarily mean that the educational systems in other lower Gulf states are better. On the contrary, Bahrain's educational tradition is older and more universally rooted than that of any other Gulf amirate, including Kuwait. Also, the analyses of labor, the press, liberal sociopolitical trends and tendencies, and public administration are not based on regional comparisons.

The second point concerns the whole question of field research in the developing countries. Like many other newly independent countries, Bahrain—government and people alike—has not yet developed a familiarity with research and the whole process of scientific inquiry. What is more disturbing, in most of these countries history is regarded as one of the banalities of life, and historical accuracy is treated, if it is thought of at all, with utter apathy. History is rarely accepted as a reflection of the truth, often altered at whim and always viewed as the property of the ruler.

Archives are nonexistent, documents frequently disappear, and national public libraries even fail to keep the country's official gazette. The result is that in many developing countries field research becomes a burdensome task in which procedure is as important as substance.

Concerning the transliteration of Arabic names and the use of terms in this book, several clarifications are in order. First, the gulf separating Iran from Saudi Arabia, the United Arab Emirates and Qatar, and in which Bahrain is situated has traditionally been known as the Persian Gulf. Iran considers the name an extension of its sovereignty and insists on it. The Arab littoral states, especially since they all have become independent, refer to this body of water as the Arabian Gulf. They view this name as an extension of their sovereignty and as a continuation of the old name *Shatt al-'Arab* to the south of Basra (Iraq). Although the Arab coastline on the Gulf is longer than the Iranian coastline, it is not the intention of the author to support either claim. This body of water will simply be referred to as the Gulf throughout this work.

Second, the Library of Congress system of transliteration is generally used here; however, the commonly used English spelling of certain names is excepted. Examples are Bahrain instead of Bahrayn and Kuwait instead of Kuwayt. Another exception to the transliteration rule are certain Bahraini names as they are used in Bahrain. Examples are Sulman instead of Salman, Kanoo instead of Kanu, and Fakhro instead of Fakhru.

A final point concerns the name of the state and the ruler's title. Prior to independence, the country was called the Government of Bahrain; after independence the title changed to the State of Bahrain. Prior to independence, Shaikh 'Isa bin Sulman al-Khalifa's title was ruler of Bahrain and its dependencies; since independence his title has been changed to amir (prince) of the State of Bahrain. However, the terms ruler and amir are user interchangeably throughout the book. An amirate is a political formation ruled by an amir; a shaykhdom is a political formation ruled by a shaykh. The Gulf shaykhdoms and amirates refer to the same political entities. Moreover, any member, regardless of age, of any one of the Gulf's ruling families bears the title of shaikh (shaykh) before his name.

Bahrain, like any other Gulf amirate, is a tribal society governed by a ruling family that only recently has begun to encourage a degree of popular participation. The remainder of this chapter, as well as the rest of the book, is an examination of this modernizing system of tribalism.

The Tribal Context of Modern Bahrain

The State of Bahrain is an archipelago of some 33 low-lying islands and islets, only 5 of which are inhabited, located in the Gulf equidistant from

Saudi Arabia and Qatar (latitude 26 N, longitude 50 30° E). The main island of the archipelago is Bahrain (Two Seas), from which the country takes its name and on which the capital of Manama is located. The island of Bahrain is approximately 217 square miles in area, and on it live over two-thirds of the entire population. The ratio of the total population (216,000) to the total area of the country (256 square miles) gives Bahrain a fairly high population density.

The second largest island in area is Hawar, but it is uninhabited. The third largest island but the second most inhabited in Muharraq. Approximately one-fourth of the population lives on Muharraq, which is connected with Manama by a causeway. The bulk of the remaining population is situated on Sitra Island, with some 300 people on the two other major islands of Nabi Salih and Um al-Na'san. Jidda Island is a penal colony.[8]

This island country is ruled by the al-Khalifa family, which originally stems from the Bani 'Utba clan of the 'Aniza tribal confederation. In centuries past the 'Aniza roamed the deserts of Iraq and the northeastern part of Arabia. The al-Sabahs of Kuwait and the Saudis of Saudi Arabia also are descended from the 'Aniza. In fact, the al-Sabahs and the al-Khalifas are both members of the Bani 'Utba clan.[i]

In 1716 the al-Khalifas and al-Sabahs settled in the town of Kuwait; 60 years later the al-Khalifas left Kuwait and headed for the western coast of Qatar, where they settled in the town of Zubara. Since the al-Khalifas were primarily pearl merchants and since Bahrain was known for its fine pearls, Zubara, which was only some 15 miles from Bahrain, proved a logical site for the al-Khalifas. The economic prosperity and rapid expansion of the town of Zubara under the al-Khalifas aroused the suspicions of both the ruling tribe of Qatar and the Persians, who were at that time in control of Bahrain. The Qatar tribe demanded a tribute from the al-Khalifas but failed to receive it, and the Persians attacked Zubara but were repulsed.

In 1782, following the Persian defeat at Zubara, Shaikh Ahmad (given the title of *al-Fatih* or *the conqueror*) al-Khalifa invaded Bahrain, and thus began al-Khalifa rule on the islands of Bahrain.[j] Since 1782 the country has remained under al-Khalifa rule except for the years 1799-1809 when Bahrain was occupied by the Imam of Muscat (Oman) and the period 1809-11

---

[i]For a more detailed popular chronicle of the al-Khalifa story see James H.D. Belgrave, *Welcome to Bahrain*, 8th ed. (Manama, Bahrain: The Augustan Press Ltd., 1973), pp. 129-137.

[j]For a thorough analysis of political conditions in the lower Gulf in the eighteenth, nineteenth, and early twentieth centuries see the following excellent volumes: Arnold T. Wilson, *The Persian Gulf* (London: Allen & Unwin Ltd., 1954); J.B. Kelly, *Britain and the Persian Gulf: 1795-1880* (London: Oxford University Press, 1968); Briton Cooper Busch, *Britain and the Persian Gulf, 1894-1914* (Berkeley, California: University of California Press, 1967) and *Britain, India, and the Arabs, 1914-1921* (Berkeley, California: University of California Press, 1971); Donald Hawley, *The Trucial States* (London: Allen & Unwin Ltd., 1970); Ahmad Abu Hakima, *Early History of Eastern Arabia: The Rise and Development of Bahrain and Kuwait* (Beirut: Khayat Book and Publishing Co., 1963).

when the Saudi Wahhabis drove out the Omanis and ruled in their stead.

Contacts between the British and the al-Khalifas of Bahrain began early in the nineteenth century, and in 1820 a "General Treaty" was signed by Bahrain and the East India Company.[k] Still another "Perpetual Treaty of Peace and Friendship" was signed with Great Britain in 1861; finally two more treaties were concluded between the two countries in 1880 and 1892 respectively. These treaties and agreements resulted in two corollary benefits: Great Britain cemented its position in Bahrain and throughout the Gulf; the al-Khalifas consolidated their rule over Bahrain. The internecine feuds, which occurred sporadically throughout the nineteenth century, gave way to a rather peaceful form of tribal rule in the twentieth century. Throughout this century tribal authority has been handed down from father to son by peaceful means; consequently Bahrain has been able to develop economically. Figure 1-1 gives an outline of the al-Khalifa rulers and their dates.

1971 proved to be a turning point in Bahrain's history, for on 15 August 1971 the British government agreed to:

1. Terminate the special treaty relations between the United Kingdom and Bahrain
2. Terminate the special agreements of 22 December 1880 and 13 March 1892 and all other special agreements between the United Kingdom and Bahrain
3. Maintain relations between the United Kingdom and Bahrain in the spirit of friendship and cooperation[9]

The ruler of Bahrain, Sheikh 'Isa bin Sulman al-Khalifa, accepted the British memoranda and declared that both memoranda constituted a new agreement between the two governments.[10]

The exchange of memoranda between the British government and the ruler of Bahrain in August 1971 was preceded by two years of diplomatic activity concerning Iranian territorial claims to Bahrain, which culminated in the recommendation of the United Nations secretary-general's personal representative that Bahrain be given independence as a sovereign Arab state. On 11 May 1970 the Security Council adopted a resolution endorsing the report of the secretary-general's personal representative and welcomed that report's conclusions, particularly in that "the overwhelming majority of the people of Bahrain wish to gain recognition of their identity in a fully independent and sovereign State free to decide for itself its relations with other states."[11]

Thus, the al-Khalifa tribal regime was recognized as the legitimate form

---

[k]For an examination of this and other treaties from an international law perspective see Husayn M. al-Baharna, *The Legal Status of the Arabian Gulf States: A Study of Their Treaty Relations and Their International Problems* (Manchester, England: Manchester University Press, 1968).

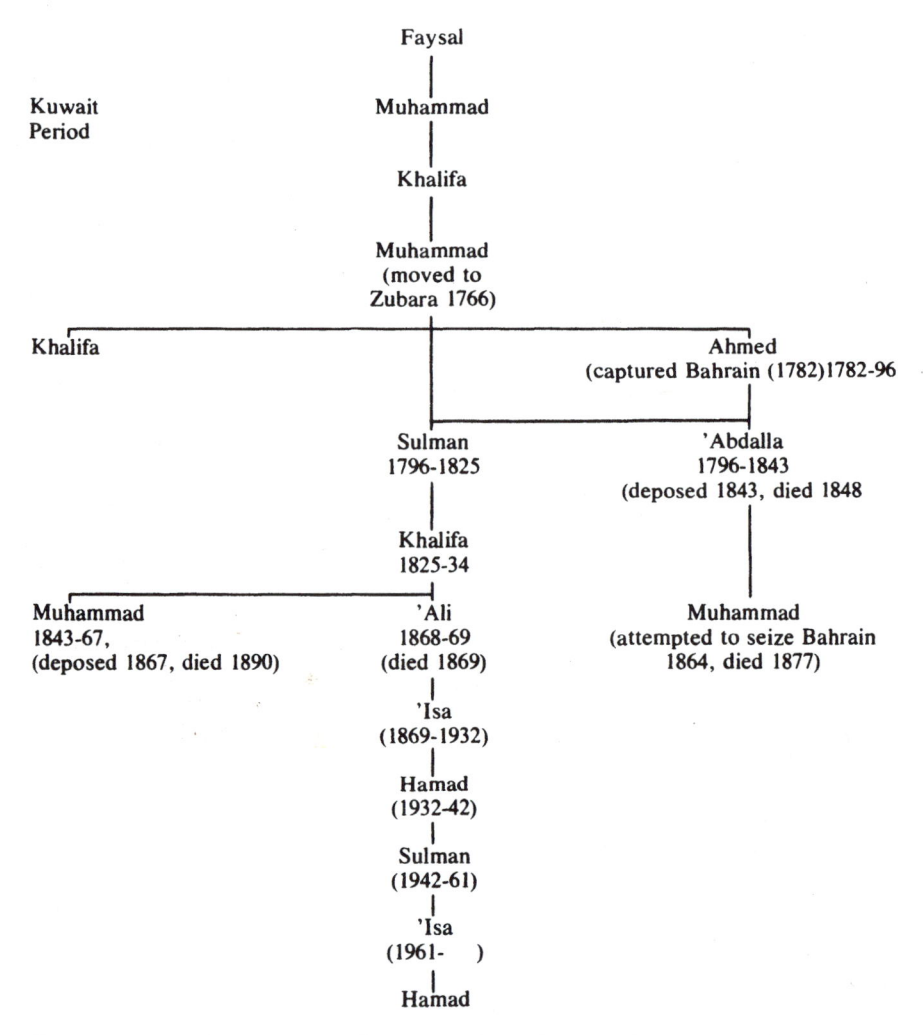

```
                        Faysal
                          |
Kuwait                 Muhammad
Period                    |
                        Khalifa
                          |
                       Muhammad
                       (moved to
                      Zubara 1766)
         ┌────────────────┴────────────────────────┐
Khalifa                                           Ahmed
                                          (captured Bahrain (1782)1782-96
                          ┌──────────────────────────┐
                       Sulman                     'Abdalla
                       1796-1825                  1796-1843
                          |                  (deposed 1843, died 1848
                       Khalifa
                       1825-34
         ┌────────────────┼──────────────────────────┐
    Muhammad            'Ali                      Muhammad
    1843-67,            1868-69              (attempted to seize Bahrain
(deposed 1867, died 1890) (died 1869)           1864, died 1877)
                          |
                         'Isa
                      (1869-1932)
                          |
                        Hamad
                      (1932-42)
                          |
                        Sulman
                      (1942-61)
                          |
                         'Isa
                       (1961-  )
                          |
                        Hamad
```

Source: James H.D. Belgrave, *Welcome to Bahrain*, 8th ed. (Manama, Bahrain: The Augustan Press Ltd., 1973), p. 143.

Figure 1-1. The al-Khalifas

of government in Bahrain, based on the hereditary succession of rulers. Regionally, the al-Khalifa family is related to Kuwait through both a tribal relationship and the ideological empathy of a semiliberal philosophy of tribal government. Their relations with Qatar are correct but strained; relations with Saudi Arabia are based on mutual interest, primarily economic.

Domestically, the authority of the al-Khalifa ruler is legitimized in the consitution adopted by the Constitutional Assembly in May 1973. Article 1, section b states: "Rule in Bahrain is hereditary; it shall be transmitted from Shaikh 'Isa bin Sulman al-Khalifa to his eldest son and from him to his eldest son and so on. . . . Unless the Ruler during his lifetime appoints some one other than his eldest son to succeed him." This form of succession is constitutionally binding and cannot be amended.[1] In addition the constitution further declares that the amir is "the head of the state"[12] and the "commander-in-chief of the defense force."[13] He is also entrusted with the responsibility of protecting the "legitimacy of rule and the supremacy of law."[14]

Functionally the ruler exercises authority through a Council of Ministers, which since independence has been headed by the ruler's brother, Shaikh Kahlifa bin Sulman al-Khalifa. At least six ministers, in addition to the prime minister, are also members of the al-Khalifa family. According to the constitution, the ministers are ex officio members of the National Assembly.[15]

It is in the context of this tribal tradition and the modern constitutional institutionalization of the al-Khalifas' hereditary rule that political development is being attempted in Bahrain. The centralized legitimate authority of the al-Khalifas is perhaps inversely related to the people's demands for popular participation in government. This much is clear: any future expansion of popular participation in government will result in a contraction of the ruling family's source and exercise of authority. Any serious attempt to democratize the regime will ultimately set the two diametrically opposed sources of authority, tribal legitimacy and popular sovereignty, on a collision course. Recent political developments in the country indicate however that the pragmatism of the Bahrainis might yet prevent such a head-on collision—an urbanizing tribalist system could become the new synthesis.

---

[1] Article 1, section c. The final draft was officially promulgated by the ruler on 6 December 1973.

2

Education and Bahrain's Political Development

Notes on Theory: Education and the Formation of a Modern Polity

In examining the primary factors contributing to the building of Bahrain's modern polity, the researcher need not engage in a thorough search before discovering that education is the leading factor.[a] The educational tradition in Bahrain is over 50 years old—a rather venerable tradition by Gulf standards—and the educational complex is obviously one of Bahrain's basic institutions. The statistics of this half-century tradition are indeed impressive, and the impact of this educational tradition in Bahraini society and its influence on the postindependence polity constitute the bases of this chapter.

Another question, which might be considered tangential to this study but which patently cannot be ignored, concerns the contribution of education to the developing economy of Bahrain. In other words, how has the educational complex aided in the formation of a Bahraini manpower supply and what changes should this complex undergo in order to build a manpower reservoir that would shortly be able to replace expatriate labor? The relationship between education and the Bahrainization of labor, though economic in scope and orientation, is in the final analysis political. For such a policy to be successful, certain political decisions must be made. For example, many seemingly technical economic decisions are basically political, such as the appropriation of funds and the allocation for education in the national budget, the authors, contents, and publishers of textbooks, the distribution of scientific equipment among the schools, the establishment of hiring priorities, the speed of the Bahrainization program in the schools, the reorganization of the adminstrative structure of the Ministry, and the admission policies of the teacher institutes. These decisions must be placed within the national decision-making apparatus, thereby transcending the boundaries of the Ministry of Education itself. This is not to say that this organic interrelationship between the educational and the political systems in the society is necessarily preferable; the intention here is merely to describe a standing relationship present in most developing societies. This interrelationship stems from two sources: In the immediate post-

---
[a] During the last ten years, the country's educational program has consistently been allotted over 20 percent of the national budget's recurring expenditures.

independence years most developing societies experience a ubiquitous presence of politics, and, second, the governments of these societies usually assign to their educational systems the primary responsibiillity for the building of the new polity. [b] In Bahrain, as in other developing societies, the relationships between education and political socialization and education and manpower must be jointly examined even though they exist on different planes.

One must at the outset recognize the contradiction between these two essentially different roles performed by the systems of education in developing societies. The school and the system of education must act as inculcators of particularistic values, especially in the realm of citizenship, yet they must also transmit a body of knowledge that reflects man's philosophical view of the universe and the universal values based on this conception.[1]

Educational planners in Bahrain have been occupied with the attempt to establish an equilibrium in which the school would act as an agent of political socialization, primarily in the 5 to 19-year-old age group, and in which the school would simultaneously produce technicians in different skills to man the country's industrializing economy. Bahrain, like other developing societies, has recognized the organic relationship between education (literacy) and participatory government. For a democratic form of government, be it traditional Islamic (*shura*) or modern Western, to remain functionally viable, a certain level of mass education must exist in the society. This is particularly true in the immediate postindependence years when the country embarks on a new form of government, requiring a new body of laws. At this point, when a country begins to convert its traditional, legally binding, and mostly unwritten customs into new laws, the country's leadership begins to place new and unprecedented emphasis on the written word. As a result, the constitutions of most developing societies require that to be eligible for membership in popularly elected national assemblies, a candidate must be literate, that is, possess a minimal knowledge of reading and writing.

Several studies have dealt with the relationship between education and political development; however, most of these studies have used the model or systems approach in an attempt to build some sort of theory. These studies have largely ignored the fact that most of these developing countries view education as a functional rather than a sociological process. In the immediate postindependence years, the presistent question asked by developing countries is how can education contribute to economic de-

---

[b] In Bahrain the director of planning in the Ministry of Education, Hamad Slayti, has served on several national manpower and planning committees. Slayti was the secretary of the National Manpower Planning Council formed in January 1971.

velopment.[c] To illustrate the developing countries' preoccupation with the link between education and economic development, let us examine Bahrain's own view of its educational system. The annual report that Bahrain submitted to the Conference of Arab Ministers of Eduction held in San'a, Yemen, 23-30 December 1972[2] stated that the eductional policy of the state was to campaign against illiteracy in order to aid the country in its development programs. Moreover, the Ministry of Education indicated a commitment to improving the quality of education in the country.

To achieve these twin goals the report identified several specific steps, which the Ministry of Education has recently undertaken:[3]

1. Continuation of the system of mass education
2. Provision of in-service training for teachers and other efforts to upgrade their qualifications
3. Constant revision of school curricula
4. Improvement of the Ministry of Education's administrative system, particularly in order to make school administrations more efficient and more responsive
5. Diversification of the curriculum, especially on the high school level, to create a system of vocational training, which would be able to meet the country's manpower needs in economic and social fields
6. Improvement of the physical facilities of the schools

In spite of these efforts of the Bahraini government in the field of education, serious inconsistencies due to lack of planning still exist within the educational policy. Like almost every other sector in Bahrain, no long-range developmental plan has yet been established.[d] As a consequence of this unorganized growth, several basic questions present themselves. Why has Bahrain's educational system, in spite of its 50-year

[c] Earlier studies on education and the polity include such works as Charles Merriam, *The Making of Citizens: A Comparative Study of Methods of Civic Training* (Chicago: University of Chicago Press, 1931); V.O. Key, Jr., *Public Opinion and American Democracy* (New York: Knopf, 1961); Gabriel A. Almond and James S. Coleman, eds., *The Politics of the Developing Areas* (Princeton, N.J.: Princeton University Press, 1960); Gabriel A. Almond and Sidney Verba, *The Civic Culture* (Princeton, N.J.: Princeton University Press, 1963). More recent studies include: James S. Coleman, ed., *Education and Political Development* (Princeton, N.J.: Princeton University Press, 1965), and Leonard Binder et al., *Crises and Sequences in Political Development* (Princeton, N.J.: Princeton University Press, 1971). Such studies as Gunnar Myrdal, *Asian Drama: an Inquiry into the Poverty of Nations*, 3 vols. (New York: Random House, 1968), and Irving Louis Horowitz, *Three Worlds of Development: The Theory and Practice of International Stratification*, 2nd ed. (New York: Oxford University Press, 1972) have taken a somewhat different approach than the one used in the preceding works.

[d] Although in 1972-73 a labor advisor, an industrial planning advisor, and a UNESCO-supported educational team were working in Bahrain, their efforts were on a departmental level, without any common objective for a national plan.

tradition, failed to reach large numbers of people outside the two major urban centers of Manama and Muharraq? Why has this system to date failed to staff Bahrain's developing economy, thereby amplifying the problem of foreign labor in Bahrain? Why has there not been any effective coordination between the educational system and the country's social and economic needs? Finally, has education actually contributed to the development of a Bahraini citizenry, that is, has education contributed to the Bahraini polity in general? The following sections of this chapter attempt to answer some of these questions.

A Statistical Profile of Education in Bahrain

Almost 60 percent of Bahrain's population (Bahrainis only) is under 20 years of age, 70 percent is under 30, and 80 percent is under 40. Bahrain is a nation of young people, which places the educational system under a tremendous strain in trying to serve the large numbers of children who are of school age. (See table 2-1.) Also the annual population increase, as in most Middle Eastern countries, is over 3 percent, which means that the country's population will double in a generation's time. (See table 2-2.) This demographic reality creates the need to reassess the entire system of education in approach, methods, and long-range objectives, particularly since any comprehensive system of mass education would constitute a heavy drain on the financial resources of the country. Also, Bahrain is not in need of a mediocre educational system that would graduate students barely qualified to fill the middle level of the government's bureaucracy.

Bahrain has not yet acknowledged this problem, but it will not be long before its full range of symptoms will begin to be felt. Either the decision makers do not comprehend the magnitude of the detrimental impact that an inadequate or a mediocre system of education usually has on the entire polity or they might be consciously interested in preserving the present system, hoping that disparate short-range solutions will in the end dissolve away the long-range problem. Unfortunately the facts of an increasing population, limited resources, and educational mediocrity are real disabilities and must be faced.

Upon close examination of the official statistics of education, one perceives a discrepancy between rhetoric about the educational tradition and the achievements of the educational system. Although the first primary school for boys was opened in 1919, Bahrain's public education system on a mass level for both sexes is still in the budding stage. The first primary school for girls did not open until 1928, and it was not until 1939 that the first secondary school for boys was opened. The first secondary school for girls was opened in 1951. The two-year teacher training institutes (one for men

Table 2-1
Population by Five-Year Age Groups and Nationality, 1971

Age Groups	Bahraini	Non-Bahraini	Total
Under 1	5,356	669	6,025
1-4	22,399	2,847	25,246
5-9	31,001	3,409	34,410
10-14	27,590	2,369	29,959
15-19	19,839	2,350	22,189
20-24	12,254	4,223	16,477
25-29	10,190	5,724	15,914
30-34	8,506	4,801	13,307
35-39	9,254	3,930	13,184
40-44	7,109	2,814	9,923
45-49	6,639	1,804	8,443
50-54	5,943	1,345	7,288
55-59	3,153	535	3,688
60-64	3,581	504	4,085
65-69	1,734	188	1,922
70-74	1,788	214	2,002
75 and over	1,857	159	2,016
Total	178,193	37,885	216,078

Source: State of Bahrain, Ministry of Finance and National Economy, *Statistical Abstract, 1972*, p. 8.

Table 2-2
Population Increase in Bahrain, 1941-71

Nationality	1941	1950	1959	1965	1971
Bahraini	74,040	91,179	118,734	143,814	178,193
Non-Bahraini	15,930	18,471	24,401	38,389	37,885
Total	89,970	109,650	143,135	182,203	216,078

Source: State of Bahrain, Ministry of Finance and National Economy, *Statistical Abstract, 1972*, p. 6.

and the other for women) were opened in 1966 and 1967 respectively.[e] A technical institute, The Gulf Technical College, was opened in 1968-69 and is run jointly by Bahrain, Abu Dhabi, and the British government.

One must also consider the high percentage of illiteracy among the population, especially in rural areas. This indicates that, in spite of the fact that over 25 percent of the entire population is enrolled in the public school system, the schools have failed thus far to halt the growth of illiteracy. One possible explanation is that the schools have existed mostly in the towns

---
[e] State of Bahrain, Ministry of Education, *Educational Statistics, 1971-1972*, 1973, p. 10. The teacher training institutes were expanded into four-year institutes under the auspices of UNESCO and the United Nations Development Program in 1974-75.

and cities; also, public education is free but not compulsory. A third factor is that the prevailing cultural view against women's education has kept many school-age girls out of the educational system.

Table 2-3 shows that even among school age groups (10-19 years old), the percentage of illiteracy as compared to the total population over 10 years of age is greater than 25 percent. Also, the older the age group, the higher the percentage of illiteracy. A comparison of the percentages of illiteracy in urban and rural areas shows a marked difference between the two groups. Fifty percent of the school-age children in rural Bahrain are illiterate, especially in the 10-14 and 15-19 age groups; roughly 22 percent of the urban school age children are illiterate in the same age groups. This means that, the small size of Bahrain notwithstanding, the rural population has not benefited from the country's educational system. (See table 2-4.)

Also, Bahrain's small size and the geographic distribution of its population add to the significance of the high percentage of illiteracy in the rural areas. An examination of table 2-5 indicates that 47,000 (or 22%) of the (1971) population lived in what are officially known as rural areas. Moreover, unlike other industrializing societies and again because of its small size, the rural population has not experienced any mobility in the last decade. No population migration into the cities has occurred, although rural workers who had been previously employed in agriculture did seek industrial employment with the advent of the two major industries of oil and aluminum. However, they were able to remain in their own villages and commute to work; therefore, these workers and their families have not benefited, and will not benefit, from the improved school system in the towns and cities. This means that the rural educational system must be improved in order to become effective in combating illiteracy.

The level of illiteracy in the rural areas has also been detrimental to the development of participatory government. In 1972 the government of Bahrain initiated a series of steps, in particular the Constitutional Assembly, to bring about some degree of popular participation in the governing process. It was precisely the election to this Assembly that revealed Bahrain's 50-year old educational tradition was not as widely spread as had been believed. In fact, the level of illiteracy in rural areas negatively influenced the country's first national election in that rural representatives in the Constitutional Assembly were generally underqualified for serving in such a body.

As a final point, it should be noted that the majority of village dwellers are native Bahrainis and not expatriate laborers who might eventually leave the country.[f] The problem will not vanish of its own accord; the rural population is Bahraini, and the low level of education in the rural areas has

---
[f]The 1971 population census shows that the vast majority of the 38,000 resident non-Bahrainis lived in the capital city area and in 'Awali, the BAPCO town.

Table 2-3
Percentage of Illiterate Population by Age Groups and Sex, 1971

	Percentage of Illiterate Population		
Age Groups	Male	Female	Total
10-14	16.7%	34.4%	25.4%
15-19	15.5	38.7	26.5
20-24	31.7	55.8	41.8
25-29	45.7	67.7	55.1
30-34	53.9	76.5	63.2
35-44	63.0	86.6	73.1
45 and Over	77.6	95.6	85.3
National Mean	44.6	63.3	52.9

Source: State of Bahrain, Ministry of Education, *Educational Statistics, 1961-1971*, 1972, p. 18.

Table 2-4
Percentage of Illiterate Population in Urban and Rural Areas by Age Groups, 1971

Age Groups	Urban	Rural	Total
10-14	20.9%	51.7%	25.4%
15-19	23.0	49.2	26.5
20-24	39.8	57.1	41.8
25-29	52.4	76.6	55.1
30-34	60.8	83.3	63.2
35-44	70.8	89.6	73.1
45 and Over	84.0	93.7	85.3
National Mean	50.3%	70.6%	52.9%

Source: State of Bahrain, Ministry of Education, *Educational Statistics, 1961-1971*, 1972, p. 19.

an unwelcome effect on the country as a whole. The preceding three points, that is, illiteracy and the immobility of the rural population, illiteracy and democratization, and illiteracy and the national educational level, highlight the awesome responsibility of the country's educational system. They also point to the stresses under which this educational system has labored.

The statistics of the student population, apart from the general population statistics discussed in the preceding pages, tell yet another side of the story of education in Bahrain, especially the demands that the modern polity places on the educational system. The Bahraini government has not yet instituted a compulsory system of education because it simply cannot

Table 2-5
Population of Major Civil Divisions by Urban-Rural Residents

		Population	
Geographic Division	1959	1965	1971
Manama Division	62,266	79,705	89,399
Manama Town	61,726	79,098	88,785
Rural	540	607	614
Muharraq Island	36,742	46,373	49,540
Muharraq Town	27,115	34,430	37,732
Hidd Town	4,440	5,230	5,269
Rural	5,187	6,713	6,539
Jidhafs Division	11,579	14,571	19,521
Jidhafs Town	5,591	7,941	11,152
Rural	5,988	6,630	8,369
Northern Division (Rural)	5,933	8,610	10,614
Western Division (Rural)	5,044	6,760	8,689
Central Division	3,738	5,230	14,228
'Isa Town	—	—	7,501
Rural	3,738	5,230	6,727
Sitra Division	7,315	8,872	11,323
Sitra Town	3,926	5,071	6,663
Rural	3,389	3,801	4,658
Rifa' Division	10,295	11,970	12,633
Rifa' Town	6,623	9,403	10,731
'Awali	3,123	2,097	984
Rural	549	470	918
Other Islands (Rural)	223	112	131
Total	143,135	182,203	216,078

Source: State of Bahrain, Ministry of Finance and National Economy, *Statistical Abstract,* 1972, p. 9.

afford it.[g] Noncompulsory education has relieved the pressure on the public school system, at least temporarily, in terms of the total number of school-age children who do not attend school and in terms of the especially large number of female students who because of their conservative social and religious traditions have been kept out of school. Table 2-6 indicates that between 5 and 24 years of age over 48,000 children of Bahraini nationals attended school in 1971. In this context school attendance included

---
[g]On 23 January 1973 the Constitutional Assembly passed article 7 of the draft constitution concerning education. Section a of this article stipulated that elementary education should be compulsory and free. See *Minutes*, Constitutional Assembly Debates, Tenth Session (23 January 1973). During the debate on this article several Assembly members advocated a compulsory and free system of education throughout the public school system and on all levels. The government's response was that although education in Bahrain was free, the country could not yet afford a free *and* compulsory system of education at all grade levels.

Table 2-6
Attending School Population 5 to 24 Years of Age by Single Years of Age and Nationality (Bahraini and Non-Bahraini), 1971

Age	Bahraini	Non-Bahraini	Total
5	234	207	441
6	1,410	356	1,766
7	3,944	515	4,459
8	4,724	573	5,297
9	4,502	479	4,981
10	5,084	560	5,644
11	4,150	381	4,351
12	5,138	455	5,593
13	3,874	303	4,177
14	3,767	261	4,028
15	3,002	208	3,210
16	2,571	173	2,744
17	1,829	107	1,936
18	1,771	93	1,864
19	818	42	860
20	644	36	680
21	238	16	254
22	216	12	228
23	89	7	96
24	65	3	68
Total	48,070	4,787	52,857

Source: State of Bahrain, Ministry of Finance and National Economy, *Statistics of the Population Census,* 1971, p. 123.

elementary schools, intermediate schools, high schools, and the teacher training institutes.

Table 2-7, on the other hand, indicates that by not having compulsory education almost as many school-age children in 1971 were out of school as were attending school. Moreover, the table shows the tremendous number of school-age girls that were kept out of school. In the 8-16 age group, three to four times as many girls as boys did not attend school. Taken together, the two tables demonstrate that the voluntary nature of education has been a mixed blessing—something that will not last indefinitely. Although the pressure on the schools has been kept to a manageable level, the rate of illiteracy has burgeoned, especially within the female school-age population. Drastic reforms must be taken in order to break this circle of rapidly increasing population and leaping illiteracy. Such steps will have to go beyond just building more schools and marshalling a bigger teaching staff. Such a solution breeds educational mediocrity—a chronic disability in most developing countries. What is needed is a serious coordinated reform of the quality of education in the light of the quantity of school age children.

Table 2-7
Nonschool Attending Population 5 to 24 Years of Age by Single Years of Age and Sex (Bahraini Nationals), 1971

Age	Males	Females	Total
5	3,113	3,033	6,146
6	2,330	2,399	4,729
7	1,143	1,408	2,551
8	546	1,053	1,599
9	243	919	1,162
10	276	955	1,231
11	148	663	811
12	257	1,011	1,268
13	183	712	895
14	314	1,058	1,372
15	428	948	1,376
16	611	1,123	1,734
17	708	983	1,691
18	1,320	1,737	3,057
19	1,026	964	1,990
20	1,790	2,102	3,892
21	850	669	1,519
22	1,276	1,246	2,522
23	885	665	1,550
24	777	742	1,519
Total	18,224	24,390	42,614

Source: State of Bahrain, Ministry of Finance and National Economy, *Statistics of the Population Census*, 1971, p. 124.

Focusing on school-attending children, one can see that the student enrollment has shown a marked annual increase. Student enrollment in elementary and secondary schools between 1940-41 and 1960-61 showed only a gradual increase (see table 2-8); however, the annual increase in student enrollment took a dramatic rise in the sixties. Between 1940-41 and 1960-61, student enrollment increased by approximately 18,500, but between 1961-62 and 1971-72 alone the enrollment rose by over 28,000 students. (See table 2-9.)

Although the dropout rate is very low in the public school system,[4] at the other end of the academic spectrum very few students have attempted a college education or graduated with a college degree. Table 2-10 shows that only 426 Bahrainis received advanced degrees (college and above) between 1950 and 1972, over 75 percent of whom were men.[h] By far the largest

[h] There have been no more than a dozen who earned masters' degrees and half a dozen who earned doctorates. It is also interesting to note that the present minister of development and engineering services in Bahrain, Yusuf al-Shirawi, was the first Bahraini ever to graduate from college (American University of Beirut, 1950, chemistry). In April 1973 al-Shirawi became a member of the American University of Beirut's Board of Trustees, the first board member to come from the Gulf region.

Table 2-8
Student Enrollment from 1940-41 to 1960-61 in Elementary and Secondary Schools

Academic Year	Elementary Boys	Elementary Girls	Secondary Boys	Secondary Girls[a]	Total
1940-41	1,188	667	45	—	1,900
1941-42	1,149	763	45	—	1,957
1942-43	1,295	822	55	—	2,172
1943-44	1,360	1,167	50	—	2,577
1944-45	1,423	1,178	47	—	2,648
1945-46	1,714	1,193	36	—	2,943
1946-47	2,028	1,310	56	—	3,394
1947-48	2,299	1,283	88	—	3,670
1948-49	2,663	1,285	122	—	4,070
1949-50	3,081	1,356	125	—	4,562
1950-51	3,659	1,763	133	—	5,555
1951-52	3,806	1,952	162	11	5,931
1952-53	4,413	2,250	167	17	6,847
1953-54	5,240	2,299	220	14	7,773
1954-55	6,239	2,618	305	22	9,184
1955-56	6,912	3,274	462	39	10,687
1956-57	7,950	3,911	556	30	12,447
1957-58	9,122	4,020	645	71	13,858
1958-59	10,378	4,909	716	110	16,113
1959-60	11,581	5,315	883	152	17,931
1960-61	12,677	6,236	1,246	250	20,409

Source: Based on 'Abd al-Malik al-Hamir, *Development of Education in Bahrain: 1940-1965* (Manama, Bahrain: Oriental Press, 1969), pp. 44-45. Originally written as a Master's thesis for The American University of Beirut.

[a]The first secondary school for girls was opened in 1951-52.

number of graduates has been in the fields of commerce and business, a fact that reflects Bahrain's entrepôt, service-oriented economy. Medicinal and pharmaceutical sciences and legal studies occupy the second and fourth positions in the number of graduates; these fields have always been respected in the traditional Arab view of education. The study of literature, which comes third on this list, also falls into this traditional category. In 1971 and 1972 the number of college graduates soared: 62 graduates in 1971 and 64 in 1972, almost 30 percent of all Bahraini college graduates. Also, in the last two years, more secondary school graduates than ever before have enrolled in colleges in various Middle Eastern countries. In the fall of 1972 alone over 120 Bahrainis enrolled as freshmen on scholarships in several universities. Table 2-11 gives the distribution of freshman Bahraini students, excluding self-supporting students.

In order to complete this statistical profile of education, additional items should be mentioned: the structure of the Ministry of Education and

Table 2-9
Student Enrollment on All Levels, 1961-62 to 1972-3

Academic Year	Elementary	Intermediate	Secondary	Technical	Commercial	Religious	Teachers' Inst.[a]	Total
1961-62	21,154	1,326	318	146	65	81	—	23,090
1962-63	25,257	1,691	471	162	151	106	—	27,839
1963-64	28,563	2,361	739	271	215	117	—	32,266
1964-65	30,345	3,089	1,146	461	229	133	—	35,403
1965-66	30,811	3,838	1,736	420	197	133	—	37,135
1966-67	32,829	4,893	2,739	513	255	146	25	41,400
1967-68	35,167	4,923	3,690	476	252	146	103	44,757
1968-69	34,746	5,354	4,905	544	332	130	189	46,200
1969-70	34,416	6,562	5,022	470	348	141	234	47,193
1970-71	36,113	7,288	5,242	439	490	150	289	50,011
1971-72	36,953	7,264	5,332	601	632	138	312	51,232
1972-73	38,156	7,727	5,898	614	772	139	355	53,661

Sources: State of Bahrain, Ministry of Education, *Educational Statistics, 1961-1971*, pp. 25,35,41,50,56,60,64; *Educational Statistics, 1971-72*, pp. 7,23,25,26,31,34; State of Bahrain, Ministry of Information, *al-Bahrain al-Yom* [Bahrain Today], December 1972, a special annual issue, pp. 340-41; and personal interviews with Ministry of Education officials.

[a]The first Teachers' Institute was opened in 1966-67.

the educational ladder and the government's annual expenditures for education. The educational system is Bahrain is administered by the minister of education,[1] under whom the Ministry's seven departments direct the progress of education in Bahrain.

A few private schools (nurseries, kindergartens, primary and secondary schools) operate in Bahrain with a 1972 enrollment of around 4,500 students. These schools are generally governed by the 1961 Private Schools Ordinance, which gives the Ministry of Education the power to inspect the curricula and textbooks of these schools. However, these schools primarily serve non-Bahraini nationals, and they tend to play a negligible role in the process of political development.

The public school educational ladder consists of a primary level of six grades, beginning with age six, an intermediate level of two years and a secondary level of three years. The secondary level is divided into three branches: general (arts or sciences), commercial, and technical. In addition, two two-year teacher training institutes presently exist in Bahrain, one for men, established in 1966, and one for women, established in 1967. These institutes offer courses on a postsecondary school level.[5] The Gulf Technical College was opened in 1968-69 and is operated jointly by Bahrain, Abu Dhabi, and the British government. The college offers a three-year course in several engineering fields.

Education on all levels is free, which understandably means that the Ministry of Education has consistently received the lion's share of the national budget. According to table 2-12, the educational budget during 1965-70 had consistently been allotted over 20 percent of the national budget. Although this percentage has dropped slightly since then, it still is one of the top three expenditures in the budget. However, when the recurrent expenditures on education are considered separately, the annual percentage is still over 20 percent.[6] These facts indicate the need to reexamine the entire educational program. The following two sections of this chapter, education and manpower and education and political socialization, also clearly illustrate this need.

Education and Manpower

Although the study of manpower as it relates to education is technically outside the scope of this work, a brief presentation of the problems facing Bahrain in this area is in order. This interrelationship demonstrates anew the ubiquity of politics; in order to forestall a possible national crisis that

---

[1]For several years the Ministry (formerly Department) of Education was headed by Ahmad al-'Umran, a long-time educator. In December 1972 he retired and was appointed special advisor to the ruler of Bahrain, Shaikh 'Isa bin Sulman al-Khalifa. al-'Umran was replaced as minister of education by Shaikh 'Abd al-'Aziz al-Khalifa. See State of Bahrain, *Official Gazette*, 14 December 1972, pp. 5-6.

Table 2-10
Bahraini College Graduates and Their Fields of Specialization, 1950-72

	1950	1952	1953	1954	1955	1956	1957	1958	1959	1960
Agriculture	—	—	—	—	—	—	—	—	—	—
Commerce[a]	—	—	—	—	—	1	—	2	2	—
Economics[b]	—	—	—	—	1	—	1	—	—	—
Education[c]	—	—	1	1	—	—	1	1	—	—
Engineering[d]	—	—	—	—	1	—	—	—	—	—
Fine arts	—	—	—	—	—	—	—	—	—	1
Geography	—	—	—	—	—	—	—	—	—	—
History	—	—	—	—	—	—	—	—	—	—
Journalism	—	—	—	—	—	—	—	—	—	—
Law[e]	—	1	—	—	—	1	—	4	1	1
Literature[f]	—	—	—	—	—	1	—	1	—	—
Medicine[g]	—	—	—	—	—	—	—	2	2	2
Military Science	—	—	—	—	—	—	—	—	—	—
Philosophy relig.	—	—	—	—	—	—	—	—	—	—
Political science[h]	1	—	—	—	—	—	—	3	3	2
Science[i]	1	—	—	1	—	—	1	1	—	—
Sociology[j]	—	—	—	—	—	—	—	—	—	—
Men	2	1	1	1	2	3	3	14	8	6
Women	—	—	—	—	—	—	—	—	—	—
Total	2	1	1	1	2	3	3	14	8	6

Source: Based on information, published and unpublished, obtained from the Ministry of Education.

[a]Includes secretarial science, management, and business administration.
[b]Includes statistics, accounting, and home economics (only 2).
[c]Includes teaching methods, child psychology, psychology of education, physical education, and general psychology.
[d]Includes civil, mechanical, automotive, electrical, chemical, refrigeration, wireless and health engineering, and wood craftsmanship.

might be caused by a lack of coordination between education and manpower requirements, serious national political decisions must be made in the immediate future.[j]

In making these decisions, the Bahraini government will have to consider several facts:

1. The population of Bahrain continues to increase at an annual rate of

---
[j]For a useful analysis of education and manpower planning in the Gulf see Robert Anton Mertz, *Education and Manpower in the Arabian Gulf* (Washington, D.C.: American Friends of the Middle East, 1972). Chapter I of this mimeographed study covers Bahrain.

1961	1962	1963	1964	1965	1966	1967	1968	1969	1970	1971	1972	Total
—	—	—	—	2	—	2	—	3	1	—	1	9
1	1	4	1	5	4	8	5	5	3	7	8	57
—	—	—	—	7	6	4	2	3	—	3	2	29
1	1	—	—	1	8	5	—	2	—	2	2	26
1	4	1	2	1	6	4	3	—	1	—	3	27
—	—	—	1	—	—	1	—	—	1	—	—	4
—	—	—	—	—	—	1	—	1	1	—	2	5
—	—	—	—	1	1	—	1	3	6	4	6	22
—	—	—	—	—	—	—	—	—	2	3	—	5
2	4	3	1	1	4	2	3	3	2	—	6	39
5	1	3	1	1	4	2	1	3	4	6	9	42
2	—	1	—	2	4	6	3	4	2	12	1	43
2	—	1	1	—	3	2	—	—	—	—	—	9
—	1	1	—	—	—	—	2	5	4	—	2	14
—	—	—	—	—	—	2	—	1	1	7	1	21
—	1	—	—	—	1	4	3	2	2	8	14	39
—	1	1	3	1	3	3	2	—	6	9	7	36
12	14	13	8	19	39	39	19	29	18	39	41	331
2	—	1	2	3	5	7	6	6	17	23	23	95
14	14	14	10	22	44	46	25	35	35	62	64	426

[e]Includes Shari'a.
[f]Includes Arabic language and literature and English language and literature.
[g]Includes public health, veterinary medicine, dentistry, pharmaceutical science, and general medicine.
[h]Includes public administration.
[i]Includes chemistry, physics, mathematics, geology, zoology, botany, and laboratory technicians.
[j]Includes child care.

over 3.5 percent, which means that in the next two decades the demand for education will rise sharply.

2. Between 1961-62 and 1972-73 primary school enrollment grew from 21,154 to 38,156 or 80 percent; intermediate school enrollment in the same period increased from 1,326 to 7,727 or 485 percent. Secondary school (general) enrollment rose from 318 to 5,898 or 1,755 percent. (See table 2-9). The technical and commercial education branches have shown marked increases also, especially since in 1970-71 girls were admitted into commercial education, such as offered at the Gulf Technical College.

Table 2-11
Distribution of First-Year Bahraini College Students in Middle Eastern Universities, 1972-73

University	City/Country	Bahraini Freshmen
al-Azhar University	Cairo, Egypt	3
American University	Beirut, Lebanon	10
Cairo University	Cairo, Egypt	5
Islamic University	Madina, Saudi Arabia	2
King 'Abd al-'Aziz University	Jidda, Saudi Arabia	5
Kuwait University	Kuwait, Kuwait	45
Petroleum College	Dhahran, Saudi Arabia	2
Riyad University	Riyad, Saudi Arabia	40
Miscellaneous (under Abu Dhabi grants)		10
Total		122

Source: Based on information obtained from the Ministry of Education. This table includes only scholarship students.

Table 2-12
Ministry of Education Budget Compared to the National Budget, 1965-73
(Bahraini Dinars)

Year	National Budget	Recurrent	Nonrecurrent	Total	Percent of National Budget
1965	10,268,100	2,127,420	169,697	2,297,117	22.4%
1966	11,184,000	2,332,748	102,207	2,434,956	21.1
1967	12,104,200	2,726,682	47,122	2,773,804	22.9
1968	13,031,212	2,934,521	95,533	3,030,055	23.3
1969	13,272,716	3,287,039	90,294	3,377,333	25.4
1970	15,000,000	3,500,000	147,000	3,647,000	24.3
1971	24,000,000	3,850,000	375,000	4,225,000	17.6
1972	26,000,000	4,200,000	460,000	4,660,000	17.9
1973	32,500,000	4,650,000	450,000	5,100,000	15.7%

Sources: State of Bahrain, Ministry of Education, *Educational Statistics, 1971-72*, p. 6; Government of Bahrain, *1970 Budget; 1971 Budget;* and State of Bahrain, Ministry of Finance and National Economy, *State Budget,* 1972; and *State Budget,* 1973.

3. The enrollment of girls on all educational levels during the last decade has risen twice as fast as the enrollment of boys. (See table 2-13.) This means that by 1980 unprecedented numbers of women with secondary and vocational educations will be seeking employment, especially in areas

Table 2-13
Enrollment Increase by Sex, 1961-62 to 1971-72

Level	Females 1961-62	1971-72	%	Males 1961-62	1971-72	%
Primary	7,394	15,757	113%	13,760	21,290	55%
Intermediate	258	3,219	1,148	1,068	4,045	279
Secondary	112	2,897	2,487	216	2,435	1,027

Source: State of Bahrain, Ministry of Education, *Educational Statistics, 1961-1971*, 1972, and *Educational Statistics, 1971-1972*, 1973.

that had been traditionally reserved for men and expatriate women. Hence, the Bahraini government should create new employment opportunities and hasten the Bahrainization of labor.

4. No comprehensive steps have yet been taken to update the educational curricula, the teaching staff, the laboratories, audiovisual aids, or the physical facilities. In 1971-72 the country's 43 elementary schools for boys had only three laboratories and/or workshops, and these three were officially termed inadequate. The 32 schools for girls had no laboratories or workshops at all. Even the women's teacher training institute in 1971 had no laboratory, and the students had to use the laboratory of the men's teacher training institute. (See table 2-14.)

5. Finally, there has been a lack of high-level guidance on the type of college specialization that prospective Bahraini collegians should enter. This type of guidance, especially since most students are supported by state scholarships, should serve a two-fold purpose: college graduates should be able to find employment opportunities, and by encouraging specialization in the right fields, the government could insure that the national economy would be served by trained Bahraini manpower, thereby arresting the money outflow caused by expatriate labor.

Higher education statistics are also telling. The first observation based on these statistics is that the small number of college graduates has always meant that those who sought employment were quickly and completely absorbed into the country's civil service or other public sector positions. Those who did not choose the civil service have found employment in the commercial sector. In other words, Bahrain has not yet experienced the problem of unemployment among the intelligentsia—an enviable position in the Third World. However, this state of affairs will be short-lived due to at least three factors: the limited nature of the Bahraini economy and the employment opportunities in the public sector; the number of expected college graduates in the next 5-10 years and the lack of coordination

Table 2-14
Schools by Type, Level, and Availability of Laboratories, Workshops, and Libraries, 1971-72

Level	Type	No. of Schools	Libraries Adequate	Libraries Inadequate	Labs & Workshops Adequate	Labs & Workshops Inadequate
Primary	Boys	43	5	8	—	3
	Girls	32	13	7	—	—
Primary & Intermediate	Boys	12	2	—	—	1
	Girls	8	4	2	—	3
Primary, Intermediate, Secondary	Boys	1	—	—	1	—
	Girls	—	—	—	—	—
Intermediate	Boys	—	—	—	—	—
	Girls	1	1	—	—	—
Intermediate Secondary	Boys	2	1	—	2	2
	Girls	3	1	2	1	4
Secondary, (General, & Commercial)	Boys	3	3	—	3	—
	Girls	3	3	—	3	—
Technical Schools	Boys	2	2	—	2	—
	Girls	—	—	—	—	—
Religious Education	Boys	1	—	—	—	—
	Girls	—	—	—	—	—
Teachers' Institutes	Boys	1	1	—	1	—
	Girls	1	1	—	—	—
Total	Boys	65	14	8	9	6
	Girls	48	23	11	4	7
	Total	113	37	19	13	13

Source: State of Bahrain, Ministry of Education, *Educational Statistics, 1971-1972*, 1973, pp. 45-46.

between the direction of higher education, that is, the type of college majors most likely required; and the country's short-range manpower needs.

Two possible corrective measures can be taken to preempt this expected problem. The Ministry of Education should develop effective guidelines for prospective college students to establish some degree of correlation between college specialization and future manpower needs. When developing these guidelines for prospective college students, the Ministry of Education should take into consideration the short-range and long-range manpower needs of the oil-rich neighboring states, Qatar, Abu Dhabi, Dubai, and the Sultanate of Oman. Bahrain's educational tradition is more advanced than that of these states and therefore could be of benefit to these countries in their modernization efforts. Since Bahrain imports practically all of its necessities, it should be able to develop a manpower export of highly-trained college graduates.

A possible long-range corrective measure is a reexamination of the educational curriculum with a view toward a radical systemic overhaul—the ultimate elimination of a concern with numbers and the deliberate cultivation of a new concern with the quality of education. Otherwise, the government will find itself in the position of creating more civil service positions in order to absorb large numbers of college graduates, thereby creating an oversized, nonresponsive bureaucracy.

The major target of this educational reform should be the curriculum. New material should be introduced, not newly printed editions of old textbooks. Modern pedagogical methods and subjects such as the new mathematics should be encouraged. In-service teacher training programs should be put into effect; poorly trained teachers should gradually but surely be weeded out. The long-range impact of such steps on the Bahraini polity cannot be overstated, especially in the area of political development. For, as has so often been stated, there is a direct link between the curriculum and the formation of the child's political culture, a relationship that is disucssed in the following pages.[k]

Education and Citizenship

Education since time immemorial has been viewed by thinkers and political leaders alike as a tool of citizenship. Twenty-five hundred years ago in his *Republic* Plato relied heavily on education for the formation of the good society. More recently, states of all ideologies have employed education to form the type of political perception and imagery that would perpetuate and glorify a specific political culture. This process of preserving and transmitting a political culture through childhood socializing experiences is called *political socialization*, which in the final analysis is the formation of a method of valuing the political system. The school's role in this process is to form the mind of the child in such a way that he will attach certain universal values to the political system within his environment. This incul-

---

[k] For a further examination of more concrete recommendations on curricular changes in Bahrain's educational system see Mertz, *Education and Manpower in the Arabian Gulf*, pp. 169-181.

cation of values fosters emotions of loyalty, love, respect, and pride in regard to the political system.

Bahrain, like other societies, both developed and developing, has viewed education as one means of political socialization by which the child is inducted into citizenship. In his 1972-73 annual message to the students, the former minister of education, Ahmad al-'Umran, ascribed several roles to education.[7] He viewed education as a process of civilization and as a basis for man's progress. He asserted that education must incorporate two facets of man's culture—the spiritual and the material. al-'Umran maintained that any revision of the educational curricula and policies of the country must have as its ultimate goal the will to search within the society's collective self for a new synthesis which could be based on the nation's history and modern technological progress.

al-'Umran strongly attacked those who desire a complete emulation of Western cultures; instead he envisioned rearing a generation that would not imitate the West but that would be concerned with spiritual, moral, and cultural values. His emphasis on traditional values did not imply that the new generation should stagnate or fall behind modern civilization. In a national context, the minister believed that the responsibility for the attainment of national goals falls squarely on the academic curriculum.

In the context of Bahrain, al-'Umran stated that the academic curriculum, in particular history and geography, must consider the realities of three concentric circles: the Bahraini environment; the Gulf environment; and the Arab environment. Of course, the curriculum must obviously relate to world affairs, and Bahrains's educational system has already produced, according to al-'Umran, a sophisticated, open, reasonable, orderly, and pragmatic people.[l]

In order to assess translation of the relationship between education and political socialization into actual school curricula, one should survey the entire primary school (grades 1-6) academic program, in particular those parts that directly relate to political socialization.[m] The textbooks actually used in the primary schools should then be examined, bearing in mind the official policy and goals of the national curriculum, in order to evaluate the level of realization of objectives, or goal attainment.

As stated in table 2-15, the primary school curriculum consists of 9 subjects for each of the first and second grades, 10 subjects for the third grade, and 11 subjects for each of the fourth through sixth grades. The class schedules consists of 34 periods per week for each grade.[8] The subjects,

---

[l]al-'Umran expressed similar views in a personal interview conducted on 23 October 1972. This basic philosophy has also been expressed by the new minister of education, Shaikh 'Abd al-'Aziz bin Muhammad al-Khalifa.

[m]Obviously similar studies can be made on the curricula of other school levels in Bahrain, that is, intermediate, secondary, and postsecondary. However, because of its paramount importance, the primary level is the focus of this analysis.

which are directly related to political socialization, and officially viewed as such, are Arabic language (all grades), history (grades 3-6), geography (grades 4-6), chorus (patriotic songs) (grades 1-4), and selected readings (grades 1-2).[n] Of the 34 weekly class periods subjects inculcating political socialization constitute 47 percent of the total hours of instruction in the first and second grades, 50 percent in the third grade, 41 percent in the fourth grade, and 38 percent in the fifth and sixth grades.

Table 2-15
Primary School Curriculum in Bahrain, 1972

Subject	1st Grade	2nd Grade	3rd Grade	4th Grade	5th Grade	6th Grade
1. Religious education	4	4	2	2	2	2
2. Arabic language	12	12	12	10	9	9
3. English language	—	—	—	6	7	7
4. Arithmetic	6	6	7	6	6	6
5. Geometry	—	—	—	—	1	1
6. History	—	—	1	1	2	2
7. Geography	—	—	—	2	2	2
8. Science hygiene	—	—	2	2	2	2
9. Drawing	2	2	2	1	1	1
10. Crafts	2	2	2	1	1	1
11. Physical education	3	3	2	2	1	1
12. Chorus (patriotic songs)	2	2	2	1	—	—
13. Selected readings (stories)	2	2	2	—	—	—
14. Nature studies	1	1	—	—	—	—
Total	34	34	34	34	34	34

Source: Government of Bahrain, Department of Education, *Primary School Curriculum*, 1969, p. 5.

At this juncture it would be helpful to look at the officially stated goals and purposes of some of these courses of instruction. Instruction in the Arabic language on the primary level is designed to help the student:

1. Realize that the national language is the primary bond between the members of the Arab nation everywhere

---
[n] Although religious education is a required subject in all grades, it has been excluded from this analysis.

2. Develop a deep love for the language because it is the language of the Qur'an, of the Muslim religion, and of the common history of the Arab countries
3. Acquire and nurture sincere Arab characteristics
4. Cement his ties with his local environment and strengthen his pride in belonging to it
5. Begin to respect manual labor and manual laborers[9]

The teaching of stories and chorus in the first, second, and third grades is another case in point. In this instance the instruction strives to fulfill the following general objectives:

1. To give the student a true picture of his environment through simple and interesting stories
2. To give the student a picture of events from Arab history and of Arab achievements
3. To foster the national and religious spirit[10]

Instruction in the social studies, by which is meant mainly history and geography, in primary schools develops political awareness in several areas. In this part of the curriculum the student is guided into building a political perspective of his history, country, society, and people. History and geography are primarily taught in the fourth, fifth, and sixth grades. The social studies curriculum deals with both the universal aspects of man's existence on earth and the more particular situation of the Bahraini-Arab heritage. More specifically, the social studies curriculum is designed to fulfill the following objectives:

1. To lead the students into a correct perception of their environment
2. To inculcate patriotism and nationalism thereby deepening their attachment to their country
3. To emphasize the political, economic, social, and strategic significance of Arab civilization and to point out the Arabs' cultural contribution to medieval European civilization
4. To constantly remind the student that his Arab heritage teaches tolerance, fidelity, courage, heroism, and sacrifice for the nation[11]

Moving away from the officially stated purposes of the subjects, which relate to political socialization, one notes the discrepancy between the curriculum and the textbooks. Quite aside from any deficiencies of the curriculum itself, the textbooks are inadequate, badly conceived, and poorly written. The problem is compounded by the fact that most primary school teachers in Bahrain, as in many developing societies, are inadequately trained for the teaching profession in either subject matter or pedagogical methods. Therefore, the textbook is the primary tool of classroom instruction. The primary schol school teacher usually does not use outside sources for the course; hence, a bad text is doubly detrimental.

In the Bahraini school system, a college degree is not required to teach on the primary level, and in fact a majority of primary school teachers in 1971-72 had only high school training. Of the entire administrative and teaching staff of the primary through secondary levels, 17 percent had a college degree; most of those with degrees were teachers or administrators in secondary schools. (See table 2-16.)

Table 2-16
Administrative and Teaching Staff of Primary, Intermediate, and General and Commercial Secondary Schools by Qualification and Sex, 1971-72

Academic Qualifications	Male	Female	Total
Less than primary	8	6	14
Primary	20	49	69
Intermediate	32	64	96
General secondary	593	392	985
Secondary teacher training	278	155	433
Commercial secondary	36	—	36
Technical secondary	16	—	16
Higher diploma	127	84	211
Higher educational diploma	39	95	134
Bachelor of science (B.S.)	59	43	102
Bachelor of arts (B.A.)	90	103	193
B.S. + educational diploma	21	14	35
B.A. + educational diploma	23	42	65
Master of arts (M.A.)	4	1	5
M.A. + educational diploma	2	—	2
Total	1,348	1,048	2,396

Source: Based on State of Bahrain, Ministry of Education, *Educational Statistics, 1971-1972*, 1973, pp. 48-49.

Turning to the actual textbooks, the first grade reader[12] was written by Egyptian teachers, published in Egypt, and originally designed for Egyptian schools. The book introduces the student to simple verbs such as to weigh, to jump, to plant, to sow, to plough, to bake, to dig, to harvest, to thrash, and to grind.[13] The action appropriate to each of the verbs is illustrated by an adjacent drawing. All of the illustrations give a primitive, premechanized picture of the actions involved. The verb to jump is illustrated by a soldier in full military gear crossing a barbed wire fence (p. 9).

The second grade uses the second volume of the same reader.[14] However, instead of verb study, the second grade reader emphasizes short stories describing everyday life in Egypt as it should be, not as it is. The book's 36 lessons include such stories as "The Home" (p. 3) describing a spacious house with many rooms in a large city, "The Family" (p. 5) showing a wealthy family with a servant living in another spacious house, "The Field" (p. 10) depicting a primitive little farm on the Nile, and "Su'ad and Her Chickens" (p. 20) showing a little girl feeding her chickens—the story leaves the reader confused as to whether the chickens are raised as pets or for food.

A thorough examination of these first and second grade readers leads the reader to conclude that no political socialization occurs inside the classroom. The two books have no mention of nation, state, country, people, government, progress, science, or modern technology. In addition, the two books, especially volume II, present very atypical stories to the average child, stories involving well-appointed houses cared for by servants and lived in by wealthy families.[o] Still more damaging, however, is the social philosophy that these textbooks advocate (a similar case can be made concerning the other primary school readers). Several readings, perhaps inadvertently, teach the principle that the strong have natural authority over the weak and that trickery and cunning are sure safeguards against all dangers.

The readings dealing with Bahrain in the higher primary grades are few, poorly written, sentimental, and lack rational presentation. The third grade reader endeavors to implant a love of country by comparing patriotism to the love of a bird for its nest.[15] Lesson 2 of the fourth grade reader teaches that Bahrain is known for pearls, oil, palm trees, hospitality, and noble people.[16] Lesson 18 of the same reader ingeniously discusses the geography of the Gulf by pointing out that most of the countries on its shores are Arab countries, such as Bahrain, Oman, al-Shariqa, Dubai, and Kuwait.[17] The author's evident intention to ignore the presence of Iran is understandable in the light of Iran's former territorial claims to Bahrain. However, this is a serious omission, especially when Iran's 36 million people are compared with Bahrain's 216,000!

In a related context, the reader should consider a random selection of sixth grade students throughout Bahrain who were polled by Miss La'ali' Zayani as a part of her master of arts' thesis. The questionnaire, which was used to help Miss Zayani develop a selection of meaningful and environmentally relevant English language readings, produced some interesting sidelights on the traditional cultural patterns of the students.[18] The

---

[o] In 1971 almost 35 percent of all one-room houses and 60 percent of all two-room houses in Bahrain were inhabited by five or more persons. Moreover, these two categories of housing constituted 45 percent of all housing in Bahrain. See State of Bahrain, Ministry of Finance and National Economy, *Statistical Abstract*, 1972, p. 14.

results revealed a confrontation between the universal and the parochial in education that is very interesting in the context of political development. On the questions, which asked the students to list their greatest desires, 19 percent wanted to be doctors, 18 percent teachers, and another 18 percent would simply settle for secure employment. On the question dealing with the student's chosen future profession, 31 percent chose teaching and only 5 percent chose any manual profession, such as carpentry or mechanics.

Miss Zayani concluded that the students possessed a traditional approach to life. Few were attracted to such nontraditional professions as being an artist, an airline pilot, or an astronaut.[19] Also, since traditional societies normally hold that manual labor is beneath the dignity of the intelligentsia (primarily considered to be the high school educated), a minimal attraction was shown toward the mechanical and building trades.

The analysis in this chapter of Bahrain's educational system points to a serious gap between the rhetoric and the reality of the educational process. It is clear that the entire curriculum, including the textbooks, should be reexamined thoroughly. The philosophy of the educational system should also be updated. Judging from his actions on the high school student boycott in February 1973,[p] the recently appointed minister of education is determined to review the entire educational policy of Bahrain in a spirit of reason and civility.[q] The educational system, like any other system, cannot successfully operate in a vacuum, isolated from its environment. The educational system must be responsive to society's needs and desires, for it is the producer of the society's greatly needed technicians and technocrats, and it is the channel through which future leaders are selected.

---

[p] See the developments of the student boycott and their meeting with the minister of education in *Sada al-'Usbu*, 6 February 1973; *al-Adwa'*, 8 and 22 February 1973; and *al-Mujtama' al-Jadid*, 19 February 1973. See also the letter that the minister of education sent to the parents on 22 February 1973 concerning the boycott in *Akhbar al-Bahrain*, 22 February 1973.

[q] For an interview with the minister of education, see *Sada al-'Usbu'*, 13 April 1973, pp. 8-11.

3 Communication and Political Socialization: The Role of the Clubs and the Press

Notes on Theory: Functions and Media of Socialization

Bahrain's modernizing political system is still in the process of delineating its domestic boundaries, and therefore it has not yet defined its priorities or the demands with which the system must cope during the formative years following independence.[a] In attempting to build a theoretical construct of the new Bahraini polity, one must examine at least one activity or function inherent in the new system—the political communication function.[b] Two questions are included in this function: how are interests articulated among different policy-oriented groups and how are these interests communicated to the decision makers? A third question, how are the citizens socialized into different political roles and how are potential leaders recruited, which in a more developed political system normally helps to define the political socialization function is in this case dependent on and an integral part of the first two questions and the functions they generate. The two media that are directly related to these questions and that usually perform the two resulting functions in the Bahraini context are the clubs and the press.

Upon examining the function of political communication as performed by the clubs and the press, it becomes obvious that a distinction must be drawn between the traditional role of communication as it relates to political development in other, more established and larger transitional societies and as it relates to the Gulf states, including Bahrain. Primarily because of the small size of Bahrain and the limited nature of the press as a medium of communication and because of the unstructured political function of the clubs, it seems logical to discuss both the clubs and the press jointly under the function of communication. Concerning the clubs, as in the case of

---

[a] It should be remembered that none of the functions, that is, the articulation, aggregation, and communication of interests, in Bahrain's political structure have developed beyond a personalized tribal form of authority.

[b] Professor Almond has established four input functions that he viewed as being common to all political systems: interest articulation; interest aggregation; political communication; recruitment and socialization. These four functions, which can be defined only through raising functional questions, cannot yet be clearly discerned in the Bahraini political system, but it is possible to detect certain salient features in the system that would indirectly render the use of the political system method of input, output, and feedback plausible. See Gabriel A. Almond and James S. Coleman, eds., *The Politics of the Developing Areas*, (Princeton, N.J., Princeton University Press, 1960), pp. 16-17. Page reference herein is made to the 1970 paperback edition.

olitical parties, the type of leadership, the method of selection, ...nal and professional level of the leadership, the general level of education of the membership, the type of social and cultural activity of the club, and the method that the club uses to communicate its views to the decision maker—all of these factors determine the clubs' contribution, individually and collectively, to political socialization.

By the same token, the influence and effectiveness of the communication function as performed by the Bahraini press, as in the case of other media of mass communication in larger societies, can only be assessed through a study of the size of the press, the background and political orientation of the editors, the material published, the frequency and circulation of the newspaper, and, most importantly, the restrictions placed on the media.[c] The communication process of the press in Bahrain is very limited if it is compared to the basic functions of this process in the developing countries that have already been established by students of the subject.

Professor Wilbur Schramm has maintained that communication performs at least six basic functions:[1] The first function is that communication contributes to the building of the psychological image of the nation. This function is primarily performed during the crisis of identity. Second, communication gives embodiment and shape to national planning, especially in disseminating basic information on planning. In turn, the press relays the popular response to national planning to the decision maker. The third basic function of communication is to foster necessary skills, which invariably means, especially in most developing countries, mastering the basic tools of literacy. The necessary technical skills usually follow. The fourth function of communication is to develop and expand an effective economic picture of the society, that is, business, trade, commerce, marketing, private enterprise, and industrialization. This function is primarily important to Bahrain's entrepôt economy. The fifth function is that communication contributes to the development of political socialization. In this case, communication performs a dual function: the selection and recruitment of potential leaders; and the assignment of societal roles to the people. In other words, the citizens of the newly independent country are socialized through communication into their new and developing political system. As a corollary to the previous point, the press performs the sixth function of socializing the people into the international political system. This means that the communication function in this case connects the roles played by the people in their own society to the role played by their state in world affairs.

---

[c] For an excellent analysis of this point see Professor Wilbur Schramm's study of communication and development in Lucian W. Pye, ed., *Communication and Political Development* (Princeton, N.J.: Princeton University Press, 1963), pp. 30-57. Page reference herein is made to the 1969 paperback edition.

Though limited in scope and effectiveness, the Bahraini press over the last half decade has contributed significantly, in Bahrain's proper perspective and within the limits of the six basic functions which Professor Schramm attributed to communication, to the process of political socialization. The articles and editorials, which have appeared in the press during the last five years, both prior to and since independence, have consistently addressed themselves to Bahrain's political existence (identity), its economic structure (distribution), and the citizens' political roles in the system (participation and integration).

In most societies, political parties constitute the medium that translates the issues developed through the political communication function into the input factors of supports and demands. In Bahrain, however, the clubs, as shown in the following section, have acted in this area, albeit on a limited basis, as a substitute for political parties.

The Clubs and Politics

In the absence of political parties, the clubs and societies, whose memberships include a majority of Bahrain's elite public, have played the essential functions performed by political parties in other political systems, that is, the articulation of interests and the recruitment of leaders. Although none of the clubs and societies was established for political reasons or to perform an explicit political function, they have all provided the milieu for the elite public to develop political opinions and to articulate them. The minister of information, Shaikh Muhammad bin Mubarak al-Khalifa, noted that the clubs have acted as gathering places for political opinions and as a place for their young men to gather. However, he believed that their role would diminish as the democratic experiment developed.[2]

In discussing the role of the clubs as a substitute for political parties, two significant points must be considered: The first is that whether or not the clubs function according to the traditional role of political parties in other political systems is irrelevant to our purposes. What is significant is that they have performed a political role and that both the ruling family and the elite public have perceived them as agents of political socialization.[d] The second consideration is that the phenomenon of clubs and societies is not unique to Bahrain; it is common to the rest of the region's modernizing

---

[d] In their discussion of political parties, Professors J. LaPalombara and M. Weiner identified certain criteria that would justify calling any association a political party: that the association have a continuous organization; that this organization have an interdependent pyramidal structure; that the primary goal of the organization's leadership is to possess power, not only to seek it; and that said organization would always strive to build a popular base through the democratic method. Joseph LaPalombara and Myron Weiner, eds., *Political Parties and Political Development* (Princeton, N.J.: Princeton University Press, 1966), p. 6. Page reference herein is made to the 1969 paperback edition.

tribal systems. Still a third point of consideration is that the clubs in Bahrain are not a new phenomenon, appearing on the horizon only after independence, nor is this phenomenon an attribute of modernization. That is, these clubs should not be viewed or studied as just a variant formation of political parties. They are not political parties; they are not organized political formations of any type. However, they do perform a political function, and hence they are directly related to political socialization.[e]

The relationship between political parties and political development has generally been viewed from a circular cause-effect perspective. That is, parties could be viewed as the culmination of a development process cutting across the entire society. On the other hand, as an organized power base—elite controlled and popularly supported—political parties definitely influence political development. Admittedly, this traditional role of political parties does not apply to the clubs in Bahrain; the clubs have been organically connected to political development only through their being a gathering place for the elite public. The social nature of the clubs has contributed to the spontaneity of political opinions—something that political parties are at times incapable of achieving due to their formalistic, heirarchical structure.[f]

As a final thought on the role of the clubs in Bahrain as compared to the role of traditional political parties in either developing or developed socieites, it should be emphasized that, structurally or formally, the clubs have not played a direct role in the resolution of the crises of nation building, especially those crises of identity, legitimacy, and integration. Yet, it is clear that the clubs have directly influenced the entire Bahraini polity. As an example, the clubs played an essential and sometimes crucial role in establishing the Arab nature of Bahrain and in convincing the United Nations' special envoy in March-April 1970 to recommend that Bahrain be granted independence. This is particularly important when one reviews Iran's persistent territorial demands for sovereignty over Bahrain during the previous half century.[3] Sir Charles Belgrave, advisor to the ruler of Bahrain between 1926 and 1957, wrote that the increase in the number of clubs and the intensification of their political role were directly related to the emerging political consciousness since World War II. As they were the places where the educated met, the clubs, though strictly nonpolitical, became in reality centers for things political.[4]

According to the 1971 *Statistical Abstract*, over 90 clubs and societies

---

[e] This discussion points to a major difference between the political systems that exist in what are generally accepted as Third World developing countries and the tribal political systems of the Gulf's Arab States. The theories, hypotheses, and assumptions established in standard research on comparative politics concerning the developing countries require substantial alterations if they are to be of any use as tools of analysis for tribal political systems.

[f] For an excellent examination of this functional relationship see LaPalombara and Weiner, *Parties and Political Development*, especially pp. 3-42 and 399-435.

exist in Bahrain whose functions cut across the entire social and cultural spectrum of the society. Table 3-1 indicates that a majority of the clubs are athletic and cultural, which simply means that most of the clubs have their own soccer teams[g] and that the prominent ones sponsor annual plays and panels on social and cultural questions. The clubs are scattered throughout the country in practically every town and village, but obviously the most active ones are those in the two major urban centers of Manama and Muharraq.

Table 3-1
Bahrain Clubs and Associations by Type, 1967-71

Type of Club	1967	1968	1969	1970	1971
Literary & cultural	13	13	15	16	18
Sports & cultural	61	65	68	63	69
Women's welfare societies	2	2	2	5[a]	5[a]
Music clubs	3	3	3	6	2
	79	83	88	90	94

Source: Taken from State of Bahrain, Ministry of Finance and National Economy *Statistical Abstract*, 1971 and 1972, and State of Bahrain, Ministry of Information, *Huna al-Bahrain*, December 1971, special issue.

[a]Includes Bahrain Red Crescent Society.

Of the 94 clubs and societies, only 4 are women's societies; 2 are mixed in membership. The rest of the clubs are for men only. The sampling of clubs and societies in table 3-2 shows that over one-third of the clubs are found in Manama and Muharraq. The women's societies are distributed in Manama (2), Muharraq (1), and Rifa'(1). The two mixed societies, that is, the Society of Writers and the Red Crescent Society, are located in Manama.

Legally, the clubs and societies are controlled by the 1959 Bahrain Licensing of Societies and Clubs Ordinance, which is administered by the

---

[g]Soccer is Bahrain's national sport, and the people's intense interest in this game is by all indications out of proportion to Bahrain's small size. To illustrate, one of the biggest athletic-social events of 1973, and the most expensive for soccer fans, was the game that Bahrain's National Team played against the renowned Santos of Brazil on 16 February 1973. Santos' victory (7-1) was not lamented by Bahrainis, for the country was intensely proud of the one goal that its team entered against Santos. The Santos visit and the sum ($27,000) that Bahrain had to guarantee the visiting team became a national controversy, especially when *Sada al-'Usbu'*, one of the country's two Arabic-language newspapers, called for a boycott of the game (*Sada al-'Usbu'*, 6 and 13 February 1973). The other newspaper supported the visit, although the result of the match was a foregone conclusion with Pele playing on the Santos team (*al-Adwa'*, 15 February 1973).

Table 3-2
A Sample of the Clubs and Societies in Bahrain

Men's Clubs	Location
Ahli Club	Manama
Alumni	Manama
'Arabi Club	Manama
'Asifa Club	Manama
Bahrain Club	Manama
Firdawsi Club	Manama
Islah Club	Manama
Ittifaq Club	Manama
Ittihad Club	Manama
Jaza'ir Club	Manama
Jufair Club	Jufair, Manama
Lulu Club	Manama
Na'im Club	Manama
Nil Club	Manama
Nusur Club	Manama
Qudabiyya Club	Manama
Shu'a Club	Manama
Shuruq Club	Manama
Taj Club	Manama
Tirsana Club	Manama
Umm al-Hasam Club	Manama
'Uruba Club	Manama
Watani Club	Manama
Wila' Club	Manama
Yarmuq Club	Manama
Yaqatha Club	Manama
Basatin Club	Muharraq
Dayr Club	Dayr, Muharraq
Hala Club	Muharraq
Jazira Club[a]	Muharraq
Jil Club	Muharraq
Khalij Club	Muharraq
Muharraq Cultural Club	Muharraq
Murrikh Club	Muharraq
Nahj Club	Muharraq
Nasr Club	Muharraq
Qalali Club	Qalali, Muharraq
Shat al-'Arab Club	Muharraq
Shu'lat al-Shabab Club	Muharraq
Ta'aruf Club	Muharraq
Taqaddum Club	Muharraq
East Rifa' Club	Rifa'
West Rifa' Club	Rifa'
'Ali Club	'Ali
Barbar Club	Barbar
Budaya' Club	Budaya'
Dayh Club	Dayh
Daraz Club	Daraz
Daraz Sa'iqa Club	Daraz
Dar Kulayb Club	Dar Kulayb
Hidaya Club	Samahij
Hidd Nahdha Club	Hidd
Intaj al-Rif Club	Jidhafs
Irshad Club	Bani Jamra

Men's Clubs	Location
'Isa Town Club	'Isa Town
Ittihad al-Rif Club	Shaharakkan
Jidhafs Club	Jidhafs
Karzakkan Club	Karzakkan
Khamis Club	Khamis
Ma'amir Club	Ma'amir
Malkiyya Club	Malkiyya
Nabi Salih Club	Jazira
Nuwaydrat Club	Nuwaydrat
Safa' Club	Dayh
Samahij Club	Samahij
Sanabis Club	Sanabis
Shabab al-Daraz Club	Daraz
Sitra Club	Sitra
Tubli Club	Tubli
Zallaq Club	Zallaq
Women's Societies[b]	
Jam'iyyat Awal al-Nisa'iyya	Muharraq
Jam'iyyat Nahdat Fatat al-Bahrain	Manama
Jam'iyyat al-Rifa' al-Nisa'iyya	Rifa'
Jam'iyyat Ri'ayat al-Tifl wa al-'Umuma	Manama
Mixed Societies	
Jam'iyyat al-Hilal al-Ahmar (Red Crescent Society)	Manama
'Usrat al-'Udaba' wa al-Kuttab fi al-Bahrain (Society of Writers)	Manama

Source: Based on United Nations Security Council Document S/9772, Annex, with modification by the author.

ᵃThese two clubs merged in March 1973 under the name of al-Hala Club. Like its predecessors, the Hala Club is located in Muharraq's Seventh Ward and is supported to a great extent by Jasim Murad, the Seventh Ward's representative to the Constitutional Assembly.

ᵇIn April 1973 a fifth women's society, Jam'iyyat Fatat al-Rif [Rural Women's Society], in the town of Jidhafs.

ministry of labor and social affairs.[h] The ordinance states that to form a society or a club written permission must be obtained from the Ministry of Labor and Social Affairs. Even after such a club or society has been established, activities such as showing a play or sponsoring a panel must receive prior approval from the Ministry. The following ordinance offers further details.

[h] On 20 February 1973 the Constitutional Assembly passed article 25 in the Draft Constitution, which deals with unions and societies. Article 25 states: "The freedom to form societies and unions, so long as they have a patriotic basis and aim at lawful goals and operate by peaceful means, shall be guaranteed according to the conditions specified by law; on one shall be coerced into joining a union or a society or into continuing his membership in said society or union."

*The Bahrain Licensing of Societies and Clubs
Ordinance–1959, Notice No. 5/1959*

Article 4. No person shall form, organize, manage, control or take part in the management or control of any society or club unless a permit in writing has been obtained from the Government for such society or club.

Article 5. An application for such a permit shall be made through the Secretary to the Government by sending or delivering to him in his office a statement in writing containing the following particulars:

a. the names, addresses and nationality of the promoters;
b. the name and address of the society or club;
c. the objectives and purposes of the society or club;
d. the name, address and nationality of the secretary to the society or club;
e. the name, address and nationality of the managing members;
f. the number and general description of the persons who have agreed to become members of the society or club;
g. the name, address and nationality of any other person who (whether because he has provided or is providing capital for the society or club or for any other reason) is financially interested in the success of the application, together with a statement of the nature and extent of his interest.

Article 10. The Government may grant or refuse to grant a permit under this Ordinance, or it may grant it subject to such conditions as it may think fit, which conditions shall be complied with.

Article 11. (i). The Government may withdraw, cancel or revoke any permit issued under this Ordinance. . . .

(ii). Any society or club whose permit has been withdrawn, cancelled or revoked shall be immediately dissolved.

*The Exhibition of Plays, Theatrical Shows and Musical
Performances Ordinance–1960*

Article 2. No society or club shall exhibit to the public any play, theatrical show or musical performance unless a permit in writing is first obtained from the Director [later minister of labor and social affairs] in respect of such play, theatrical show or musical performance.

Article 4. The Director may grant or refuse to grant a permit under this Ordinance, or may grant it subject to such conditions as he may deem fit, which conditions shall be complied with. He may also cancel, withdraw or suspend any such permit.

Article 5. The Director may attend or cause to be attended any rehearsal of a play, theatrical show or musical performance before issuing a permit in respect thereof. . . .

For the purposes of this study, a selected sample of clubs was analyzed:

The al-Khirrijin [Alumin] Club, Manama

The al-'Uruba [Arabism] Club, Manama

The al-'Arabi [Arab] Club, Manama

The al-Bahrain Club, Muharraq

The Intaj al-Rif [Rural] Club, Jidhafs

Three women's societies were also studied:

Jam'iyyat Ri'ayat al-Tifl wa al-'Umuma [Children and Mothers Welfare Society], Manama

Jam'iyyat Nahdat Fatat al-Bahrain [Bahrain Young Ladies Society], Manama

Jam'iyyat Awal al-Nisa'iyya [Awal Women's Society], Muharraq

One mixed society was included in this sample, namely, the 'Usrat al-'Udaba' wa al-Kuttab [Society of Writers], Manama.

These clubs and societies were interviewed using the following questionnaire format as a general guideline: [1]

A Sample Questionnaire

(Questions were asked in Arabic.)

1. Name:
2. Location:

---

[1] The questionnaire approach rarely produces satisfactory results for field researchers in the developing countries. However, it may be used to collect some basic and pertinent information.

3. Year of establishment:
4. Number of members:
5. Qualifications for membership (from the constitution):
6. Average age of members:
7. Average level of education of members:
8. Profession of majority of members:
9. Objectives of the club (from the constitution):
10. Community services provided by the club:
11. Major events sponsored by the club in the past year:
12. Club views on current issues:
13. Researcher's notes:

The main consideration governing the selection of this particular sample of clubs and societies is that each of them represents a specific line of thought, subscribes to a particular set of social concepts and expresses a certain background. To illustrate, the Alumni Club is the social bastion of the college-educated and the intelligentsia. Its past contributions to the formation of the Bahraini polity and its future role within the whole modernization process obviously reflect the concepts of the whole elitist class in Bahrain. The 'Uruba Club is one of the oldest and most established clubs in Bahrain. It is an establishment club and reflects the continuous and gradual process of social, cultural, and political modernization in the country within the last generation. Therefore, the 'Uruba Club is a true representative of such other well-established clubs as al-Ahli Club. The Bahrain Club of Muharraq has played a role similar to that of the 'Uruba Club in Manama.

By way of contrast, the 'Arabi Club is composed mostly of workers, and it stands for a definite ideology, which is partly political and partly economic. Rural clubs have their own problems too—usually economic. The Intaj al-Rif Club is the best representative of this group of clubs. The women's societies constitute the best barometer for measuring the social, cultural, and educational progress of women in Bahrain's conservative cultural and religious milieu. The individual comments on each of these societies help to deliniate that society's position on political issues, its perception of social issues, and its contribution in turn to society. Similar individual analysis follows each of the other clubs herein examined.

The Alumni Club (Manama) was founded in 1966 and currently enrolls 150 members. A bachelor's degree or its equivalent is required for membership,[5] and most members are in their thirties. They are mostly civil servants, which includes teachers and self-employed. The club's stated objectives are to provide a gathering place for Bahraini college graduates and to strengthen the cultural, social, and intellectual ties among them. Also, the club wishes to share in raising the intellectual, social, and health levels of the citizen through social services, lectures, and scientific and intellectual panels.[6] The club has primarily served its own members and has brought several prominent speakers to lecture on various subjects. It supported the country's move toward a written constitution and the establishment of the Constitutional Assembly to write the constitution. The club supported the move toward a democratic political life.

The Alumni Club is the club par excellence for the intelligentsia in the country. It is frequented by college graduates who are for the most part high-level civil servants in various ministries. It is these people who will set Bahrain on whatever future course is decided upon by the country's leadership. On the other hand, the Alumni Club has been criticized, often by its own members,[7] for its elitist attitude toward the rest of the society and for its failure to contribute to the development of Bahrain as a whole, especially during these formative years just preceding and since independence. Over the last two decades the Alumni Club paradoxically brought to Bahrain new liberal ideas, both social and political, and simultaneously produced men and women to staff Bahrain's basically conservative bureaucracy. Those members of the club who are the sons of the al-Khalifas or of large merchant families (Zayani, Kanoo, al-Mu'ayyad) have not produced any radical changes in the country—either in the governing of Bahrain or in its commercial life.

For the past two decades the club has been able to maintain its prestigious status mostly because of the limited number of college graduates—300 between 1950 and 1970, However, the number of graduates has risen in the last three years to over 50 per year, and the number is rising dramatically. Therefore, the role of the Alumni Club as an elitist institution is expected to diminish over the next few years for at least two reasons: The increase in the number of graduates and the new trend toward specialized professional societies. As a final point, graduates have traditionally found employment because of their small numbers, which meant that the club membership was economically satisfied. In the next 5-10 years, however, the economy—both public and private—will probably not be able to absorb the projected number of graduates, which will lead to unemployment of the intelligentsia. This phenomenon will create new political tensions and unrest.

al-'Uruba Club was founded in 1939 and is located in Manama. It has a membership of 250, and applicants for membership must be Arab, literate, of good character and reputation, and at least 18 years old.[8] Most members are in their thirties, have achieved a high school education, and are merchants and civil servants. The goals of the club are to spread the spirit of cooperation, to raise the level of social and nationalist consciousness, to guide minds along the path of Arab nationalism, to spread public education, and to participate in all areas of social reform.[9] The club has established a library and conducted and sponsored a number of literary panels, Arab-Islamic festivals, and adult education courses. As a charitable activity, the club also helps the aged and disabled. On the political side, the club advocated participation in the elections to the Constitutional Assembly, and on constitutional issues the club supported the inclusion of a bill of rights in the constitution, women's suffrage, labor unions, constitutional gvernment, and the right of the accused to be considered innocent until proven guilty.

This is the second oldest club in Bahrain, and its membership roster reads like a "Who's Who" of Bahraini merchants and civil servants. Ministers, professionals, and self-employed are also part of the list. Arab nationalism in its Bahraini context is the raison d'être of the club and continues to be the basis of the constitution. Also, like the other clubs, al-'Uruba has provided its members a forum where political ideas are brought together and debated. Several of the members ran in the election to the Constitutional Assembly from several districts. Although the majority of the membership is of the high school level, several members are college graduates and professionals who also hold membership in the Alumni Club. al-'Uruba Club is the most outstanding example of the unique role that the clubs play in Bahrain. Political ideas are discussed freely inside the club, and one can clearly see how the clubs function as substitutes for the political parties that do not exist in Bahrain.

al-'Arabi Club in Manama was founded in 1962 and has a total membership of around 250. To be eligible for membership a man must be at least 18 years old and a Bahraini citizen. Most of the members are comparatively young, in their twenties, and have a high school education. All of them are workers, and the goals of the club are to spread the ideas of Arab nationalism among its members, to unify the youth of the country, to raise their cultural and educational levels, and to serve society.[j] The club boasts a soccer team, which competes vigorously in interclub soccer matches, and it has also sponsored several political panels, somewhat along the lines of "meet-the-candidate" forums. The club strongly advocated a move toward democracy, although club members have not been entirely convinced of the effectiveness of the constitutional experiment.

The 'Arabi Club represents a definite political ideology, basically nationalistic and labor oriented. Most of its members are politically conscious workers who are primarily drawn from Manama's Hura district—"hotbed" of politics in the country. Like other clubs, the 'Arabi Club is enjoined by its constitution from engaging in political activities, but more than any other club, everything about the 'Arabi Club is political: the monthly wall newspaper, the issues discussed, and the activities of its

---

[j]The author was unable to obtain a copy of the club's constitution.

individual members. Most of the members are young and political; on occasions some of them have been detained under the Emergency Law for political reasons.

The 'Arabi Club is the best supportive example of the premise that clubs in Bahrain have acted as substitutes for political parties—albeit with some differences. The questions that club members raised during the several "meet-the-candidate" panels held at the club on the eve of the Constitutional Assembly election reflected two characteristics of the club: the members were not afraid to bring up sensitive political issues, and they showed a high level of political awareness.

In commenting on the country's move toward a constitutional government, members of the 'Arabi Club expressed several opinions. First, most members held a cynical attitude toward the Khalifa family's intentions to go domocratic. Second, most members believed that the country's government required a more radical systemic change than just an assembly and a constitution inspired and written from above. Third, they desired some recognition on the part of the ruling family of the need to grant individual freedoms and to stop the harassment of political dissidents. Fourth, club members wanted an unequivocal commitment on the part of the ruling family to the right of labor to unionize.

The Bahrain Club was founded in Muharraq in 1936 and has a total membership of about 350. An applicant for membership must be at least 18 years old, an Arabic-speaking person, and a citizen of Bahrain.[10] Most members are in their thirties and possess an elementary to high school education; most of them are workers, clerks, and merchants. As stated by their constitution, the goals of the club are to unify the people of the country, to spread culture among them, to promote athletics and sports among its members, and to develop a viable social and cultural program.[11] The club sponsors cultural and literary panels, art shows, soccer matches, and panels on topical social issues, for example, women's rights. The club supported the country's move toward a constitutional government, and it strongly endorsed women's suffrage and individual political rights.

The Bahrain Club is one of the oldest and most well-established clubs in Bahrain. It is situated in Muharraq, but its membership does include several people from Manama who are either from Manama originally or who moved there from Muharraq. For the last three years, the Bahrain Club has offered its premises as headquarters for the Awal Women's Society. Like other clubs in both Manama and Muharraq, the Bahrain Club provides a meeting place for its members to congregate and exchange views on political and social issues. In addition, the club signed the petition, which the women's societies presented to the government prior to the Constitutional Assembly election, supporting women's right to vote.

The Intaj al-Rif Club is the best representative of the clubs located in the villages of Bahrain. It is located in Jidhafs, and it was founded there in 1969. Its current membership numbers around 70; an applicant must possess good character and be at least 18 years old. Interestingly, the club offers a special membership for children. Most of the members have an elementary to high school education and are employed as workers. The club has no written constitution, but in an interview with the members they stated that the club's goals were to provide a meeting place for the members, to raise the level of sports, to improve the cultural level of the members, and to offer guidance to young people and children. The club sponsors soccer matches, trips to different parts of Bahrain, plays, and religious activities. The club supported the country's move toward democracy and strongly advocated granting the common man basic freedoms, such as the right to unionize.

The Intaj al-Rif Club is a typical small club of the countryside. It is a poor club by the standards used for the other clubs, and it receives no assistance from the government or from wealthy merchants. It is financed primarily by its membership dues and by donations from members on religious occasions. The club rents its headquarters in a small house on the outskirts of Jifhafs, a little town between Manama and Budaya' on the northern tip of Bahrain. Its members are workers, but they show sincere and unpretentious desires to improve the lot of the young people in their village and in the surrounding villages.

The members' cultural, social, and religious outlook is much different from that of urbane Manama—some 10 miles away. Members of the Intaj al-Rif Club are generally religious conservatives and belong to the Shi'a sect. In the Constitutional Assembly election held 1 December 1972, a majority of the members supported and, by their own admission, voted for a conservative religious Shi'a mulla against a more liberal college-educated candidate. The liberal graduate lost the election by a substantial margin. Several meetings were held at the club on the eve of that election to discuss the candidates and the issues, and a general political position was adopted. The problems that the club faces and the issues it raises are primarily rural; yet, because of the small size of the country the rural population includes a large percentage of workers who are manual laborers and a very small percentage who are agricultural workers.

Women's societies have played a different role from that of the men's clubs, whose activities have been primarily for the benefit of their membership. The women's societies have instead concentrated on helping the poor and the needy and on fighting illiteracy through charitable projects and adult education classes. These women's societies are not as widespread or as influential as the clubs, yet they too have had their part to play as gathering places for the wealthy and educated where the woman's role in Bahraini society can be freely discussed and debated.

Jam'iyyat Ri'ayat al-Tifl wa al-'Umuma [Children and Mothers Welfare Society] is the most prominent of the women's societies. It is located in Sulmaniyya Road in Manama, founded in 1960 and currently has a membership of around 120. An applicant for membership must be at least 18 years old, a Bahraini Arab, and of good reputation.[12] Most of the members are housewives in their thirties and forties, and most of them have a high school education. The goals of the society are to help the poor and the needy and to comfort those in distress.[13] Their most outstanding project is a very successful day care center established especially for the children of working mothers. Their charitable activities include money-raising bazaars, distribution of clothing during Ramadan, and visiting the villages during Health Week to demonstrate basic hygiene techniques. Also, the members visit the sick and the aged, and courses in English and basic Arabic are offered on the club premises.

The society supports the principle of women's suffrage and of the right of women to participate in the political life of the country. Its membership is drawn from the aristocratic class in the country, mainly the Khalifa family, influential business and merchant families, and very high level civil servants—mostly on the ministerial level or very close to it. The ladies of the society are energetically and sincerely committed to helping the poor.[k] The goals of the society were further detailed in a brief report, *Bayan Mujaz*, about the activities of the society. In this report the goals of the society were elaborated as follows:

1. To help the poor and the needy and to comfort those in distress
2. To raise the cultural and intellectual levels of Bahraini mothers so that they may successfully raise the new generation
3. To lead the able Bahraini women to implement the principle of social cooperation scientifically and to positively participate in the service of their country

As previously mentioned, the society runs a very successful day care center for the children of working mothers, and several of the 185 pupils, 3 to 6 years of age, are kept free of charge. In addition to their other activities, the society regularly gives financial support on a monthly basis to 18 poor families; the funds come from members' contributions and bazaars. Politically the society is composed of ladies who are the direct beneficiaries of the status quo. They are wives, daughters, sisters, or cousins of cabinet members and various other government officials. Therefore, the society's commitment to political issues, such as women's rights, is understandably moderate, albeit sincere. The society tends to be more understanding than other women's societies of the government's position—even in depriving

---

[k] For example, the proceeds from their yearly bazaar and fashion show are donated to poor families.

the women of their right to vote in the election to the Constitutional Assembly.

Jam'iyyat Nahdat Fatat al-Bahrain [The Bahrain Young Ladies Society] is another active society in the community. It is the oldest women's society in the country and indeed in the Arabian Gulf region. It was founded in Manama in 1955 and currently enrolls 75 members. To be a member a woman must be at least 18 years old, literate, nonpolitical, of good character, and willing to participate in the activities of the society.[14] Most members are in their thirties, have an elementary or secondary education, and are housewives or civil servants. The goals of the society are to elevate the social and educational status of women, to fight illiteracy by conducting adult education classes, to help the poor and the needy, to serve the country and to advance its name in social areas, and to create cooperation, compassion, and honesty among individuals and groups.[15] To accomplish its goals, the society sponsors bazaars, plays, folk dances, serious cultural panels, lectures, and concerts. The society actively supports women's right to participate in the political life of the country, and the group had argued strongly against disenfranchising the women in the election to the Constitutional Assembly.

The Bahrain Young Ladies Society is composed of women from well-established merchant families (al-Mu'ayyad, Zayani, etc.). Members are strongly committed to the basic goal of the society—the fight against illiteracy. The society conducts regular adult education classes for women on the society's premises. The society has participated in several national celebrations and has visited the Gulf countries and advised them on organizing women's societies. The society has sponsored several panels, concerts, and lectures, and it has contributed to various charities.

The society occupies a median position between the other two societies in social status, and it strongly supported women's rights and the right of Bahraini women to participate in the political life of the country. The society rejected the government's arguments for disenfranchising women in the Constitutional Assembly elections; the society collaborated with Awal Women's Society and the Rifa' Women's Society in petitioning the Ministry of Labor and Social Affairs for a permit to collect signatures and present a petition to the Council of Ministers supporting women's rights (See chapter 8). The society also canvassed the candidates for the Constitutional Assembly election and asked their support for women's suffrage. Some members of the society campaigned unofficially for or against certain candidates in the light of their position on women's suffrage.

The third women's society incorporated into this study is Jam'iyyat Awal al-Nisa'iyya [Awal Women's Society]. This society is located in Muharraq and was founded in 1969. The 50 members are young, unmarried women, mostly in their twenties. They have a high school or university education, and the great majority of them are teachers. Their stated goals are to perform charitable works, to cement the ties of cooperation among Bahraini women, to raise the social and cultural level of Bahraini women, to train the members to assume an administrative and organizational role within the society, and to create awareness of and raise the status of women in rural areas.[16] An applicant for membership must be at least 18 years of age and a Bahraini citizen.[17]

The society conducts classes in basic Arabic for adult women on a regular basis, and they frequently sponsor plays and panels on social questions. They have supported women's rights, especially the right to vote, and the general move toward democracy; they have also expressed concern over the rising cost of living in the country. The Awal Society comes very close to the Western concept of a women's liberation group. It is composed of young, educated, energetic, socially conscious women who are not daughters of the Khalifas, high civil servants, or wealthy merchants. They are committed to the work of their society and especially to elevating the position of women. They are actively dedicated to the principle that the Bahraini woman can and must share in the building of Bahrain side by side with the Bahraini man and that therefore woman should have the same rights and responsibilities as the men.

In common with the other women's societies, the Awal Society has deplored the fact that women were denied the right to vote in the election to the Constitutional Assembly. The Awal Society joined with the other women's societies in presenting a petition to the government demanding that women be given the right to participate in the political life of the country. Like other clubs and societies, Jam'iyyat Awal al-Nisa'iyya provides a forum for its members to debate and formulate political opinions, which, although on a limited basis, acts as a political input. This is especially true in the absence of organized political parties.

'Usrat al-'Udaba' wa al-Kuttab fi al-Bahrain [Society of Writers in Bahrain] is a different kind of society, and yet the literary activities of its members have provided a direct link to politics. It is located in Manama and was founded in 1969. Its 27 members are mostly poets and writers of short stories. To be eligible for membership, a candidate must be a Bahraini citizen, and he or she must have had some literary output or a serious interest in literature; the applicant must also be at least 18 years old.[18] Most members are in their twenties, have a high school education and are employed as civil servants, primarily in the public library, the radio station, the Ministry of Information, and in teaching.[1] The goals of the club are to raise the level of the literary and intellectual movement in Bahrain, to

---

[1] The public library falls under the jurisdiction of the Ministry of Education, as does the entire public school system; the radio station falls under the Ministry of Information, as does the monthly magazine *al-Bahrain al-Yom* [Bahrain Today] and its entire staff.

support and sponsor literary creativity, to foster close relations with the literati in the Arab world, to encourage research in Arabic culture and heritage both in Bahrain and outside of it, and to represent Bahrain in literary conferences locally and internationally. To achieve its goals the society sponsors periodic panels in poetry, the arts, and related topics. Also, the society has maintained international contacts with literary societies in Arab and Afro-Asian regions, and for the past three years it has been a member of and attended the annual conference of the Arab Writers' Union and the Afro-Asian Writers' Union. On the political level, the Writers' Society endorsed the general turn toward democracy, and it strongly urged that the new constitution include such points as a bill of rights, labor unions, women's suffrage, a constitutional government, and "innocent until proven guilty."

The society's 24 men and 3 women are the most significant literature-producing cadre in Bahrain; many of them have published collections of either poetry or short stories. The society itself has produced a collection of short stories; 9 members contributed to *Sirat al-Ju' wa al-Samt* [The Story of Hunger and Silence] published in Beirut in 1971. The society does not interfere in political matters,[19] but it is nonetheless political and is viewed as such by the authorities. It is the only society whose license is renewed annually, and the society's request for a permit to publish a literary journal has been refused. Several of its members have been arrested and interrogated for alleged political acitivities; these detentions and interrogations have been carried out by the Special Branch of the Public Security Department under the State of Emergency Law. The political nature of this society may stem from its poetry and short stories, which describe the common man's frustrations in trying to earn his daily bread. Like other societies and clubs, the members of the Writers' Society are sensitive to the shortcomings of their environment, particularly social injustice, colonial remnants, and tribal rule. It is this bias in their writings that makes the Writers' Society political.

In the light of the above, several concluding remarks may be made on the nature, present function, and future direction of the clubs in Bahrain. First, in order to exist and operate the clubs must be licensed by the government. They also must obtain a government permit for every activity sponsored by the club. Over 90 clubs and societies exist in the country, 1 in practically every neighborhood. By law these clubs are not political organizations, yet all of them provide a meeting place for the men and women of the community, and thus collectively of the country, who are actively concerned about such social issues as illiteracy, education, health, athletics, and literary activities. Together, the membership of the clubs and societies constitutes the elite public—that stratum of the population which is attentive to policy issues and to the factors that influence the formulation of these issues and the execution of policy related to these issues. Most clubs and societies are enjoined by their own constitutions from interfering in political affairs and political organizations. Yet, in contributing to the process of nation building, these clubs and societies cannot convincingly claim to have assumed an apolitical position. The ubiquity of politics in Bahrain is nowhere more consciously felt than inside the walled buildings that house these clubs.

Interestingly, club membership is not noticeably divided along class or social status lines, with the possible exception of the women's societies. A club may count among its members ministers, teachers, merchants, and workers. This cross section of the community, or the public policy-oriented segment thereof, renders the club an efficient marketplace of ideas, opinions, and news. A club usually perceives two functions: service to its members and service to the community. To its members a club usually offers a reading room with books, magazines, and newspapers, a recreation room, and a large meeting room. Also, they frequently have either an athletic team or a theatrical group. For the community the club sponsors cultural events, shows, panels, art shows, concerts, and lectures.

In their unofficial, albeit recognized, political role the clubs reached their peak of influence in the fifties and sixties. In these two decades, Bahrain experienced a series of political activities that were primarily of a confrontation nature, usually between popular movements and the authorities. The confrontations of 1954-56 ultimately forced the ruler, at that time the late Shaikh Sulman bin Hamad al-Khalifa, to dismiss his British advisor, Sir Charles Belgrave. This coupled with the political developments of 1956 throughout the Arab world and particularly in the Gulf, greatly enhanced the sociopolitical role of the clubs.

In the coming few years one can foresee a decline in the traditional role of the clubs in Bahrain's sociopolitical sphere for two reasons: There is a new tendency, especially among the college educated, to form professional societies, such as an Engineering Society established in August 1972 and a Medical Society and an Accountants' Society formed in March 1973. It is true, however, that this development will have the most direct impact on the Alumni Club; nonetheless it is symptomatic of future trends. Also, the election to the Constitutional Assembly and the discussion of the constitution have started a serious debate over two constitutional issues: labor unions and political parties. If the democratization process will allow, constitutionally or extraconstitutionally, the development of labor unions and political parties, the clubs will definitely lose their traditional role as the only meeting place for the politically aware and the socially conscious members of the community. In order to survive as viable and relevant entities for the future, the clubs must rid themselves of their traditional image of being a reading room for the members. Commented a younger club member, "Nowadays newspapers and magazines may be purchased everywhere; a member need not go to the club just to read the newspaper." Moreover, any tendency toward popular participation in the governing process inevitably fosters new political loyalties and political conflicts that transcend traditional club loyalties. Any democratic trend in form or substance will put in motion new supports and demands, which will require different social formations than those that functioned in an era when the system of government was static and no change was tolerated.[m]

The Press and Political Socialization

The press in Bahrain, at least in its present form, is a recent phenomenon, limited in circulation, staff, and coverage. Its contribution to political socialization has been limited by such factors as a high illiteracy rate, a narrow readership, and close government supervision. According to Professor Daniel Lerner's model of communications theory,[n] six factors should be considered by social researchers if they wish to assess the impact of the news media, especially the press, on political socialization in the developing countries. The first three factors define the capacity to produce information: the physical plant in which the news is produced, the equipment, and the professional personnel. In other words, Professor Lerner's main contention in citing these points is that the mass communication revolution is primarily technological-managerial. However, these particular points of the model are not especially applicable to Bahrain because this communications revolution has not yet occurred in Bahrain and will not occur in the foreseeable future.

Therefore, it is more advantageous to study the press and political socialization in Bahrain in the light of Professor Lerner's other three factors, which are related to the consumption rather than the production of news. These three factors are the availability of cash, the level of literacy, and the degree of motivation. Put differently, one should look into whether the potential reader can afford the newspaper, whether he can read it, and whether he wants to read it.[o] These three factors act to restrict severely the consumption of news via the press in Bahrain.

The cash factor is crucial, since in 1972-73 the price per issue of a Bahraini newspaper was 100 fils (BD0.100 = US$0.26, approximately), which was also the price of a one-pound loaf of the so-called foreign bread

---
[m] See *al-Nahar* (Beirut), June 1970, pp. 48-49, a special issue on Bahrain, for further analysis.

[n] Pye, *Communication and Political Development*, pp. 336-342. Professor Lerner's article, pp. 327-350, should be studied in its entirety.

[o] Ibid., p. 339. The study of political socialization in this chapter concentrated on the role of *privately owned* media.

or 10 loaves of the local bread (about two pounds) made of second-grade flour.[p] In addition, the relatively low level of wages of the majority of the people have acted with the steadily rising prices—practically all consumer goods, including such staples as flour, rice, sugar, oil, and milk, are imported—to put an additional demand on the availability of cash. To illustrate, at a special press conference held on 3 March 1973 to deal with rising prices, the deputy minister of finance and national economy stated that in its study of personal expenditure in Bahrain, the Ministry discovered that people with monthly incomes between 30 and 250 Bahraini dinars (BD1 = US$2.60) spend 51 percent of their income on food and 17 percent on housing. The remainder of the family budget (32 percent) covered all other items.[q] When one realizes that the legal minimum wage is BD0.900 per day and that the national average monthly salary is BD65, the cost of newspapers per month becomes considerable, especially in the low-income group (30-60 dinars per month).

Table 3-3 shows that the sum of cash left after the two major allocations for food and housing are deducted is very limited. Add to that the fact that most of the workers in the low-income brackets have to use public transportation (a monthly sum of BD1-2) to commute to work, and the strain becomes even more severe.

Table 3-3
Distribution of Personal Income for Major Items by Income Levels

Monthly Income	Food (51% of Budget)	Housing (17% of Budget)	All Other Items (32% of Budget)
BD 25.000	BD 12.750	BD 4.250	BD 8.000
30.000	15.300	5.100	9.600
40.000	20.400	6.800	12.800
50.000	25.500	8.500	16.000
60.000	30.600	10.200	19.200
70.000	35.700	11.900	22.400
80.000	40.800	13.600	25.600

Note: This table was constructed by the author to illustrate the variation in spending on different levels of income based upon the percentages of spending obtained from the Ministry of Finance and National Economy. 1 BD (Bahraini Dinar) = $2.60.

---

[p]In February 1973 the government of Bahrain fixed the price of local bread, made of second-grade flour, at BD0.010 per loaf with the condition that the standard 4-pound weight unit did not make more than 21 loaves. State of Bahrain, *Official Gazette*, 1 February 1973, p. 5.

[q]The deputy minister of finance and national economy gave the following breakdown: groceries 51%; housing 17%; clothing 6.8%; furniture 6.5%; transportation 5.3%; household goods 4.7%; cigarettes and refreshments 3.8%; miscellaneous expenses (telephone, hairdresser, domestic help, medicines and medical care, glasses) 4.9%. For a full report of this press conference see *Akhbar al-Bahrain*, 5 March 1973, pp. 4-5.

As for the second factor inhibiting widespread news consumption via the newspapers, the illiteracy rate, several facts ought to be considered with regard to the demographic structure of the general Bahraini population and of the illiterate population in particular. Demographically, the population of Bahrain is primarily composed of young people. According to the 1971 population census, the total population is 216,078 of which 178,193, or 82.5 percent, are Bahraini citizens (see table 3-4). Of this last total, 58,756, or 33 percent, are under ten years of age. Of the remaining 119,437 Bahraini citizens ten years of age and over, 63,179, or 53 percent, are illiterate[r] (see table 3-5).

Table 3-4
Population by Five-Year Age Groups and Sex (Bahraini Only)

Age Groups (Years)	Males	Females	Total
Under 1	2,752	2,604	5,356
1-4	11,108	11,291	22,399
5-9	15,487	15,514	31,001
10-14	13,911	13,679	27,590
15-19	9,990	9,849	19,839
20-24	6,408	5,846	12,254
25-29	4,846	5,344	10,190
30-34	4,158	4,348	8,506
35-39	4,462	4,792	9,254
40-44	3,489	3,620	7,109
45-49	3,551	3,088	6,639
50-54	3,263	2,680	5,943
55-59	1,770	1,383	3,153
60-64	1,919	1,662	3,581
65-69	941	793	1,734
70-74	878	910	1,788
75 & over	839	1,018	1,857
Total	89,772	88,421	178,193

Source: Based on State of Bahrain, Ministry of Finance and National Economy, *Statistics of the Population Census*, 1971, p. XIII.

When the total population of Bahrain is considered, the above percentages do not show any appreciable difference. For our purposes, the age groups 10-14 and 15-19 could be excluded from this discussion because the press plays only a minimal and indirect role in the inculcation of political ideas about the system and the polity in these age groups. The school, the

---
[r] The 1971 *Statistics of the Population Census* defines literacy "as the ability both to read and to write. A person is literate who can, with understanding, both read and write a short simple statement on his everyday life" (p. III).

family, and peer groups play a much more basic role in political socialization at this age level, which for the most part consists of both elementary and high school age children. If these age groups in question (47,429) are deducted from the total number of Bahraini citizens 10 years of age and over (119,437), we are left with 72,008, of which 51,313, or 71 percent, are illiterate. Although this percentage of illiteracy measures favorably with many other developing countries, it is amply clear that large numbers of Bahrainis cannot read the printed word.

Table 3-5
Illiterate Population Ten Years of Age and Over by Age and Sex (Bahraini Only)

Age Groups (Years)	Males	Females	Total
10-14	2,249	4,862	7,111
15-19	849	3,906	4,755
20-24	945	3,452	4,397
25-29	1,560	4,159	5,719
30-34	2,058	3,792	5,850
35-44	5,349	7,887	13,236
45-54	5,399	5,616	11,015
55-64	3,123	2,993	6,116
65 & over	2,282	2,698	4,980
Total	23,814	39,365	63,179

Source: Based on State of Bahrain, Ministry of Finance and National Economy, *Statistics of the Population Census*, 1971, p. 68.

Concerning the third factor determining the consumption of media news, motivation, the preceding discussion of the cash and literacy factors definitely reveals that the limited availability of cash and the low literacy rate are directly related to motivation. Whenever a literate worker must decide as to whether he should spend his 100 fils[s] on a newspaper or a few loaves of bread, the choice becomes a foregone conclusion. In this category of wage earners, it takes a highly motivated person to spend his limited cash on newspapers. For this purpose, a highly motivated person can be defined as one who is literate and who shows a definite inclination toward reading. Because of the strong hold that the spoken word has over the Arab person, even a highly motivated person must often make a serious effort to rely on a source, in this case the newspaper, other than the radio.

Another factor limiting the consumption of news via the press is the fact that the two Bahraini newspapers under discussion are weeklies; they are oriented toward analytical articles, investigative reports, and editorials

---
[s] 1 Bahraini dinar (BD) = 1,000 fils.

rather than news per se. These two weeklies are neither able to nor attempt to publish all the news. By being weeklies and not dailies, the local newspapers have not enabled or encouraged the Bahraini reader to form a daily habit of reading. Also, the analytical orientation of these weeklies presupposes a higher understanding quotient on the part of the reader, which means a higher level of motivation, than if he were to read a straightforward daily news journal.

With the above limitations (cash, literacy, motivation) in mind, the only two privately owned, Arabic-language weeklies with political coverage, *al-Adwa'* and *Sada al-'Usbu'*, have still played a central role in political communication, especially as it related to political development.[t] The process of nation building, in particular the search for identity, relies heavily on the communication function to provide the basic supports of the political system. The press in Bahrain is an integral part of this communications process, although it has strong competition from such oral means of communication as broadcasting.[u]

It must be pointed out, however, that the standard studies of communication processes in other developing and developed societies appear to be inadequate when applied to such traditional, yet modernizing political systems as the Gulf states. The approach common to these standard studies is basically sound, but it does require methodological modification. To illustrate, Professor Lucian W. Pye assigns several functions to the communication process:

1. It sheds light on the entire spectrum of social processes.
2. It contributes to the understanding of political behavior.
3. It provides a forum for individuals to develop a societywide dimension for their actions.
4. It injects mass politics with a measure of rationality, especially when the new society is emotionally engaged in establishing its political identity.
5. Through rationally debating the issues, the process of communication also provides the political system with a sense of pragmatism—a method of sifting the plausible from the implausible.[20]

The following two statements underscore the difference between the

---

[t]The function of political communication performed by the press was noticeably intensified after the Constitutional Assembly began its deliberations on the draft constitution in late December 1972. The two weeklies published extensive, often verbatim reports on the sessions plus editorials on issues related to the Assembly. Both weeklies reported an increase in circulation after they began to publish the constitutional debates.

[u]Radio Bahrain has been excluded from this study because as a part of the Ministry of Information it is not a privately owned medium of communication. Also, it is very limited in its programming, hours of broadcasting, and staff. Personal interview with Ibrahim Kanoo, manager of Radio Bahrain, and Ahmad Sulayman, director of programming, on 30 October 1972.

academic, theoretical concept of the communications function in developing societies, such as the preceding model by Professor Pye, and the practioner's view of the role of the press and the real problems that any newspaper might face in a particular developing society, particularly during the search for legitimacy immediately following independence. The academic view of the communications process is that it structures the political process by reminding politicians that political acts have consequences and by warning practitioners that no one is omnipotent.[21]

From the journalist's point of view, the press as an agent of political socialization in modernizing societies is often subjected to legal, primarily administrative, restrictions, which often inhibit the press from becoming an effective participant in the process of political development. In a statement on the floor of the Constitutional Assembly, 'Ali Sayyar, Assembly member and owner-editor of *Sada al-'Usbu'*, addressed himself to the role of the press in a developing society. He noted that the press in Bahrain could not perform its function fully because of the restrictions imposed by the government. The 1965 Press Law gave the government the power to suspend publication, and he maintained that this power violated the most elemental right to freedom of the press.[22] At the same session, Sayyar suggested a constitutional amendment to forbid administratively ordered stoppages and to place such a procedure under the administration of the courts. The deputy-speaker of the Assembly, 'Abd al-'Aziz Shamlan, described the press as a mirror that reflected the people's wishes, that spoke for them, and that directed the decision maker into the right path.[23]

In replying to these comments, the former minister of information, Shaikh Muhammad bin Mubarak al-Khalifa, Assembly member ex officio, simply pointed out that no freedom was without limits and that such advanced countries as the United States and the United Kingdom had enacted laws restricting their press.[24]

Bahrain has had a relatively strong tradition of journalism in the last two decades, especially in comparison to other Gulf states. However, this tradition was in fact intermittent due to the numerous interruptions to which the newspapers were subjected as a result of governmental restrictions and orders, particularly during the mid 1950s. The first of these weeklies appearing in this period was *Jaridat al-Bahrain* [The Bahrain Newspaper], which was published during the World War II years. *Jaridat al-Bahrain* began publication in 1939 and ceased appearing in 1944. Financial, political, and administrative reasons led to the newspaper's eventual demise.

The politically active journalistic tradition in Bahrain developed and ended in the first half of the fifties. It was obviously short-lived, but it left a definite mark on the political life of the country. The first of these politically oriented newspapers was a monthly called *Sawt al-Bahrain* [Voice of

Bahrain], which was printed in Beirut, Lebanon. It began as a literary journal, but it later assumed a definite political posture. *Sawt al-Bahrain* published articles, literary reviews, and critiques by the leading literati of Bahrain; such prominent poets as 'Ibrahim al-'Urayyid and such teachers as Hasan al-Jishshi contributed regularly to it.[v] When *Sawt al-Bahrain* first appeared in 1952, it proudly carried in its first issue a statement of support and encouragement by the ruler of Bahrain, then Shaikh Sulman bin Hamed al-Khalifa, but early in 1955 it was ordered by the government to cease publication.

al-Qafila [The Caravan] was a political weekly that was also being published in Bahrain at this time. It began publication in 1953 under the editorship of 'Ali Sayyar and Mahmud al-Mardi, presently the owners and editors-in-chief of *Sada al-'Usbu'* and *al-Adwa'* respectively, *al-Qafila* began as a political weekly, and from the beginning it took a sympathetic attitude toward the nationalist forces in the country, especially the Committee of National Union. Such a position understandably angered the Khalifa family, the ruler's advisor, the late Sir Charles Belgrave, and the British Agency.

Not surprisingly, in late 1955 *al-Qafila* was ordered to halt publication, but shortly thereafter it was given permission to reappear on three conditions: (1) that it appear under a new name; (2) that the new version should not carry the names of the editors and owners, in particular that of 'Ali Sayyar; and (3) that its material be subject to censorship prior to publication. Later in that year (1955), *al-Qafila* actually did reappear under the new name of *al-Watan* [The Homeland]. The newspaper was able to continue for about a year, but in late 1956 it was ordered by the government to cease publication.[w]

Also, in late 1956 another newspaper was started by Mahmud al-Mardi under the name of *al-Shu'la* [The Torch]. Only one issue ever came out, and then like the others it was ordered to close. *al-Mizan* [The Scales] was only a little more fortunate. Owned by 'Abdalla al-Wazzan, *al-Mizan* came out weekly and adopted a moderate political position on public issues. It was oriented more toward news coverage than news analysis; it appeared early in 1954, but like all other Bahraini publications, it was ordered to close in late 1956.

To complete this historical synopsis of the Bahraini press in the fifties, a

---

[v] al-'Urayyid was later elected speaker of the Constitutional Assembly. al-Jishshi has since 1972 been employed by Aluminum Bahrain as the director of public relations. On 7 December 1973 al-Jishshi was elected to Bahrain's first National Assembly, and during the Assembly's first meeting on 16 December 1973, he was elected speaker.

[w] It is interesting to note that the editors of *al-Watan* offered one page in their publication to the editors of *Sawt al-Bahrain*, which was closed early in 1955, to continue the tradition, albeit on a limited basis, of *Sawt al-Bahrain*. However, with the closing of *al-Watan* this, too, came to an end.

mention must be made of one other weekly, *The Gulf*, an English-language newspaper that appeared in mid 1956. *The Gulf* was an affiliate of *Iraq Times*, which supported the Hashimite monarchy then in power. However, as a reaction to British participation in the Anglo-French invasion of Egypt in October-November 1956 and as a protest against its support of the pro-Western regime in Iraq, *The Gulf* offices were attacked in early 1957 by Bahraini demonstrators. Shortly thereafter, *The Gulf* closed, and with its closing the independent press in Bahrain ended, not to reappear until almost a decade later.

Although the political press in the fifties was short-lived, the press played an important role in that tumultuous decade of modern Bahrain. Several factors can be singled out as contributing to the widespread influence of the press in that period: One factor was that the newspapers were widely read.[x] These newspapers commanded a wide readership because they addressed themselves to the major issues of the society, that is, the British presence in the country, governmental reform, the demand for unions and the improvement of labor conditions, and the insistent demand for individual freedoms. In other words, the press reflected the major concerns of the people; it was a definite medium through which the general public expressed its position on national issues. Moreover the press offered a collective presence of the community's demand and desires; consequently the average politically aware person bought the newspaper and read it.

Another factor entering into this unity of interest between the producers of news (the press) and the consumers of news (the reading public) was the general Arab political situation in the Middle East, especially the rise of Arab nationalism under the leadership of Jamal 'Abd al-Nasir of Egypt. Between 1953, when the 1952 Egyptian revolution began to assume an Arab character transcending the borders of Egypt, and 1956, the year in which Nasir nationalized the Suez Canal administration and the Anglo-French forces invaded Egypt, the tide of Arab nationalism surged to its height, and the Bahraini press and a majority of the Bahraini people responded exultantly, as did most peoples throughout the entire region. In Bahrain, as in most Arab countries that were not yet independent, the call for independence became loud and insistent.

The British forces were always present on the island, and they used their naval base at Jufair, just outside Manama, as a springboard for military activities in the region, especially during the Suez war. In addition, the British advisor, Sir Charles Belgrave, was an influential figure. These two facts led the Bahraini public and press alike to clammor for the

---

[x]*al-Qafila*, for example, had a circulation of 4,000 to 5,000 per week—more than the 1972 circulation of either *Sada al-'Usbu'* or *al-Adwa'*.

eradication of Britain's presence and the elimination of the advisor's grip on the country.[y]

In the 1954-56 period the Committee for National Union was established in Bahrain, which was the first such political formation in the country. The committee became more vocal, the strikes more massive, the issues more polarized, and the political situation more tense; Belgrave's security forces struck with ruthlessness. By late 1956 the Bahraini press was closed, and three of the committee's leading figures were exiled to St. Helena.[z] This ended the first chapter in the history of Bahrain's independent press. It was not until 1965 that a new press law was enacted and the first political, privately owned newspaper of the 1960s, *al-Adwa'*, was published.

Since 1965 the dailies, weeklies, and monthlies read in Bahrain may be grouped into three categories: Bahraini privately owned publications; Bahraini government-owned publications; and non-Bahraini publications read regularly in Bahrain. The first category embraces both the political press and the social or nonpolitical press. Table 3-6 indicates that of the five privately owned newspapers and magazines, four are weeklies and one is monthly; also one monthly, *al-Haya al-Tijariyya*, and one weekly, *al-Mujtama' al-Jadid*, are nonpolitical. The *Gulf Weekly Mirror*, the only English-language newspaper, is owned by 12 leading merchants in Bahrain and is basically Gulf oriented. *al-Adwa'* and *Sada al-'Usbu'* are the only two privately owned political publications that have serious relevance to political socialization in Bahrain.[aa]

Like most developing countries, Bahrain has a Ministry of Information, which publishes two weeklies and one monthly. Obviously *al-Jarida al-Rasmiyya* [Official Gazette] is the most important of the Ministry's publications, and the monthly *al-Bahrain al-Yom* [Bahrain Today] is the only monthly of its kind in Bahrain. *al-Bahrain al-Yom* publishes critiques and literary and cultural articles; moreover, it has met a definite need in the country's cultural life. However, it is definitely not a political publication. (See table 3-7.)

---

[y] For a clear picture of conditions in Bahrain during this period see 'Abd al-Rahman al-Bakir, *Min al-Bahrain ila al-Manfa* [From Bahrain to Exile] (Beirut, Lebanon: Maktabat al-Haya, 1965); and Charles Belgrave, *Personal Column*, 2nd ed. (Beirut, Lebanon: Librarie du Liban, 1972).

[z] The three were 'Abd al-Rahman al-Bakir, 'Abd al-'Ali al-'Alaywat, and 'Abd al-'Aziz Shamlan. The three were later released on the order of a British court in St. Helena in 1961. Although the first two died in exile, Shamlan returned to Bahrain early in 1972. Sir Charles Belgrave's services in Bahrain were terminated, and he left Bahrain early in 1957.

[aa] In October 1969 Mahmud al-Mardi, editor-in-chief of the weekly *al-Adwa'*, started a new four-page daily called *Adwa' al-Khalij* [Gulf Lights], which concerned itself primarily with international politics and only secondarily with Bahraini issues. However, the newspaper constantly operated with a deficit, which led to its demise seven months later. In 1974 a new weekly, *al-Mawaqif*, began publication. However, because of its limited circulation and the conservative, Shi'a religious orientation of its editor and owner, the new weekly has so far failed to compete with the generally liberal Sunni press.

Table 3-6
Bahraini Privately Owned Newspapers/Magazines

Newspaper/ Magazine	Founded	Frequency	Circulation	Full-time Staff	Editorial Position
al-Adwa' [Lights]	1965	weekly	3,500	6	Independent, moderate
Sada al-'Usbu' [Echo of the Week]	1969	weekly	3,500	6	Independent, moderate
The Gulf Weekly Mirror (English)[a]	1971	weekly	3,300[b]	6	Supports Gulf governments
al-Mujtama' al-Jadid [New Society]	1969	weekly	3,000	5	Nonpolitical (social, cultural)
al-Haya al-Tijariyya [Commerce Review]	1962	monthly	2,500	5	Chamber of Commerce

[a]Owned by 12 merchants in Bahrain.
[b]Total circulation throughout the Gulf is 4,100.

Table 3-7
Bahraini Government-owned Newspapers/Magazines

Newspaper/ Magazine	Founded	Frequency	Circulation	Full-time Staff	Editorial Remarks
al-Jarida al-Rasmiyya [Official Gazette]	1946	weekly	450	2	By subscription
al-Bahrain al-Yom[a] [Bahrain Today]	1972	monthly	5,000	4	Literary & cultural; by subscription
Akhbar al-Bahrain [Bahrain News]	1972	weekly	4,000	2	Government news releases; no charge

[a]Prior to 1972, this publication was issued under the name *Huna al-Bahrain* [Bahrain Calling].

It is essential that the third category, non-Bahraini publications, be included in this brief survey of the press because, as a small country, Bahrain is interested in and reacts to developments in other Arab countries with more than usual concern. Bahrain cannot possibly produce communications media in the foreseeable future that would be able to compete with the newspapers and magazines published in Cairo, Beirut, and Kuwait. Moreover, by reading the major Arab press, the Bahraini elite public keeps abreast of events and trends throughout the region. Table 3-8 indicates that *al-Nahar* of Beirut is the most widely read daily (circulation 200), followed by *al-Siyasa* of Kuwait (circulation 100) and *al-Ahram* of Cairo (circulation 80). *al-Hawadith* of Beirut, which had recently moved into a leading position in comparison with other weeklies throughout the Arab world, is also the most widely read non-Bahraini political weekly in Bahrain (700 issues per week). *al-'Arabi* of Kuwait is a social-cultural publication.

For the purposes of this study of the role of the press in political socialization, only the Bahraini privately owned, political press is of interest. More specifically, *al-Adwa'* and *Sada al-'Usbu'* are the only two publications to which this study is applicable. The laws and regulations governing the press and the conditions under which both *al-Adwa'* and *Sada al-'Usbu'* have operated determine to a large extent the effectiveness of this news medium in contributing to the building of the political identity of the country. The editors of both publications agreed that the implementation, or threat of implementation, of the administrative restrictions against the two newspapers have definitely limited the communication function of the press.

The press law under which the press operates was promulgated in 1965,[bb] and since that time it has been in effect without revision. Consider the following articles excerpted from the 1965 Press Law:

Article 6(a). No newspaper shall be published until after a written license has been obtained from the Director of Information.[cc]

Article 9(1). Whenever a license for publication is granted, the owner of the newspaper must deposit the following amount in the banks:
a) 2,000 rupees [dd] if the newspaper is monthly;
b) 4,000 rupees if the newspaper is bi-weekly;
c) 6,000 rupees if the newspaper is weekly;
d) 8,000 rupees if the newspaper is to be published more than once a week.

Article 9(2). A bank guarantee may substitute for the actual cash deposit.

Article 14.[ee] The press shall not publish the following:
1) Criticism of the Ruler of the country or his family and statements attributed to him without permission from his office;

[bb] "The Law of Printed and Published Material—1965," State of Bahrain, *Official Gazette*, 29 July 1965, pp. 6-7. On 2 February 1973 the Constitutional Assembly approved article 24 of the constitution, which reads: "The freedom of the press, printing and publishing is guaranteed according to the conditions stipulated by law." Constitutional Assembly, *Minutes*, 16th session, 2 February 1973.

[cc] Later minister of information.

[dd] 1 Bahraini dinar = 10 rupees. Bahrain used the Indian rupee as currency until 1965, when the Bahraini dinar was introduced as the unit of currency.

[ee] It is this article that has been invoked when the government has warned a newspaper, suspended it, or brought legal action against it.

Table 3-8
Non-Bahraini Newspapers/Magazines Read Regularly in Bahrain

Newspaper/ Magazine	Country of Origin	Frequency	Circulation (Bahrain)	Editorial Position
al-Siyasa [Politics]	Kuwait	Daily	100	Independent
al-Nahar [The Day]	Lebanon	Daily	200	Independent
al-Ahram [The Pyramids]	Egypt	Daily	80	Semiofficial
al-Hawadith [Events]	Lebanon	Weekly	700	Independent; pro-Dubai in the Gulf
al-'Usbu' al-'Arabi [The Arab Week]	Lebanon	Weekly	150	Independent
al-'Uruba [Arabism]	Qatar	Weekly	100	Cult-oriented; independent
al-'Arabi [The Arab]	Kuwait	Weekly	1,500	Social, cultural
Shu'un Falastiniyya [Palestine Affairs]	Lebanon	Quarterly	40	Scholarly journal on the Palestine case

Note: The author is indebted to Faysal 'Alaywat, proprietor of the Arab Agencies and Distribution Company.

2) The confidential minutes of the meetings of governmental councils and the confidential official communications;

3) Treaties and agreements concluded by the government of Bahrain prior to their publication in the *Official Gazette*, unless specifically permitted by the Director of Information;

4) The minutes of closed court sessions and trials relating to divorce, separation and children;

5) News items which might harm the value of domestic currency or create confusion in the economic situation of the country;

6) Criticism of foreign heads of state or whatever statements which might harm the relations between Bahrain and other Arab and friendly countries;

7) Statements contrary to public morality or the dignity of individuals or to their personal freedoms, which include the revelation of a secret harmful to that individual's reputation, livelihood or credit, or threat of blackmail;

8) Statements which would incite to riot and to criminal actions or which would spread hate and divisiveness in society;

9) False accusations of civil servants, unless the writer shows through

good intentions that he was reasonably certain of the truth of these accusations and that the publication of said accusations was intended to serve the public interest;
10) Statements which advocate the overthrow of the government by force, the spread of communism or which insult or belittle religion.

Article 15. If any newspaper publishes any of the items stated in the previous Article, both the editor of the paper and the writer of the article will, if found to have committed a crime, be punished according to the penal code of Bahrain. Otherwise, each of the two will, upon a first offense conviction, be imprisoned for no more than six months and/or fined 1,000 rupees. Further convictions will each result in a prison sentence of no more than 1 year and/or a find of 2,000 rupees. In any of these cases the court may revoke the license of the newspaper in question or order it to cease publication for whatever period the court deems necessary and order the confiscation and destruction of the original copy.

Article 16. The Director of Information, upon obtaining a court order, may halt the distribution of a newspaper if in his opinion it includes an article which violates Article 14 until the case is decided upon in court. . . .

Article 18. The Director of Information may stop the newspaper or revoke its license for a period not to exceed 1 year, if it has been verified that said newspaper serves the interests of a foreign country contrary to the national interest.

Article 20(1). In order to protect public order and morality and the sacredness of religion, the Director of Information may, with the approval of the Secretary of the Government, ban the circulation of foreign publications in the country.

Article 22(2). The editor of the newspaper shall publish in his newspaper the statements and official announcements sent to him by the Director of Information or the Secretary of the Government.

Article 24. This law shall not apply to official government newspapers and publications, and the Secretary of the Government may exempt any other newspaper from all or a part of the provisions of this law.

Both *al-Adwa'* and *Sada al-'Usbu'* have on several occasions been warned by the Ministry of Information under the 1965 Press Law concerning articles they had published. In the last two years, *al-Adwa'* was warned several times that court action might be taken against it. *Sada al-'Usbu'* also received several warnings and was actually ordered to halt publication twice. In the fall of 1971 *Sada al-'Usbu'* was stopped for the first time for a two-week period by an administrative order because of an article that the government alleged insulted some religious practices (Press Law, article 14, section 10).

The stoppage of *Sada al-'Usbu'* for almost two months in the fall of 1972 became a cause célèbre for the freedom of the press as regulated by the 1965 Press Law. Citing this case serves a two-fold purpose. It sheds some light on the process of decision making in the country, in the words of Harold Lasswell who gets what, when, how, and it illustrates the restrictive conditions under which the press has operated. What magnifies the impact of these restrictions is the fact that the 1965 Press Law lends itself easily to interpretations inspired by political considerations that are separate from the legality of a case under this law. Put differently, the press must constantly face a host of political considerations (both domestic and foreign) of which the Bahraini government takes cognizance whenever a political article is published. The following case illustrates this point clearly.

On 12 September 1972 *Sada al-'Usbu'* published a column attacking King Husayn of Jordan for his stand against the Palestine resistance movement.[ff] The column did not mention Husayn's name, but the columnist's intentions were apparent.[gg] The Bahraini government considered this attack on the head of a friendly state as a violation of the 1965 Press Law and halted publication of the newspaper.

The article had dealt in a very sensitive area and government officials acknowledged that the government's subsequent decisions were based on political considerations. Several factors influenced the government's swift reaction to the column: Bahrain's heir apparent, Shaikh Hamad bin 'Isa al-Khalifa, minister of defense and commander-in-chief of the Bahraini Defense Force, had just returned from a private visit to Jordan, and he has continued to remain on very friendly terms with Jordan's crown prince. Also, several high-ranking Jordanian military officers have been seconded to Bahrain as trainers and advisers for Bahrain's defense forces.[hh] Finally, the Bahraini government was, by all available accounts, out to "get" both 'Ali Sayyar, the editor-in-chief of *Sada al-'Usbu'*, and 'Aqil Swar, the author of the column in question.

In commenting on this case, the public prosecutor stated that the government did not intend to curtail the freedom of the press in that

---

[ff] *Sada al-'Usbu'*, 12 September 1972, p. 8. For information on this case the author drew on personal interviews with the editor-in-chief of *Sada al-'Usbu'*, newspaper articles and the court records of the trial. The first of these personal interviews began on 21 September 1972.

[gg] King Husayn's name was stated in the columnist's rough draft, which was confiscated from the newspaper offices and introduced in trial as evidence.

[hh] For example, the head of Bahrain's Criminal Investigation Department (CID) is a Jordanian national.

particular case nor did it intend to harrass *Sada al-'Usbu'*. Rather, the government was interested in seeing that the laws of the land were obeyed. The government felt that the article in question would have, if no action had been taken, harmed the relations between Bahrain and Jordan.[ii] Moreover, the timing of the article was offensive in that the heir apparent had just returned from Jordan and that he and Jordan's crown price were on very good terms.[25] The director of information, Shaikh 'Isa bin Muhammad al-Khalifa, also felt that *Sada al-'Usbu'* had been warned previously and that the article did include a threat to King Husayn; he stated that in this article the newspaper had not heeded its journalistic responsibilities.[26]

The time sequence of the case's development is of interest to researchers because it gives some insight into the method of decision making within the Khalifa family. The article appeared on Tuesday, 12 September 1972, and at its regular meeting on the following day, the Council of Ministers discussed the article and decided to move against *Sada al-'Usbu'*. On Wednesday, 16 September 1972, the prime minister, Shaikh Kahlifa bin 'Isa al-Khalifa, officially requested the acting minister of information to halt the publication of the newspaper in question. Following is a translation of this letter: [jj]

Prime Minister
14 September 1972

His Excellency the Acting Minister of Information

Greetings,

The column "In Passing" which appeared in the last issue of *Sada al-'Usbu'* (12/9/1972) and which was signed by Badriyya Fu'ad[kk] is unacceptable to me and to the Ministers, since said column contained insult and attack on the head of an Arab state which will harm the friendly relations between Bahrain and the Hashimite Kingdom of Jordan.

The Cabinet has discussed this subject and has decided that this column constitutes a clear violation of Article 14, Section 6 of the 1965 Press Law. Therefore, in accordance with Article 16 of said law, we suggest that measures be taken to stop the publication of this newspaper, after obtaining permission from the Minister of Justice, until we have the opportunity to take other necessary legal measures.

Sincerely,
Prime Minister

Since the Acting Minister of Information, Shaikh Muhammad bin Mubarak, was out of the country at the time, the Director of Information, Shaikh 'Isa bin Muhammad al-Khalifa, acted upon receiving the Prime

---

[ii] In fact, the Jordanian ambassador in Bahrain did protest the article to the Bahrain government.

[jj] The original Arabic version of this letter was obtained from the trial folder of *Sada al-'Usbu'*.

[kk] A pseudonym used by 'Aqil Swar.

Minister's letter. Two days later, he sent a letter to the editor-in-chief of *Sada al-'Usbu'* ordering him to cease publication. Following is a translation of this letter. [ll]

16/9/1972

Editor-in-Chief
Sada al-'Usbu'
Greetings,

In its issue No. 149 of 12/9/1972, *Sada al-'Usbu'* published a column entitled "In Passing" by Badriyya Fu'ad. I consider the publication of this article a clear violation of Article 14, Section 6 of the 1965 Press Law. Therefore, based on Article 16 of said law and upon the approval of the Minister of Justice, I hereby order your newspaper to halt publication immediately until further notice.

        Sincerely,
        'Isa Muhammad al-Khalifa
        for the Acting Minister
        of Information

That same week the editor-in-chief of *Sada al-'Usbu'* and the author of the column "In Passing" were ordered to appear at the public prosecutor's office for depositions. They were released on bail awaiting trial.

The trial of *Sada al-'Usbu'* was begun on 21 October 1972, postponed to 1 November, and repostponed to 5 November, 1972.[mm] The court convicted both 'Ali Sayyar and 'Aqil Swar, levied a fine of BD50 each and ordered the newspaper to halt publication retroactively for the period originally ordered by the Ministry of Information. *Sada al-'Usbu'* reappeared on 14 November 1972, two months after the celebrated issue of 12 September.[nn]

In the light of the preceding analysis of the role of political groupings (in Bahrain's case, the clubs) and the press in modernizing societies, it is clear that the organic link between the press and political socialization reflects the press' essential contribution to democratic government. By introducing the reading public into the political system of the developing society, the press actually sets in motion the process of leadership selection—the cornerstone of participatory government and political democracy.

What is paradoxical here is that in their modernization programs most developing societies have established political democracy as their ultimate goal; yet, they have concurrently imposed such restrictions on their press that the evolution of popular participation is hampered. The explanation for

---

[ll] The original Arabic version of this letter was obtained from the trial folder of *Sada al-'Usbu'*.

[mm] See reports on this trial in *al-Adwa'*, 26 October and 2 November 1972.

[nn] Upon reading the record of this trial, one might inquire about two points: First, the 1965 Press Law applies only to material actually printed, published, and distributed; yet, the court accepted as admissible evidence the rough draft of the column. Second, one of the prosecution's chief witnesses was a Jordanian national, an officer in the Bahraini police force.

this apparent paradox can only be that the postindependence regimes in the developing societies view democracy and popular participation as a part of the prerogatives of the regimes—to be granted, expanded, or withheld from above—and not as being part of the basic rights of the people. In Bahrain itself, even after the country declared its independence, the press continued to operate under restrictions. Government officials have maintained that freedom of the press exists in Bahrain, so long as the press is constructive. Obviously destructive criticism cannot be tolerated. In this regard the fate of the press in Bahrain is not different from its fate in other developing societies.

Moreover, the preceding analysis of the availability of cash, the level of literacy of the Bahraini citizen and the type of press presently available would indicate a need for a daily, privately owned political newspaper. A place for such a publication definitely exists; however, to succeed and to avoid the fate of previous abortive attempts at daily journalism, such a newspaper should be moderately priced,°° well-managed and sufficiently staffed. It should feature issues from and about Bahrain, since it is through this orientation that the readers' level of motivation would be increased.

As a final thought, modernizing societies should realize that the freedom of the press is an essential ingredient in the process of democratization, thereby providing the country's new citizenry with the opportunity to share in the making of laws and the responsibility of voluntarily complying with them. The history of man has taught us that if the law is not understood or if the citizen does not resort to it for the preservation of order, the propensity for compliance will deteriorate, and lawlessness will surely follow. Good law is the medium through which the ruler communicates with the citizens, thereby translating his authority into abiding decisions, and the press is the medium through which the people identify with and develop their membership in the political community.

°°National income statistics for the next few years indicate that 25 fils (6½¢) would be a reasonable price for a daily newspaper.

4 Labor and Political Development

Background Notes

Labor is the one constant underpinning of politics in modern Bahrain. Since the 1930s, when a labor class began to develop due to the discovery of oil, most political crises in the country have been centered on, rooted in, and caused by the Bahraini workers' determination to unionize. In order to display a national image of calm and serenity to the outside world, the authorities have muffled labor's demands, including frequent arrests of labor leaders. The Bahraini government has apparently believed that a society free from labor troubles is the greatest inducement to international Western business.

Labor unions have been viewed as a negative force whose long-range objective was to dismantle the Khalifa regime, and therefore such a force has not been tolerated. The failure of the authorities to adopt a flexible attitude toward labor and their inability to realize that unions can contribute to economic development, national vigor, and societal harmony have forced laborers to politicize their demands. As a result, every labor strike has been considered a "crisis," and the government's response has usually been suppression.

However, the history of labor in the nineteenth and twentieth centuries, especially in the industrial Western democracies, has taught us that labor unions are viable contributors to national development, that they are essential for the growth of an open society, that they have generally acted as a stimulant within the economy, and that they can be a strong component of stability in society. This same history has also taught us that suppression is never a satisfactory solution for the ailments of the human condition. In the United States for example, labor organization in the nineteenth century contributed to rapid development, which in turn helped the economy reach the takeoff stage. Economic growth of the industrial countries in this century has been definitely accelerated by the expanding demand of the mass society—an outgrowth of the unions' pressure for higher wages.[1]

Professor Irving Louis Horowitz maintains that industrial unionism has, in contemporary American society, come to protect the interests of the bourgeoisie class, that increased productivity has been spurred by spiraling labor costs, and that unions have been fundamental in transforming the worker's status.[2] In sum, the entire developmental process in industrial democracies could not have occurred had it not been for labor unions. Recognizing the labor unions' contribution to national stability and economic development and recognizing the dictum that a dissatisfied labor is symptomatic of socioeconomic disequilibrium, Western democracies have, in this century, generally adopted a pro-labor attitude, as contrasted with their strong pro-business posture of the nineteenth century.

Bahrain has had a long labor tradition—the first and perhaps the most sophisticated in the Gulf. In the last 30 years labor has been an integral part of the country's economic and political development. Prior to independence in 1971 many factors contributed to the development and direction of Bahrain's labor tradition: the structure of government, the country's special relationship with Great Britain, the presence of a powerful British Advisor, and, most importantly, the type of employment available in Bahrain.

As an outgrowth of Bahrain's specific economic conditions and society, labor has, like the rest of Bahraini society, generally displayed an attitude of pragmatism. The economic and political demands of labor over the years have been aimed at specific goals, usually higher wages, better working conditions, and the right to unionize. Unlike the situation in many other countries, labor in Bahrain has not been ideologically oriented nor has it been influenced by any particular political doctrines. To illustrate, at no time has labor advocated the complete overthrow of the tribal system of government; in the fifties however, labor did call for the removal of the British advisor to the Government of Bahrain and for more popular participation in government. And, of course, labor has persistently demanded the right to unionize. It can be convincingly argued that the politicization of labor in Bahrain was primarily caused by the repressive response of the authorities to labor demands and by the fact that Bahrain was a protectorate, not a fully independent state.

In order to examine the intricate relationship of labor to the Bahraini polity an attempt is made to present a brief historical survey of labor strikes in the country and an overview of the laws that have so far governed labor organization. The government's efforts concerning the Bahrainization of labor also constitute an essential part of this analysis.

Historical Overview

Although several strikes have occurred in Bahrain during the past 40 years, the most active period spanned a two-year period, 1954-56. The series of strikes, which took place during those two years, especially in December 1954, together with the strikes of March 1965 and March 1972, constitute the major episodes in Bahraini labor's attempts to organize. These episodes also indicate the government's often harsh reaction to these strikes and the response pattern that the authorities have developed toward labor.

The industrial labor movement in Bahrain began in 1932 with the discovery of oil. Prior to that period, Bahrain had two primary sources of employment: the pearling industry and agriculture. A commercial center throughout the centuries, Bahrain had developed a class of individualistic, enterpreneurial merchants who roamed the high seas in their dhows searching for trade.[a] The worldwide economic depression of the 1930s hit Bahrain hard, and it was coupled with the flood of Japanese cultured pearls into world markets. Fortunately, oil was discovered, and the establishment of the Bahrain Petroleum Company (BAPCO) began the tradition of industrial labor in Bahrain. BAPCO in fact remains the biggest employer in the country. However, the limited crude oil resources and the gradual industrial development produced two very different results; on the positive side, the small crude oil discovery forced Bahraini authorities to develop more gradually, and perhaps more rationally, than similar countries with much larger oil reserves. In addition, the timing of the first oil discovery (1932) and the first marketing of oil two years later greatly helped Bahrain ride out the Great Depression. On the negative side, the limited oil production could not keep pace with the rising expectations of the new industrial labor class. To add insult to injury, the oil company did not procure its labor through direct employment but through a labor contractor, who invariably took a substantial fee from the workers' paychecks for the employment-related services he provided for them. Another negative factor was that the ruler's new oil revenues, like other national revenue, were not public; annual state budgets were not published until years later.[3]

The first labor strike in Bahrain, indeed in the entire Gulf, occurred in 1938, and it focused on two demands: a pay raise and better working conditions. It is interesting to note that prior to 1938 most of the local workers at BAPCO were Bahrainis. However, as a result of this strike, BAPCO began to employ Indian and Iranian workers extensively. Company officials reasoned that since these workers were not directly concerned with the country's political life, they would be more loyal and docile than Bahraini workers. Also, this type of non-Bahraini worker has usually accepted lower wages than his Bahraini counterpart.[b]

There is no doubt that the most active phase of political activity in the modern history of Bahrain occurred in the mid-fifties, in particular between

---

[a] Bahrain's centuries-old commercial tradition has been discussed in several archeological studies. An excellent example is Geoffrey Bibby, *Looking for Dilmun* (New York: Knopf, 1970).

[b] For a brief history of labor strikes in Bahrain see *al-Tali'a* (Kuwait), 29 April 1972, pp. 22-23. For a pro-government view see *Personal Column*, 2nd ed., (Beirut, Lebanon: Librairie du Liban, 1972). For a pro-labor view see 'Abd al-Rahman al-Bakir, *Min al-Bahrain ila al-Manfa* [From Bahrain to Exile], (Beirut, Lebanon: Maktabat al-Haya, 1965).

the fall of 1954 and the fall of 1956. In these two years Bahrain witnessed organized mass meetings, with workers demanding popular participation in government and recognition of the right to unionize. The nationalist fervor, which swept Bahrain in this period, was the same tide of nationalism then sweeping through the Arab world and the rest of the Third World, formerly colonized areas in Asia and Africa.

Although political developments during those very critical years technically fall outside the scope of this chapter, one should mention that the success of popular organization, at the time embodied in the Committee of National Union (CNU, first known as the Higher Executive Committee), was primarily the result of labor's support. The concessions, which the CNU won from the authorities, especially in the area of labor, became a landmark in the modern history of Bahrain. In practically every statement and memorandum issued by the CNU, labor demands were preeminent, in particular the right to unionize. During its short existence (13 October 1954-6 November 1956) the CNU was able to fulfill several objectives: obtain recognition from the ruler of the country, negotiate with the British political agent as the country's sole popular organization and therefore the de facto spokesman for the people of Bahrain, and force the government of Bahrain to appoint a tripartite committee representing government, management and workers to prepare a draft labor ordinance.

This popular political organization, which came into being during an open meeting held in Sanabis (to the west of Manama) on 13 October 1954, consisted of 120 members. The committee elected an eight-member Executive Council to govern the organization; among the most prominent members of the Executive Council were 'Abd al Rahman al-Bakir (secretary-general), 'Abd al-'Aziz Shamlan, and 'Abd al-'Ali 'Alaywat.[4] In April 1956 the Higher Executive Committee changed its name to the Committee of National Union. On 6 November 1956 the three leaders of the committe, al-Bakir, Shamlan, and 'Alaywat were arrested and tried for alleged sedition before a court in Budaya', a village on the northwestern coast of the island. According to what was later revealed as a predetermined verdict, the three leaders were convicted, and on 28 December 1956 they were exiled to St. Helena. The committee was ordered to disband and a state of emergency was declared.[5]

However, the persistent demands of the CNU led the Bahraini government in April of 1955 to form a tripartite Law Ordinance Advisory Committee to discuss and recommend a draft labor ordinance for the country. [c]The committee consisted of nine members. The three representing the govern-

---
[c]One of the factors that forced the government to hasten in forming the nine-member committee was that in 1954 the CNU established its own labor union without a prior permit and called it the Labor Union of Bahrain. Within three months approximately 14,000 workers had joined this union. Like the CNU itself, this union was short-lived. 'Abd al-Rahman al-Bakir, *Min al-Bahrain ila al-Manfa*, pp. 103-108.

ment were Shaikh 'Ali bin Muhammad al-Khalifa (chairman), Shaikh 'Ali bin Ahmad al-Khalifa, and G.W.R. Smith. The three representing industry were Muhammad Kanoo, Sulman Uchi, and L.A. Smith of BAPCO. The members representing the workers were Mahmud Ahmad al-'Alawi for the government workers, 'Ali Husayn on behalf of BAPCO workers, and Muhammad Qasim al-Shirawi on behalf of workers at large. The committee was assisted in its deliberations by C. Marshall, the British government labor advisor who was on official leave to Bahrain. The committee held 57 meetings between April 1955 and late July 1956 and submitted a final report, including a draft labor ordinance, on 30 September 1956.[d] A new labor ordinance was enacted on 12 November 1957, and it became effective on 1 January 1958.[6]

The state of emergency imposed on the country in 1956 produced relative quiet for a few short years; however, it was a deceptively calm facade. On 9 March 1965 a major strike erupted at BAPCO and soon developed into a national popular uprising. The BAPCO strike proved to be only the lull before the storm. The strikers were soon joined by students, and the entire country came to a halt. The strikers' demands included the following:

1. To stop the unjust dismissal of workers
2. To reinstate the workers dismissed since 1961
3. To recognize labor's right to unionize
4. To lift the state of emergency that had been imposed on the country since 1956
5. To recognize the freedoms of press, assembly and speech
6. To release political prisoners
7. To allow exiles to return
8. To halt police harrassment of the people
9. To rid the company of British and other expatriate employees[7]

The 1965 uprising was suppressed within three months. Workers were forced to return to work; strikers and other political leaders were arrested and either sent to Jidda Island or exiled without formal charges or trial. Although a State of Emergency Law was again imposed on the country, the government began to respond to some of these demands, albeit cautiously. The Press Law was promulgated, and the first major Arabic language weekly, *al-Adwa'*, was granted a permit to publish. Nineteen sixty-five seems to have been the opening salvo in a fresh round of labor strikes and demands. Approximately 400 electricity workers struck in early 1968 and

---
[d]The minutes of the committee meetings give an insight into the content and style of the discussions that took place at those meetings. For the final recommendations of the committee see a letter from the committee chairman to Charles Belgrave dated 30 September 1956.

demanded that they be permitted to form a labor union. Other demands included cost of living pay adjustments, better safety precautions, and free transportation to and from work.[8]

Several scattered labor strikes also occurred throughout 1970. Gulf Aviation workers struck in May, Health Department workers struck in June, Cable and Wireless workers and the Public Works Department workers also struck in June, and ALBA workers struck in November. The demands put forth in all of these strikes could be summarized in the following:

1. The right to unionize
2. A cost of living pay adjustment
3. Better working conditions (work hours, safety regulations, and work uniforms)
4. Transportation
5. More supervision of labor contractors

In practically all of these strikes the Ministry of Labor and Social Affairs met strike representatives, and invariably certain improvements in working conditions were introduced. However, the Ministry still remained silent on labor's basic demand—the right to unionize.

On 23 August 1971 a seven-member group of labor representatives, called *al-Hay'a al-Ta'sisiyya* [The Founding Committee] carried a petition signed by approximately 1,500 workers to the Ministry of Labor and Social Affairs asking that they be permitted to unionize in accordance with part III of the 1957 Labor Ordinance. They were told by the former minister of labor and social affairs that part III was inoperative.[e] Part III of the Labor Ordinance simply states that "each trade union shall comprise not less than twenty members"[9] and "shall apply for registration in accordance with the provisions of this Part of this Ordinance within two months of the date of its formation or of the date of coming into force of this Ordinance, whichever is the later."[10] The ordinance also states that "application for registration may be made by any five or more members of the trade union subscribing their names to the rules of the trade union. . . ."[11]

What is interesting here is the fact that since 1957 at least 14 sections or parts of sections of the Labor Ordinance have been amended, but not part III. Neither the definition[f] of a trade union nor the possibility of the

---

[e]*al-Tali'a*, 29 April 1972, pp. 22-23. Also personal interviews were conducted with some members of the committee.

[f]Part I, section 3 (p) of the Labor Ordinance defines a trade union as being "any combination of employed persons the principal purpose of which is under its constitution the regulation of the relations between employers and employed persons . . . and which is created by the employed persons to protect themselves at their work, to improve the conditions of their work through collective bargaining, and to raise their standard of living."

existence of trade unions was ever amended or deleted. Available information shows that the Ministry of Labor and Social Affairs has never submitted any legal explanation to support its position on the "inoperativeness" of part III of the Labor Ordinance. It is instructive to note that such a position has only been communicated orally.

The government's distrust of labor unions and the authorities' reaction to workers' demands for unionism were evidenced throughout 1971 and 1972 by several arrests of workers and others under the guise of public security.[g] The tension between labor and government exploded in the second week of March 1972 when a series of strikes rocked the country and practically brought the island's commercial life to a halt.[h]

The first strike began in a Gulf Aviation (now Gulf Air) hanger on Wednesday, March 8; the Sulmaniyya Hospital workers struck on Saturday, March 11; the port (Mina Sulman) industrial workers also struck on the same day; and ALBA workers struck on Sunday, March 12. On Monday and Tuesday, March 13 and 14, the strikers clashed with police, and several strike leaders were arrested. By the evening of March 14 the strikers, encouraged by the newly appointed ministerial committee and the government's promise to study their demands, ended their strike. The March 1972 labor strikes were basically an expression of the frustrations that have built up over the years within the working class of Bahrain. The failure of the government to help create an effective labor-management machinery to handle labor's demands and the government's paternalistic attitude toward the workers' stubborn desire to unionize gave rise to two damaging conditions: the 1957 Labor Ordinance was, for all practical purposes, frozen, and the absence of any effective machinery made every labor strike, no matter how limited, a crisis situation.

The demands raised during the March 1972 strikes and the government's response are very instructive in that they both indicate, contrary to the official view, that the real issue was the right to unionize. To believe, as some ministers did at the time, that the issue of unionism was a political tactic inspired from outside the country and used by strike leaders to broaden their support among the rank and file, was a poor reading of the history of labor in Bahrain. Besides, taken in the context of the 1957 Labor Ordinance, outdated as it was, such a demand could not have been more legal. The other demands dealing with pay raises, transportation, uniforms, and better working conditions expressed a real situation, and in most cases cooperation between government and management led to improvements in the working conditions. The other serious demand, which the workers

---
[g] For a report on some of these arrests see *al-Tali'a*, 17 July 1971; 24 July 1971; 31 July 1971; 7 August 1971; and 11 September 1971.

[h] For a chronology of the strikes of March 8-14 see *al-Adwa'*, 16 March 1972, and *Sada al-'Usbu'*, 14 March 1972, 21 March 1972, and 2 May 1972.

voiced, was the improvement of safety precautions at Aluminum Bahrain.[1]

The government responded to the March strikes by appointing a special committee composed of the minister of justice, the minister of municipalities and agriculture, and the minister of labor and social affairs to negotiate with labor representatives as to the proper procedures to handle the strikers' demands.[12] At the same time the government banned all assemblies or demonstrations and authorized the police to safeguard citizens in their movement to and from their places of employment.[13]

A statement issued by B.U. Fisher, resident manager, ALBA, on 17 March 1972 declared that ALBA was advised by the three-member ministerial committee not to take any action on the workers' demands on the grounds that the labor representatives who presented the demands were not true representatives of the ALBA workers.[14]

The ministerial committee held 16 meetings between 15 and 22 April 1972, all of which were attended by representatives from labor and management. On the issue of labor unions, the ministerial committee promised the workers that the forthcoming constitution would grant them the right to unionize; therefore, the committee asked the laborers to shelve the issue of unionization until the constitution could be written. The minister of justice stated that since the country was embarking on a new constitutional life, there was no need for any immediate new labor laws or unions. He added that Bahrain was small and could not withstand the tensions that unions and political parties would create in addition to a parliament. In his view, a representative form of government would be an adequate substitute for unions.

The minister of labor and social affairs, also a member of the ministerial committee, stated that the government's policy was against labor unions. He also advocated a three-step graduated policy toward unions:

1. Discussion groups (consultative committees) should be elected from among the workers under the supervision of the Ministry of Labor and Social Affairs. These groups would carry the workers' complaints to the management. Negotiations between the discussion groups and the management would be carried out under the auspices of the Ministry of Labor and Social Affairs.

2. In case of disagreement on an issue, an arbitration committee would be formed, also under the auspices of the Ministry of Labor and Social Affairs, to review the disputed issues. The structure of these arbitration committees was not spelled out.

---

[1]The absence of proper safety precautions has been one of the major deficiencies at ALBA. An inspection team from the parent Kaiser company visited ALBA early in 1973 and was appalled by safety conditions at the smelter. The team recommended that safety should be urgently improved and considered a priority issue. The team's confidential report inferred that the poor safety conditions at ALBA would never be tolerated in any Western industrial country with the most elemental safety inspection laws. Accordingly the ALBA management immediately began to strengthen its accident units, and a new program of safety awareness and safety measures was introduced.

3. If disagreement continued, the issue would be taken to the court, whose verdict on the matter would be final.[15]

It is apparent that these discussion groups, which have so far functioned only at ALBA and BAPCO, have a very limited effectiveness. They are paternalistic, and they have shied away from thorny crucial issues such as trade unions. A look at the minutes of the discussion group's monthly meetings at ALBA clearly indicated the superficiality of this system. The tension within the laboring class was still prevalent well into 1973, and the insistence of several members of the Constitutional Assembly on including an article on labor unions in the draft constitution was a further indication that the discussion groups were viewed mostly as a delaying tactic, which neither workers nor officials believed could really work.

Article 25 of the draft constitution, approved by the Constitutional Assembly on 20 February 1973, recognized the right to form unions provided they are based on patriotism, have lawful goals, and use peaceful means. Yet, the long tradition of suspicion on the part of the workers, coupled with the government's distrust of trade unions, does not promise that the new constitutional article will fare much better than part III of the 1957 Labor Ordinance. The government seems unduly concerned with the country's image. Labor unions, if properly formed, can and do act as a stabilizing factor in the country's economic and political development. The Bahraini government should realize that most major Western companies have had much experience in dealing with trade unions. Besides, at the risk of understatement, the government should first be concerned with the well-being and contentment of its own citizens. To blame every labor strike on foreign or subversive elements is detrimental to the government's credibility.

The central question is: are trade unions necessary for Bahrain? Secondarily, how would they best function in this modernizing tribal society? The three different parties directly concerned are obviously labor, management, and the government. In order to approach the whole issue of unionism rationally and effectively, the three parties must recognize the following considerations:

1. Like any other facet of political-economic modernity, unionism requires a continuous process of education, especially as to the nature, function, and purpose of unions in a free society.
2. Like all other associations of particular interests, unions can never be an omnipotent panacea for society's ills nor are trade unions an instant solution to labor's long-standing troubles.
3. Trade unions must be viewed as an *economic* arm of labor and, at least initially, not as a *political* formation of a particular segment of society.

For unions to fulfill their economic function in a free society, labor must be prepared to search for common grounds of long-range economic goals with management. By the same token, management must be prepared to do the same. The entrenchment of either labor or management or both in their respective positions, awaiting confrontation and not in flexible positions that do not patently preclude cooperation, is a sure formula for the politicization of unionism. Then the economic basis of unions yields its precedence to a new political role, or a role that is conceived as such by government and management, and the entire issue of unionism becomes a political question.

In summary, what has happened in Bahrain has been a politicization of labor organization. Government has perceived unions as a threat to the tribal order of things. Since government officials have sincerely believed that labor would best benefit from government-management agreements and that the regime knew what was best for the country, unions have been considered superfluous and even detrimental. Labor's insistence on its right to unionize has been rejection of this paternalism.

In the context of this historical overview of labor and of the newly adopted constitution, the government would do well to initiate high-level, open-minded consultations with business representatives and labor spokesmen on the future of unionism in Bahrain. The purpose of these consultations should be to synthesize a new official position, which would move the government away from its traditionally intransigent stand against unions. At the same time, these consultations should serve to give labor a new perspective on the economic raison d'etre of unions, thereby paving the way for future management-labor understanding on the entire spectrum of economic development on the island.

Manpower and the Bahrainization of Labor

Bahrainization is simply a term that describes the process of creating employment for Bahraini nationals in the economy of Bahrain. This process is based on the training of the present Bahraini labor force to fill positions currently held by expatriate employees and the concurrent devising of a long-range manpower plan by which the government could anticipate future employment needs and hence train the proper labor force for such employment. Bahrainization of employment (*bahranat al-waza'if*) is one of the most talked about projects within government—yet one of the least successful. Consequently, the phrase "Bahrainization of labor" has come to be increasingly employed by labor as an emotional rallying cry against the presence of expatriate employees in the economy.[1]

---
[1] The most recent reports on manpower in Bahrain are Robert Anton Mertz, *Education and Manpower in the Arabian Gulf* (Washington, D.C.: American Friends of the Middle East, 1972), and United Nations Inter-Disciplinary Reconnaissance Mission, *Bahrain* (UNESOB: Beirut, 1972).

As was stated in chapter 2, the proper training of Bahrain's labor force, especially since 60 percent of the populace is under 20 years of age, is critical to the country's future economic development. Proper economic development will also have a crucial impact on the country's political stability. In addition to the very significant student statistics cited in chapter 2, such as over 25 percent of the population being in the public school system (1972-73), a profile of the labor force underlines the imperativeness of long-range manpower planning. Although appreciable initial efforts have been made along these lines, such as the gathering and analysis of basic data on the country's labor force, the fact remains that Bahrain has neither a national manpower plan nor a comprehensive developmental plan. Thus, the individual attempts of such agencies as the Ministries of Education, Labor and Social Affairs, and Development and Engineering Services, sincere and imaginative as they may be, have lacked functionally effective coordination and have therefore failed in presenting a common front to deal with the basic issues of manpower planning.

According to a departmental memorandum prepared by the Ministry of Labor and Social Affairs, the three immediate problems facing Bahrain in the area of manpower are:

1. "The difficulties experienced in placing secondary school leavers in suitable employment consistent with their qualifications
2. "The need for greater emphasis to be afforded the development of vocational skills and attitudes which realistically match the actual requirements and prospects of the local employment market
3. "The high proportion of non-citizens in employment, of whom a substantial majority, having less than a primary education, are often employed at very low wage levels."[16]

In order to place manpower planning in its proper perspective, certain demographic characteristics of Bahrain's population should be considered. According to the 1971 population census, 82.5 percent (or 178,193) of Bahrain's total population of 216,078 are Bahraini. Also, most of the population falls in the 0-15 years of age group, which means that at a present annual rate of growth of 3.5 percent the demand on the employment market will by 1980 reach a record high. The population is expected to double by 1995, at which time the 3.5 percent annual rate of population increase is expected to push into the region of 4-5 percent.[17] Table 4-1 shows the increase in population over the last 30 years since 1941 when the first census was taken. The table also indicates that the increase of non-Bahrainis plateaued in 1965, and by 1971 non-Bahrainis had actually declined from their number in 1965.

The projected increase in population and the very rapid growth rate in the economically active population will, if no corrective measures are

Table 4-1
Actual and Expected Bahraini Population, 1941-86

Nationality	1941	1950	1959	1965	1971	1976	1986
Bahraini	74,040	91,179	118,734	143,814	178,193	205,523	288,675
Non-Bahraini	15,930	18,471	24,401	38,389	37,885	n.a.	n.a.
Total	89,970	109,650	143,135	182,203	216,078	n.a.	n.a.

Source: State of Bahrain, Ministry of Finance and National Economy, *Statistical Abstract*, 1972, p. 6; State of Bahrain, Ministry of Labor and Social Affairs, *Manpower Requirements and Employment in Bahrain*, 1972, p. 1. Hereafter, *Manpower Memorandum*.
Note: n.a. = not available.

taken now, create new stresses, which the economy will find impossible to handle. These stresses will be caused by two developments: growth in the traditionally male labor force and the entrance of unprecedented numbers of female workers into the labor market. The number of female laborers actually employed, which almost doubled between 1965 and 1971, reflects a rising desire on the part of younger women to have gainful employment, which is due to the expansion of education.

Statistics cited in chapter 2 graphically illustrate the phenomenal increase in female students over the last decade throughout the educational ladder, including the university level. Although approximately half the potential labor force of Bahraini citizens was economically inactive in 1971 due to sex, this picture is changing rapidly. Between 1967 and 1971 female employment among Bahraini citizens rose by 85.7 percent, or from 995 in 1965 to 1,848 in 1971. This means that in the next 5-10 years a completely new segment of the population will join the economically active population, with a higher level of educational attainment than ever before. Consequently, there is a desperate need for long-range economic planning in view of this imminent influx of workers.

One of the most important facts about the labor market in Bahrain is the dispersement of expatriate labor throughout the economy. A cursory examination of this distribution reveals a need for the training of present and potential employment seekers in the economically active population of Bahrain. This need cuts across the entire economy, from educational administrators to cobblers. Table 4-2 shows that foreign or expatriate labor is predominant in technical and professional areas, construction, processing, and management. The preponderance of expatriate labor, especially females, at the bottom of the employment pyramid in household services has not caused any serious dislocation of the economy. Culturally and because of the low wages associated with this type of employment, Bahrainis are not expected to seek employment in this area for the foreseeable future. Table 4-2 also reveals that non-Bahrainis outnumber Bahrainis in five manufacturing industries, in the restaurant and hotel businesses, in

Table 4-2
Economically Active Population by Industry and Nationality, 1971

Industry	Bahraini	Non-Bahraini	Total
Agriculture & fishing	2,995	995	3,990
Agriculture & livestock production	1,959	722	2,681
Fishing	1,036	273	1,309
Mining & manufacturing	5,614	2,902	8,516
Mining & quarrying	81	4	85
Manufacture of food and beverages	468	772	1,240
Textile, wearing apparel & leather ind.	216	621	837
Manufacture of wood, wood products, furniture	403	134	537
Manufacture of paper, paper products; printing & publishing	45	124	169
Crude petroleum production & refining	3,791	519	4,310
Manufacture of chemicals & plastic products	65	124	189
Manufacture of nonmetallic mineral products	137	238	375
Nonferrous metal basic industries	155	76	231
Manufacture of fabricated metal prod., machinery & equipment	220	169	389
Other manufacturing industries	33	121	154
Electricity, gas, & water	1,480	225	1,705
Electricity & gas	1,067	216	1,283
Water workers & water supply	413	9	422
Construction	5,639	4,765	10,404
Wholesale & retail trade, restaurants & hotels	4,851	2,855	7,706
Wholesale trade	220	107	327
Retail trade	4,300	2,039	6,339
Restaurants & hotels	331	709	1,040
Transport, storage, & communication	5,067	2,676	7,743
Transport & storage	4,482	2,382	6,864
Communication	585	294	879
Finance, insurance, real estate, & business services	740	344	1,084
Financial institutions	495	230	725
Insurance	23	27	50
Real estate & business services	222	87	309
Community, social, & personal services	10,930	7,458	18,388
Public administration & defense	3,714	1,492	5,206
Sanitary & similar services	1,045	742	1,787
Social & related community services	4,292	1,454	5,746
Recreational & cultural services	97	67	164
Personal & household services	1,147	2,494	3,641
International & other extraterritorial bodies	635	1,209	1,844
Activities not adequately defined	62	44	106
Persons seeking employment for the first time	572	139	711
Total	37,950	22,403	60,353

Source: State of Bahrain, Ministry of Finance and National Economy, *Statistical Abstract*, 1972, p. 17. The term economically active is used here to include ages 14 and above.

insurance, and, of course, in personal and household services. In such other areas as retail trade, transport and storage, finance, public administration, sanitation, and recreational and cultural services, non-Bahrainis equal approximately one-half or more of the number of Bahrainis employed in these areas.

Table 4-3 gives a further occupational breakdown of the economically active population. The table shows that non-Bahrainis outnumber Bahrainis in 19 occupations, 5 of which are in the professions and related technical fields. In 17 other occupations non-Bahrainis equalled approximately one-half of the number of Bahrainis.

Another important consideration of manpower planning is the level of educational attainment. No meaningful manpower planning can be undertaken without a thorough survey of the level of education of the present labor force and a projection of the educational attainments of the new entrants to the labor market over the next 5-10 years. Whereas a majority of the present economically active population (68.5%) has not completed primary school and only 13.5 perecent have a secondary education or above (see table 4-4), it is estimated that over 80 percent of the new employment seekers in the next five years will have completed secondary school.[18] On the other hand, the occupational distribution of secondary educated employees in 1971 shows that non-Bahrainis with a secondary education outnumbered Bahrainis in 5 of the 11 major occupations. (See table 4-5.) If one takes into account those with two or more years of postsecondary education, non-Bahrainis outnumber Bahrainis in 7 of the 11 major occupations.

Several major problems will likely be encountered in the light of the foregoing tables. It will be extremely difficult to absorb the hoards of secondary school graduates over the next 5-10 years, even if non-Bahrainis are totally replaced. Unless the work performed by a secondary school graduate under the present system of job definition is expanded, the economy will not be able absorb the rising numbers of employable Bahrainis.

The government's recognition of the need for manpower planning predates independence. On 11 January 1968 the Finance Department announced that it was charged by the ruler to conduct a comprehensive study of manpower in Bahrain, the available and projected positions and the qualifications needed to fill those positions. The Finance Department project also included the formation of a steering committee with representatives from the Departments of Education, Labor, Police, and Public Security.[19] Nothing of substance was done for nearly three years, and then in January 1971 the government established a National Manpower Planning Council (NMPC). The NMPC consisted of the ministers of finance and national economy, labor and social affairs, education, health, immigration,

Table 4-3
Economically Active Population by Occupation and Nationality, 1971

Occupation	Bahraini	Non-Bahraini	Total
Professional, technical, & related workers	2,886	1,938	4,824
Architects, engineers, & related workers	30	204	234
Chemists & physicists	15	15	30
Biologists & agronomists	10	5	15
Doctors, surgeons, & dentists	20	115	135
Nurses & midwives	393	470	863
Professional medical workers & medical technicians	83	78	161
Teachers	1,900	700	2,600
Members of religious orders & related workers	265	15	280
Jurists	46	15	61
Artists, writers, & related workers	33	29	62
Draftsmen & science & engineering technicians	44	35	79
Other professional technicians & related workers	47	257	304
Administrative, executive, & managerial workers	549	486	1,035
Administrators & government & executive officers	196	41	237
Directors, managers, & working proprietors	353	445	798
Clerical workers	3,933	1,271	5,204
Bookkeepers & cashiers	532	337	869
Stenographers & typists	254	219	473
Other clerical workers	3,147	715	3,862
Sales workers	4,043	1,211	5,254
Wholesale & retail working proprietors	3,156	580	3,736
Insurance and real estate salesmen	163	43	206
Commercial travelers & manufacturers	154	38	192
Salesmen, shop assistants, & related workers	570	550	1,120
Farmers, fishermen, hunters, & related workers	3,122	1,108	4,230
Farmers & farm managers	782	25	807
Farm workers not elsewhere classified	1,309	842	2,151
Fishermen & related workers	1,031	241	1,272
Miners, quarrymen, & related workers	173	45	218
Miners & quarrymen	102	20	122
Well drillers & related workers	20	12	32
Mineral treaters	51	13	64
Transport & communication workers	3,862	1,062	4,924
Ships officers & pilots	200	124	324
Barge crews & boatmen	330	220	550
Aircraft pilots & navigators	6	32	38
Road transport drivers	2,927	548	3,475
Postmen & messengers	70	7	77

Table 4-3 (cont.)

Occupation	Bahraini	Non-Bahraini	Total
Communication workers not elsewhere classified	88	41	129
Craftsmen & Production process workers	13,126	9,720	22,846
Spinners, weavers, & related workers	9	—	9
Tailors, cutters, & related workers	203	643	846
Shoe repairers, leather cutters, & related workers	9	22	31
Furnacemen, moulders, & related workers	226	180	406
Watchmakers, jewelers, & related workers	55	216	271
Plumbers, platers, & pipe fitters	2,703	1,310	4,013
Electricians & electrical & electronic workers	898	640	1,538
Carpenters & joiners	1,606	381	1,987
Painters & paperhangers	588	430	1,018
Bricklayers & construction workers	1,717	2,775	5,492
Pressmen & related workers	35	63	98
Potters, glass & clay formers, & related workers	10	27	37
Bakers	219	384	603
Butchers	92	15	107
Other food & beverage workers	73	196	269
Chemical & related process workers	407	49	456
Other craftsmen & production process workers	49	43	92
Packers & labelers	76	65	141
Excavating & lifting equipment operators	556	202	758
Longshoremen & related freight handlers	579	792	1,371
Laborers not elsewhere classified	2,016	1,287	3,303
Services, sports, & recreation workers	4,611	5,353	9,964
Firefighters, policemen, guards, & related workers	1,468	1,732	3,200
Cooks, maids, & related workers	749	1,709	2,458
Waiters & bartenders	142	452	601
Building caretakers & cleaners	2,085	953	3,038
Barbers, hairdressers, & beauticians	39	171	210
Launderers, dry cleaners, & pressers	68	299	367
Athletes & sportsmen	24	7	31
Photographers & related camera operators	36	23	59
Occupations inadequately described	144	39	183
Members of the armed forces	928	31	959
Persons seeking employment for the first time	572	139	711
Total	37,950	22,403	60,353

Source: State of Bahrain, Ministry of Finance and National Economy, *Statistical Abstract*, 1972, pp. 18-19. The term economically active is used here to include ages 14 and above.

Table 4-4
Economically Active Population Classified by Level of Education (Males and Females), 1971

Level	Bahrainis	%	Non-Bahrainis	%	Total	%
Primary education not completed	25,491	67.2%	15,877	70.9%	41,368	68.5%
Primary education completed	3,522	9.3	754	3.4	4,276	7.1
Secondary education not completed	5,105	13.5	1,463	6.6	6,570	10.9
Secondary education completed	3,081	8.1	2,170	9.6	5,251	8.7
Postsecondary education, minimum 2 years	751	1.9	2,137	9.5	2,888	4.8
Total	37,950	100.0%	22,403	100.0%	60,353	100.0%

Source: State of Bahrain, Ministry of Labor and Social Affairs, *Manpower Memorandum*, p. 7.

and defense. The council was served by a technical committee, which was comprised of senior government officials below the ministerial level. Hamad Slayti, director of planning in the Ministry of Education, acted as secretary of the Technical Committee.

The NMPC was charged with four major tasks:

1. "To plan for the orderly implementation of government policy that the economy of Bahrain should progressively be manned by trained and competent citizens
2. "To maintain stable conditions of employment in Bahrain
3. "To insure the optimum utilization of all human resources in Bahrain
4. "To determine the training, and developmental needs for citizens in terms of approved vocational training"[20]

Since the deliberations of the National Manpower Planning Council's meetings, the minutes of those meetings and the recommendations of the Technical Committee are treated as classified material by the Bahraini government, one must rely on available bits of information scattered throughout the bureaucracy. Of course, personal interviews play a crucial role in this area. All available information indicates that the NMPC was a positive step in the direction of manpower planning. This same information also indicates that the NMPC fell short of its goals.

Two factors contributed to this failure. Since the country had no comprehensive economic-developmental plan, the National Manpower Plan-

Table 4-5
Occupational Distribution of Those with a Secondary Education in Bahrain, 1971

Occupation	Bahrainis	Non-Bahrainis	Total	%Non-Bahrainis
Professional, technical, & related works	1,139	424	1,563	27.1%
Administrative, executive, & managerial workers	111	140	251	58.8
Clerical workers	1,030	571	1,601	35.6
Sales workers	172	146	318	45.9
Farmers, fishermen, hunters, & related workers	6	4	10	40.0
Miners, quarrymen, & related workers	—	13	13	100.0
Transport & communications workers	81	85	166	51.2
Craftsmen & production process workers	289	602	891	67.6
Services, sports, & recreation workers	65	137	202	67.3
Occupations inadequately described	7	7	14	50.0
Armed forces	80	5	85	5.9
Seeking employment for the first time	101	5	106	4.7
Total	3,081	2,139	5,220	40.9%

Source: State of Bahrain, Ministry of Labor and Social Affairs, *Manpower Memorandum*, pp. 8-9.

ning Council found itself operating in a vacuum. At the risk of proverbial triteness, the formation of a manpower council prior to a development plan was very much like putting the cart before the horse. In all fairness, the government saw this dilemma, but in all frankness, it did nothing to resolve it.

Second, some of the concerned top-level bureaucrats inside the NMPC and outside it simply did not comprehend the urgency of the matter. As an example, the NMPC had agreed quite early in its existence on the need to engage the services of a top-level manpower planner from outside the country. As early as the spring of 1971, the NMPC had even detailed the task of such a planner. He was to "undertake a detailed survey of the manpower requirements of the whole economy of Bahrain"[21] in five major occupational groups: administrative and managerial; professional; technical (subprofessional); skilled craftsmen and supervisors; and skilled office workers. For whatever reasons political or otherwise, the manpower planner did not arrive in Bahrain until February 1973.

Another indication of the NMPC's lack of success was the fate of the Technical Committee. According to the committee's secretary, the Technical Committee was initially charged with conducting a study centering around the preparation of two plans: a short-range plan, which would deal with the Bahrainization of employment, first on the clerical level and later on the technical level; and a long-range plan, which would study the country's manpower needs for the next 5-10 years. In a newspaper interview on the occasion of the first year anniversary of the NMPC, Hamad Slayti indicated that the Technical Committee was still conducting its study.[22] In January 1973 there were indications that the Technical Committee had submitted its final recommendations to the National Manpower Planning Council. The recommendations were not made public nor was there any indication that the council had acted on those recommendations. Upon being queried about the fate of the committee's recommendations and of the council itself, one member of the Technical Committee all but admitted in March 1973 that the committee's recommendations were shelved and that the National Manpower Planning Council was basically defunct.

The story of the National Manpower Planning Council and the history of the labor movement in contemporary Bahrain demonstrate that the government of Bahrain, like governments in many developing countries, has often failed to comprehend the new forces of social change that usually characterize the improving economic conditions in a modernizing community. More significantly, these governments have not yet paid sufficient serious attention to the direct relationship between economic conditions and political stability. Since the time of Aristotle, social scientists and political philosophers alike have agreed that the economic factor is a sensitive barometer of sociopolitical unrest.[23] The government of Bahrain must in the long run modify its view of labor and trade unions, for in a developing society, tribal or otherwise, the labor force is the cornerstone of modernity—the only path to a truly functional political democracy.

5

Foreign Policy and Political Development

Background Notes

In studying the process of national political development in a newly independent and strategically located country such as Bahrain, major public policy is, almost by definition, one of the main areas of investigation. Foreign policy, generally a significant part of this public policy, is therefore germane to any examination of political development, especially in that the formulation of such policy is inevitably influenced by the same political supports, demands, and pressures that govern the making of any other major domestic public policy. The factors that come into play whenever the decision maker, in this case the amir of Bahrain, contemplates a major decision concerning the country's domestic or foreign environments are known as the detaminants of policy—in this case, foreign policy.

Because of its geographic position and the rising significance of the Gulf in world affairs, Bahrain's modern foreign policy goals have never been measured by the island's pinpoint size on the world map. This disproportion between Bahrain's small size and its regional foreign policy has originated in the fact that, regionally and internationally, Bahrain has always identified with the Gulf as a whole—politically, socially, economically—and has always played a Gulf role. It is within this context that the foreign policy of Bahrain must be viewed. Because of this Gulf-oriented role, Bahrain's foreign policy has had to steer a course between the Gulf's contradictions and conflicts. However, it should be pointed out that these same tensions marring the fabric of the island's relations with other states are not restricted to Bahrain. They are common to all other Gulf political formations that use a tribal system of government.

Consider a few salient facts that influence the country's foreign policy:

1. Although relatively poor in oil itself, Bahrain floats on top of the world's largest oil lake. Such nearby countries as Saudi Arabia, Kuwait, Abu Dhabi, Qatar, and Dubai have become synonymous with the oil industry. In 1971 Bahrain's production of crude oil averaged only 75,000 barrels per day; Saudi Arabia produced in the same year 4,770,000 barrels; Kuwait, 3,198,000; Abu Dhabi, 934,000; Qatar, 430,000; and Dubai, 125,000.[1] Because Bahrain is poor in natural resources, it has developed an entrepôt, services-oriented economy; in fact the country imports virtually all of its needs. This means that international trade has had a sizeable

influence on Bahrain's foreign policy, especially as that trade applies to the top four or five countries from which Bahrain imports most of its needs: United Kingdom, Japan, Australia, United States, and China.

2. Bahrain is an Arab Muslim country; yet, it prides itself on the urbanity and middle-class pragmatism of its people. The island is buffeted by political crosscurrents representing ideologies ranging from the far right to the extreme left. Although the majority of the population is Arab, almost 15 percent are non-Arab, primarily Indian, Iranian, and Pakistani. A cursory examination of the country's economy reveals that the influence of the non-Arab minorities in the economic sector, that is, in businesses, technical positions and general manpower, is out of proportion to their numerical percentage. Bahrain's tribal system of government has also made the regime an inviting target for such Gulf revolutionary movements as the Popular Front for the Liberation of Oman and the Arabian Gulf (PFLOAG), based in Dhufar (Oman). On the other hand, the island's guarded venture into democracy has aroused certain suspicions inside Bahrain's very conservative mentor and close neighbor, Saudi Arabia. The latter closely observed Bahrain's constitutional experiment as it developed in the Constitutional Assembly during the first half of 1973.

3. Saudi Arabia has attempted to extend its religious conservatism to Bahrain through its economic support of the island. In 1971 Saudi crude oil, which is piped from Saudi Arabia to Bahrain, totaled over two-thirds of all the crude oil refined in Bahrain.[2] However, the al-Khalifa ruling family of Bahrain has been able to steer a somewhat more liberal course than that desired by the Saudi government, but in the process the al-Khalifas have had to yield to Saudi Arabia on such political issues as women's suffrage.

One stumbling block to the spread of Saudi's conservative religious influence has been the sectarian makeup of the Bahraini population. The population of Bahrain is divided equally between two major Islamic sects—the Sunnis and the Shi'as. The al-Khalifas are Sunnis, and therefore the country has been ruled by Sunnis for over 200 years. Generally the Shi'as inhabit the villages of Bahrain and the poor sections of Manama, the capital. They are usually less educated than the country's Sunnis and more conservative religiously. (See chapter 7.) Under different circumstances, the Shi'a population would provide fertile soil for the spread of Saudi religious conservatism; however, since Saudi Arabia considers itself the center of orthodox Islam (Sunnism) and since the Shi'as have traditionally been virtually excluded from Saudi society, the Saudis have not yet shown any great inclination to work with Bahrain's Shi'a leaders to arrest the sweep of modernization in the country. It is possible, even plausible, but perhaps not probable that this relationship between Saudi Arabia and the Shi'a might undergo certain changes in the future, especially if the al-Khalifas' solicitous guardianship of the constitutional experiment arouses

Saudi concern. Bahrain's future policy posture toward Saudi Arabia and the latter's continued economic support in the form of crude oil will also have to readjust to any new socioreligious relationship between the two countries.

4. Bahrain's location in the formerly British-dominated Gulf has always influenced the Island's foreign policy toward the West. In 1971 the United Kingdom severed its special relationship with Bahrain, and on the second day after Bahrain had declared itself independent, it signed a treaty of friendship with the United Kingdom. The British Ambassador to Bahrain still enjoys the special regard of the al-Khalifa family. On the other hand, the Jufair naval base in Bahrain, occupied by the British Navy for the last half century, has since December 1971 been leased to the United States Navy. It is the home port of the United States COMIDEASTFOR.[a] The government of Bahrain has never published the text of this agreement in Arabic for its people; hence, questions have persisted concerning this agreement and its economic and other benefits to Bahrain. On several occasions the government of Bahrain has found itself compelled to explain the American presence on the island to other Arab critics as well as to its own people, which is a concrete illustration of the interconnection between Bahrain's foreign policy and the Gulf region as a whole.

5. Bahrain's modest oil production has provided the country with a mixed blessing. Because of its limited oil revenues, the government of Bahrain has been forced to develop gradually a basically nonoil economy based on private entrepreneurship. At the same time, since the oil industry in Bahrain is at least 40 years old, an industrial labor class has come into being, which has in turn caused the development of a labor tradition and labor demands, first for better working conditions and later for political existence in the form of unions. The history of labor in the country has definitely influenced Bahrain's foreign policy. Domestically this labor tradition intensified the political consciousness of the workers, which in turn has constituted a persistent challenge to the traditional autocratic rule of the al-Kahlifa family. Labor's demand for the right to form unions, as was shown in the previous chapter, has been the most nagging problem of the regime for the last two decades. Neighboring countries will watch this development of labor in Bahrain with more than passing interest. The rising popular demands of a modernizing society and the ability and willingness of the regime to guarantee its people life, liberty, and economic prosperity will in the long run determine Bahrain's future foreign policy.

---

[a] The Americans are careful to refer to Jufair as the "facility" rather than the "base." The Middle East Force was established in 1949, and in terms of ships assigned it is one of the navy's smallest major commands. In announcing the termination of the Jufair agreement on 20 October 1973, the government of Bahrain granted COMIDEASTFOR one year to dismantle its onshore facilities at Jufair. Although the October 20 decision was rescinded by the Bahraini government, the United States Navy expects to leave Bahrain by mid-1977.

6. Finally, Iran's territorial claims to Bahrain over the previous half century, Bahrain's ability to neutralize these demands and declare itself an independent state, the partially successful attempts at political unity among the lower Gulf Emirates, and the traditional disputes and jealousies between the tribal rulers of these Emirates—all of these have added to Bahrain's sensitivity toward regional politics. Bahrain's relations with these different neighbors since its independence in August 1971 have reflected these pressures. The continued ability of the state to reconcile these four essentially different pressures will depend heavily on the position of the Bahraini policy-oriented elites toward the region as a whole.

A close examination of the preceding six foreign policy determinants indicates several relationships: First, there is a definite connection between Bahrain's domestic environment and its foreign environment; second, as David Easton has established in his political system model, the making of public policy, especially foreign policy, cannot be accomplished in a vacuum or in isolation from the domestic political system as well as to the components of the foreign environment.[3] Third, for the most part, Bahrain's future foreign policy will be a reaction to stresses and developments over which Bahrain will have minimal control. Fourth, ultimately Bahrain's foreign policy will not differ significantly from that of other Gulf countries, including Saudi Arabia, for such a policy will mirror Bahrain's essentially conservative family-tribal system of government.

Based on these background notes, the following sections of this chapter examine the mechanics, support, logic, and context of the foreign policy course that Bahrain has charted.

Support of Bahrain's Foreign Policy

The foreign policy of Bahrain has been defined by the country's ruler, Shaikh 'Isa bin Sulman al-Khalifa, in his official speeches and day-to-day practices. The policy itself has been carried out by a capable, college-educated member of the Khalifa family, Shaikh Muhammad bin Mubarak, who is the minister of foreign affairs. In the last half decade, he has succeeded in his efforts to establish an international personality for Bahrain, which has not always been an easy task in the complicated affairs of the Gulf.

Like other tribal governmental systems of the Gulf, Bahrain's relations with other states—Gulf amirates as well as distant countries—largely involve a personal exercise of diplomacy. The formation of policy is a personal exercise of the ruler, and the implementation of this policy is a personal exercise of the foreign minister. Obviously, the prime minister and the other members of the inner councils of the Khalifa family contribute significant inputs into the formulation of policy. In addition to the foreign minister, Bahrain's main spokesman in international conferences has been the ruler's eldest son, who is the country's heir apparent and the commander-in-chief of Bahrain's defense forces. He has, by virtue of his Western military training (primarily in the United States) and of his position, been able to establish a cordial and active relationship with Western as well as Arab defense establishments. The prime minister, Shaikh Khalifa bin Sulman al-Khalifa, is the third member of this unofficial triumvirate. His generally known conservatism has made him acceptable to such neighbors as Saudi Arabia and Qatar, and, Bahrain's liberalism notwithstanding, Shaikh Khalifa has been able to retain an economically profitable relationship with these neighbors.[b]

Since Bahrain is a newly independent country without a long tradition of policy practice and since it has a tribal form of government in which actual authority to make binding national decisions resides with the ruler,[c] official statements form the primary guidelines for the Foreign Ministry's bureaucracy. Therefore, in order to examine the principles of Bahrain's foreign policy, one must examine the statements enunciated by the ruler on official occasions since independence. In his Declaration of Independence on 14 August 1971, the ruler stated that as a newly independent country, Bahrain was committed to the following principles:

1. Adherence to treaties and agreements signed with other countries that respect Bahrain's independence and that are in accordance with the dictates of international law
2. Adherence to the Charters of the United Nations and the Arab League
3. Work for the establishment of relations with Gulf and other Arab countries on the basis of brotherhood, peaceful coexistence, cooperation, understanding, and noninterference in the domestic affairs of these countries
4. Work for the preservation of the peace, security, stability, and progress of the Gulf region through cooperation with the concerned countries
5. Promote economic, commercial, technical, and professional cooperation among the countries of the region
6. A firm belief in the rights of the Palestinian people to recover their

---

[b] The making of foreign policy is particularly interesting in Bahrain due to the centers of power within the Khalifa family. The three parties directly concerned with foreign policy include the amir and his son the heir apparent (who, unlike the situation in the other Gulf amirates, is not the prime minister), the ruler's brother, who is the prime minister, and the minister of foreign affairs.

[c] Although under the new constitution, the system of government in Bahrain is to be based on the principle of the separation of powers, the ruler heads the legislative branch in cooperation with the National Assembly. He also heads the executive branch through his cabinet, and court decisions are issued in his name (article 32). In addition, the ruler is the head of the State of Bahrain, and his person is considered to be above criticism. (article 33a).

country and in the efforts of the confrontation[d] Arab countries to recover their occupied territories[4]

Generally, the ruler's foreign policy statements have focused on Bahrain's diplomatic position vis-à-vis the three concentric circles surrounding it: the Gulf circle; the Arab circle; the international circle. The role that Bahrain has played based on this position, which is examined in the following section of this chapter, was the center of the ruler's National Day Statements in 1971 and 1972.

On 16 December 1971, the ruler discussed Bahrain's achievements in its foreign relations:

1. Through its membership in the United Nations and in the Arab League, Bahrain has become able to work for justice and peace among nations.
2. Bahrain was able in its first year of independence to establish friendly and neighborly relations with other Gulf states.
3. Bahrain's relations with other Arab countries have grown out of Bahrain's conviction that it is a part of the Arab homeland.
4. Bahrain has condemned the aggression committed against the Palestinian people.
5. Bahrain has supported the principle of pacific settlement of international disputes.[5]

Similar principles were reiterated on the 1972 National Day during the official opening of the Constitutional Assembly.[6] However, in this speech the ruler made a rather lengthy reference to Palestine and the rights of the Palestinian people.[e] The foreign policy section of the 1972 speech included the following points:

1. On Palestine, Bahrain renews its determination to offer whatever sacrifices may be necessary for this area of primary concern to every Arab nation and to offer whatever active assistance may be needed by the struggling people of Palestine. Bahrain would want to remind the world to support the usurped rights of the Palestinian people and the human rights that are being trodden upon daily by the Zionist state. Bahrain implores the international organization to take effective practical measures in accordance with its resolutions to restore justice.[f]

---
[d] Syria, Jordan, and Egypt.

[e] Whereas in the 1971 National Day speech the ruler made a scant one-line reference to Palestine, in the 1972 National Day speech a whole paragraph was devoted to the Palestine question. It also headed the list of major topics in the speech.

[f] It is interesting to note that the Palestine Liberation Organization was not allowed to open an office in Bahrain until 1974.

2. Bahrain is strongly interested in fostering its friendly and brotherly relations with the Arab and other Islamic states, especially with its neighboring countries in the Gulf.

3. Internationally, Bahrain supports world peace and strongly believes in human rights, the right of self-determination, the rejection of both local and international war, arms limitation (both nuclear and conventional, and the eradication of the remaining traces of colonialism and racial discrimination.

Another support of foreign policy is the constitutional prescription, which is embodied in several articles of Bahrain's new (1973) constitution. Consider the following articles:

Article 1a. Bahrain is an independent Arab Muslim state with full sovereignty. Its people are a part of the Arab nation; its territory is a part of the Arab homeland, and it shall not relinquish its sovereignty or a part of its territory.

Article 6. The State shall protect its Arab and Islamic heritage, contribute to the march of human civilization, and work to strengthen ties among Islamic countries and to further the Arab nation's hopes for unity and progress.

Article 10b. The State shall work toward Arab economic unity.

Article 30a. Peace shall be the goal of the State, and the safety of the fatherland is an integral part of the security of the greater Arab homeland. Protecting the fatherland is every citizen's duty, and military service, organized by law, is an honor to the citizen.

Article 36a. The waging of offensive wars shall be prohibited. . . .

Article 37. The ruler shall conclude treaties by decree; however, treaties dealing with war and peace, commerce, the country's natural resources, finances or national sovereignty must be ratified by the National Assembly.

Although the Foreign Ministry was established in 1969[7] under Shaikh Muhammad bin Mubarak al-Khalifa,[8] it was not until after independence was declared (August 1971) that the Ministry of Foreign Affairs was restructured in its present form. Decree No. 3 (1971) assigned to the Ministry of Foreign Affairs the following specific functions:

1. To secure relations with other countries and to organize the exchange of consular and diplomatic representation with these countries

2. To prepare instructions and directions for Bahraini diplomatic missions abroad
3. To prepare studies and collect information to assist the State of Bahrain in formulating foreign policy and to provide other governmental departments with information relating to Bahrain's international relations
4. To secure Bahrain's participation in international organizations, conferences, and exhibits in conjunction with other ministries and departments
5. To carry out necessary contacts and negotiations for the conclusion of treaties and international agreements between Bahrain and other countries
6. To facilitate necessary contacts between governmental agencies and ministries in Bahrain and foreign governments[9].

In its attempt to establish an international personality for Bahrain, the Ministry of Foreign Affairs has chosen a traditional approach in both Arab and international relations. Bahrain has been recognized by all Gulf and Arab countries, all of the major powers, the League of Arab States, the block of nonaligned countries, and the United Nations. Bahrain has also ratified the 1961 Vienna Convention on Diplomatic Relations, concluded a treaty of friendship with Britain, and leased its naval facilities at Jufair to the United States Navy. The specific role that Bahrain has performed in its Gulf, Arab, and international contexts, especially in view of the recent prominence of the Gulf in world affairs as a major source of energy, is examined in the following pages. It is apparent that Bahrain has already been given a certain niche in the long-range policy planning of the major powers in their attempts to secure access to the Gulf's black gold.

Setting of Bahrain's Foreign Policy

Bahrain's foreign policy since 1968, the year in which the British government announced its intention to withdraw from East of Suez, has striven for two essential accomplishments: to be born as an independent state and to survive as such. The fruition of the first objective in August 1971 meant the liquidation of Iran's long-standing territorial claims to the islands of Bahrain. The second objective has necessitated that Bahrain, as a newly independent, small-sized, and family-ruled country, walk a tightrope and play a cautious diplomatic role among the littoral states of the Gulf. In doing so, Bahrain has had to be cognizant of both its Arab character, and hence its strong ties to other Arab countries, and the omnipresence of Iran, a large non-Arab country, on the eastern coast of the Gulf.

Bahrain's regional policy has also had to consider the Gulf's traditional strategic location and, most importantly, the fact that the Gulf is the world's largest source of energy.

Without any doubt the greatest diplomatic achievement of the Khalifa family in recent years has been the attainment of independence for Bahrain as an Arab state and its acceptance by the international community as such. The story of Bahrain's independence, which culminated in the 1970 visit to Bahrain of Vittorio Winspeare Guicciardi, the personal representative of the United Nations secretary-general, and his subsequent report recommending that Bahrain be granted independence as an Arab State,[10] is a complex one. It is an accepted fact that the United Nations' action in this matter and at that time was primarily a face-saving formality.[g] Iran's agreement to relinquish its territorial claims to Bahrain had already been attained during a series of meetings held in 1968 and 1969 between representatives from Saudi Arabia, Iran, Kuwait, and Britain. The mediation of Saudi Arabia and Kuwait in this question proved successful; significantly, the Shah of Iran had paid a visit to both countries in November 1968.

While Saudi mediation on the issue of Iranian claims to Bahrain was taking place in 1968 and 1969, Bahrain, Qatar, and the seven amirates of the Trucial Coast[h] were attempting to form a political union of the nine amirates. The agreement announcing the birth of the "Federation of Arab Amirates" was signed in Dubai by the nine rulers on 27 February 1968. The "federation" collapsed two and one-half years later. Although the formation of the Federation of Arab Amirates falls outside the scope of this study, it must be pointed out that the whole idea of the federation was doomed to failure from the outset for several reasons:

1. The federation was a reaction on the part of the concerned rulers to the announcement of imminent British withdrawal. These leaders were hastily searching for a means to protect their rule.

2. The generations-old jealousies and suspicions among the rulers of the different amirates could not be easily eradicated by a quickly arranged agreement to unite.

3. The disparities in population, influence, education, and wealth between the different amirates rendered cooperation within the federation difficult.

4. The border disputes between Abu Dhabi and Saudi Arabia and between Abu Dhabi and Dubai, coupled with Bahrain's desire to assume a position of leadership within the federation and Qatar's close relations with

---

[g] Both Iran and Britain had agreed to abide by the findings of the secretary-general's personal representative concerning the wishes of the people of Bahrain even before the mission was undertaken. Both countries knew full well that a vast majority of the population was Arab and that they would support an independent sovereign status for the island.

[h] Abu Dhabi, Dubai, Umm al-Qaywayn, al-Shariqa (Sharja), Ra's al-Khayma, al-Fujayra, and 'Ajman.

Saudi Arabia, proved to be difficult issues to resolve during the meetings of the nine rulers.

5. Iran's claims to sovereignty over Bahrain posed a grave danger to Bahrain, which the other amirates did not have to face and which they did not really appreciate. The other rulers of the federation were primarily interested in a method by which they could preserve a very particularistic status quo, without any real understanding or appreciation of the far-reaching dimensions of a federal undertaking or of the magnitude of the collective responsibilities that would be placed on their shoulders.

The Dubai agreement was finally shelved, the nine-member federation collapsed, and Bahrain and Qatar, the two non-Trucial Coast amirates, decided to work toward their own independence. By 1971 a different picture had emerged: Bahrain had declared its independence on 14 August 1971; Qatar was declared independent on 1 September 1971; and on December 2 of the same year, the Trucial Coast shaykhdoms (excluding Ra's al-Khayma) had joined together to form the United Arab Emirates (U.A.E.). Ra's al-Khayma joined the U.A.E. on 10 February 1972.[i] It is against this background that Bahrain, through the good offices of the United Nations, acquired its independence.[j]

Bahrain's foreign policy since independence has operated within three concentric spheres: the Gulf sphere, the Arab world sphere, and the international sphere. The Gulf sphere includes and directly concerns Iran, Iraq, Kuwait, Saudi Arabia, Qatar, the United Arab Emirates, Oman, and the island of Bahrain itself. Within the Gulf's sphere of existence there are five major factors that affect the peace and security of the region:

1. Oil, economic development, and international trade
2. Arab nationalism, Iranian nationalism, and expatriate minorities [k]
3. Intra-Gulf politics, especially among the amirates
4. Internal security and domestic opposition[l]
5. Conservative status quo and Gulf revolutionary movements [m]

---

[i] For an analysis of the whole question of the ill-fated federation and the stand of each of the shaykhdoms on the federation see Salim al-Lawzi, *Rasasatan fi al-Khalij* [Two Bullets in the Gulf] (Beirut, Lebanon: Manshurat al-Hawadith, 1971), and Riyad Najib al-Rayyis, *Sira' al-Wahat wa al-Naft* [Struggle of Oases and Oil] (Beirut, Lebanon: al-Nahar, 1973).

[j] For a historical perspective on Bahrain's independence see Amal Ibrahim Zayani, *al-Bahrain min al-Himaya ila al-Istiqlal* [Bahrain from Protectorateship to Independence] (Cairo, Egypt: University of Cairo, 1972), an unpublished master's thesis.

[k] The term expatriate minorities is used in this context as referring to Iranian, Pakistani, and Indian minorities, usually economically influential, that are present in such Gulf Arab countries as Bahrain, Qatar, the United Arab Emirates (primarily Abu Dhabi and Dubai), and the Kurdish minority in Iraq. The term also applies to Arab and Baluchi minorities in Iran.

[l] In such lower Gulf countries as Bahrain, Qatar, the United Arab Emirates, and Oman the responsibility of preserving internal security, especially in the realm of political activities, has so far been placed in the hands of British and Jordanian officers.

[m] Among these movements are: the Popular Front for the Liberation of Oman (directed against

These five factors must be taken into consideration whenever foreign policy is made by any Gulf country or by any other country concerning the Gulf. Bahrain, like any other Gulf state, is influenced by these factors, which are essentially international in scope.

The second major sphere of Bahrain's foreign policy incorporates the Arab world, with all of its problems, aspirations, and frustrations. Geographically, this vast territory, which stretches from the Atlantic to the Gulf, encompasses such heterogeneous regions as North Africa, the Fertile Crescent, and the Arabian Peninsula. In this domain the factors affecting political stability include the following:

1. The Palestine problem, the Palestine resistance movement and the Israeli response.[n]

2. Oil, the industrial world's energy crisis, and the advent of Arab economic influence in international economics.[o]

3. Traditionalism vs. change and the regimes' individual responses to this conflict. This factor is significant because Arab governments have often based their inter-Arab and foreign relations on that regime's own domestic ideology.[p]

4. Major powers' long-range objectives vis-à-vis the Arab world and future conflict-detente among the superpowers. The twin issues of oil and Israel have forced the major powers, especially the United States, to intensify their interest in the region, which means, as is shown below, that a country such as the United States has by this forced involvement limited its policy options and therefore its effectiveness as a contributor to regional conflict resolution.

---

the tribal regimes in the Sultanate of Oman and the Amirates; it is primarily supported by the People's Democratic Republic of Yemen); the Popular Front for the Liberation of Baluchistan (directed against Iranian and Pakistani rules in the Baluchi area on the border separating Iran and Pakistan; it is primarily supported by Iraq and, to a much smaller extent, by India); and the Eritrean Liberation Movement (directed against the Ethiopian rule in Eritrea at the entrance of the Red Sea; it is primarily supported by Somalia and to some extent by the People's Democratic Republic of Yemen). This last movement is only indirectly related to the lower Gulf. In addition, some Iranian dissent groups have often operated out of Iraq against the Shah's regime in Iran.

[n] It is true that Palestine affects only a few Arab states directly; however, the issue of Palestinianism, especially in its social, economic, political, and military dimensions, is an Arab question lock, stock, and barrel. Reference to Palestine, much to the dislike of several Arab leaders and regimes, has come to permeate Arabic folklore and high-level policy planning alike.

[o] The Arab oil embargo against the major industrial powers, especially the United States, in October 1973 marked the first time that the traditionally conservative Arab states have ever used economics as a political weapon. The embargo gave the oil-producing countries an unprecedented posture of power.

[p] The result of this ideological melange is all too evident: Arab countries have so far failed to exhibit anything resembling a unified Arab diplomatic-political front. Never in history has Arab unity been so talked about or so far from realization. The Arab solidarity since the October 1973 war has been maintained due to external pressure and will probably not endure once this pressure is removed.

5. Intra-Arab conflicts, aside from the Palestine question, and the role of ideology.

6. The most important factor affecting political stability in the Arab world in the long run is the absence of freedom and therefore of its corollaries—creativity and hope. Political dissent is equated with treason, a student's inquiry with trouble making. Bahrain is a microcosm of the Gulf and of Arab society. The factors affecting stability in the Gulf, the first sphere, and stability in the Arab world, the second sphere, by definition apply to Bahrain, and these factors are organically linked to any rational foreign policy.

The third sphere of Bahrain's foreign policy is international in geography and scope. Bahrain's policy operates in this setting only insofar as the actors within this sphere are actively concerned with the two other spheres. The factors affecting the first and second spheres, spearheaded by the Palestine conflict and oil, are the same factors that affect the making of policy on the international level, as far as this policy relates to the first two spheres. In this perspective, the action-reaction policy paradigm on the international level is a synthesis of the activities within the first two spheres, Gulf politics and Arab politics.

In terms of geopolitical consideration, Bahrain's international relations have encompassed five main subdivisions within the Middle East:

1. The Gulf Basin: Iraq, Kuwait, Saudi Arabia, Bahrain, Qatar, the United Arab Emirates, Oman, Iran, and Pakistan
2. The Cauldron: Palestine/Israel, Lebanon, Syria, Jordan, and Egypt (Iraq may also be included in this subdivision)
3. Africa's Northern Tier: Egypt, Libya, Tunisia, Algeria, and Morocco (Sudan and Mauritania may also be included in this subdivision)[q]
4. The Red Sea States: Egypt, Sudan, Ethiopia, Somalia, the People's Democratic Republic of Yemen (Aden), the Republic of Yemen (San'a), and Saudi Arabia[r]
5. The Eastern Mediterranean Hub: Turkey, Greece, Cyprus, Syria, and Iraq[s]

[q] In April 1973 Bahrain was visited by an official Moroccan delegation headed by King Hasan's brother and a Mauritanian delegation headed by the minister of foreign affairs. The Moroccan visit fell within the Arab-Islamic context while the Mauritanian visit was only within an Islamic context.

[r] Although Israel is not a Red Sea state, it is vitally interested in the security of the region especially in regard to its international trade. For an analysis of the strategic importance of the Bab al-Mandab strait at the entrace to the Red Sea see John Duke Anthony, *Middle East Problem Paper No. 13—The Red Sea: Control of the Southern Approach* (Washington, D.C.: The Middle East Institute, January 1975).

[s] Since this subdivision borders on the southeastern wing of NATO, it is directly related to

The interactions of these five subdivisions are best illustrated in figure 5-1. This illustration gives a clear picture of the interaction between geopolitics and issue politics and their joint relevance to the making of foreign policy. The linkages of these different states in figure 5-1, the realities of power, the territorial-national disputes involved, and the pressures brought to bear by the major powers in the outer circle have volatilized the entire region.

It seems that the Western powers, primarily the United States, have assigned the police-keeping (mistakenly equated with peace-keeping) responsibility to two non-Arab states: Iran in the Gulf and Israel in the Eastern Mediterranean. Iran is rapidly becoming the world's most profitable market for American military products. Concerning Israel, the United States government, and more recently President Nixon himself, has often maintained that a strong Israel is a guarantee for peace in the Middle East.[t]

Pax Persiana and *Pax Judaica*, as their zealous proponents tell us, would insure the continued existence of a status quo favorable to the United States.[u] The fallacy of this logic lies in the fact that in the history of modern diplomacy and spheres of influence, nonindigenous power vacuum fillers or those who command by force alone have always failed to provide a long-term solution to the root problem of the vacuum. The tension between an imposed peace and the inability of the region's inhabitants to act independently favors the development of radicalism—which in turn is the cornerstone of political instbility.[v]

Caught in the midst of the Gulf and international cross currents, Bahrain has adopted certain policies in its international relations that are worthy of consideration. These policies have dealt with three principal relationships: Bahrain and the Gulf (including Iran); Bahrain and the Arab world; Bahrain

---

European security systems. For an examination of the position of the Persian Gulf in the international balance of power system see Enver M. Koury, *Oil and Geopolitics in the Persian Gulf: A Center of Power* (Washington, D.C.: The Institute of Middle Eastern and North African Affairs, 1973).

[t] Even such academicians as Professor J.C. Hurewitz have also come to assign such a role to Iran. *The Annals*, vol. 401 (May 1972), p. 115. A special issue on the Middle East entitled "America and the Middle East" and edited by Parker T. Hart, former president of the Middle East Institute.

[u] The first flexing of Iran's military muscles since her anointment as the peace keeper for the Gulf's littoral states was the military occupation of the three Gulf islands of Abu Musa, the Greater Tunb, and the Lesser Tunb in December 1971, the month in which Britain's military presence was finally dismantled in the Gulf. On the other side of the Peninsula, the chronicle of Israel's militarism is too well known to detail.

[v] In the present context of the Gulf it is possible to concede that Iran's role as a defender of a pro-Western status quo might be effective for yet a few years to come, since Saudi Arabia, as the major Arab state in the Gulf, is basically interested in the same status quo for which Iran, a non-Arab state, has become responsible. The present regimes in the majority of the Gulf shaykhdoms share these ideological inclinations with Iran and Saudi Arabia.

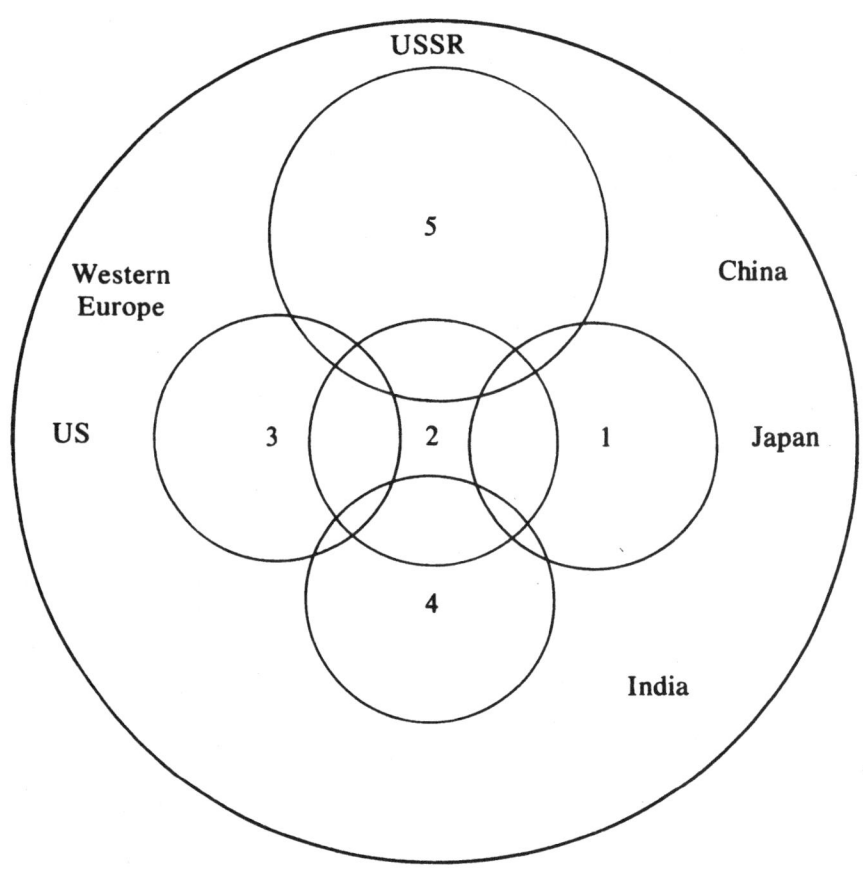

1 = The Gulf Basin
2 = The Cauldron
3 = Africa's Northern Tier
4 = The Red Sea States
5 = The Eastern Mediterranean Hub

Figure 5-1. Interaction of Conflict on a Regional Level (The Middle East)

and the West. It can be safely stated at the outset that Bahrain's attitude toward these relationships has generally been compounded of cautious pragmatism and guarded openness. As a Gulf state, Bahrain has called for closer economic, social, and even political cooperation among the Gulf states and amirates. In the spring of 1973 several attempts were made to intensify economic cooperation between Bahrain and other amirates, particularly Qatar and Abu Dhabi. A Bahraini commercial delegation visited Qatar from 4 to 7 March 1973 and concluded a seven-point agreement with the Qatari Chamber of Commerce calling for closer economic ties between the two countries.[11] Bahrain has also held discussions with Qatar and Dubai on such large-scale industrial projects as an aluminum plant[w] and a dry dock project.[x]

Politically, the Khalifas of Bahrain have not been overly zealous in their call for Gulf unity, save for economic cooperation. In the upper Gulf, Bahrain's close relations with Kuwait—economically, socially, and politically—led Bahrain to stand by Kuwait in its border clash with Iraq in March 1973. In the lower Gulf, any political unification of Bahrain, Qatar, and the United Arab Emirates seems only a remote possibility. The Bahraini press has consistently supported a future political union, basically urging that Bahrain and Qatar join the federation of the coastal amirates. However, it is generally believed among the advocates of such a union that political unification must be preceded by close economic and cultural cooperation on specific projects, such as a joint currency and a joint educational system.[y]

Bahrain's relations with Iran have also reflected the Bahraini government's realistic cognizance of its very limited resources and capabilities. The government has liquidated Iran's territorial claims to Bahrain, thanks to England, Saudi Arabia, Kuwait, Iran, and others, and it even cautiously condemned Iran's military occupation of the three Gulf islands of Abu Musa, the Greater Tunb, and the Lesser Tunb. In June 1971, two months before Bahrain declared its independence, the foreign minister of Iran visited Bahrain and stated that Iran had four demands concerning Bahrain:

1. Iran desired to lease the Muharraq air base following the withdrawal of British forces.
2. Bahrain should refrain from entering into any form of federation or similar arrangement with Kuwait.
3. Bahrain should not interfere in Iran's claim to the three Gulf islands (which Iran in fact later occupied).
4. Bahrain should open its doors to Iranian immigrants and its markets to Iranian goods.[12]

---

[w] Since Bahrain already has an aluminum smelter, it had asked Qatar not to construct a similar smelter, which Qatar had shown some interest in building. Qatar agreed temporarily.

[x] Bahrain had received the approval of the Organization of Arab Petroleum Exporting Countries (OAPEC) to build a multimillion dollar dry dock in Bahrain. Dubai objected to this decision and decided to construct its own, larger dry dock. Obviously this lack of cooperation hurt the Bahraini project, although Bahrain's minister of development and engineering services denied in a newspaper interview that the Dubai project would have any detrimental effects on Bahrain's dry dock. *al-Adwa'*, 29 March 1973, p. 2.

[y] *al-Adwa'*, 15 March 1973, p. 1, and *Sada al-'Usbu'*, 20 March 1973, pp. 12-13. It is interesting to note that the prime minister of Bahrain attended Qatar's National Day celebrations on 22 February 1973 commemorating the first anniversary of the assumption of power by Qatar's new ruler, Shaikh Khalifa bin Hamad al-Thani.

However, the air base at Muharraq was not leased to Iran,[z] and Bahrain did condemn, though very guardedly, Iran's occupation of the islands.[aa] Other countries' reactions to the occupation ranged from protest (Britain) to severance of diplomatic relations (Iraq) to rejection (Syria) to lamentation (Ra's al-Khayma and Abu Dhabi) to approval (al-Shariqa). Saudi Arabia stated that although King Faysal had persuaded Iran to relinquish its claims to Bahrain, he could not persuade the Shah to act similarly towards the three islands.[13]

Since 1972 relations with Iran have been friendly;[bb] Iran maintains a busy embassy in Bahrain. About 5 percent of the island's population is Iranian, and a much larger percentage of Bahrain's nationals are of Iranian extraction. The Shah of Iran is determined that neither Bahrain nor any other Gulf amirate will deter Iran from becoming the Gulf's *defensor pacis*.

Bahrain's relations with the Arab world have been an extension of the oft-repeated official statements that Bahrain is a sovereign Arab country and that it is part of the greater Arab homeland (see the constitution and other statements). As a member of the Arab League, Bahrain has usually attended the league's sessions, as well as all other league-sponsored meetings. Bahrain has, at least in its official statements, supported the "confrontation" Arab states, condemned Israeli occupation of Arab lands, and constantly advocated a unified Arab position. Concerning Palestine, Bahrain, like most Arab countries, has given the Palestinian people moral and financial support.[cc]

At least four factors have influenced Bahrain's relations with the Palestine resistance movement:

1. As a conservative tribal society, Bahrain has ideologically been inclined to support regimes that are status-quo oriented. Bahrain is on very good terms with Jordan and tacitly supported King Hussein's actions against the Palestine resistance movement.[dd]

2. As a Gulf amirate, Bahrain has in the last two years been an enticing

---

[z] Reports circulated in November-December 1971 to the effect that Kuwait had agreed to lease the Muharraq air base by the end of 1971 in order to provide the Kuwaiti air force with a training base. Kuwait denied the reports. *Sada al-'Usbu'*, 30 November 1971, p. 15.

[aa] On 1 December 1971 Bahrain issued a statement calling on Iran to review its action in terms of justice and regional security. *Sada al-'Usbu'*, 7 December 1971, pp. 12-14.

[bb] In September 1972, Bahrain received a present of three large tractors from Iran, and in the winter of 1972-73 the week-long Iranian Trade Exhibit in Bahrain was officially opened by the prime minister.

[cc] *Sada al-'Usbu'*, 25 January 1972, pp. 4-5. About 2,000 Palestinians were living in Bahrain in 1972, one-third of whom were employed in the Ministry of Education.

[dd] Several Jordanian military officers have been seconded to Bahrain, as well as to other Gulf amirates, for training purposes. The internal security departments in most of the amirates have also employed Jordanian officers.

target, together with the other amirates, for the activities of the revolution in Dhufar (the Popular Front for the Liberation of Oman—PFLO). Several Bahraini leftists have fought for PFLO against the Gulf's tribal regimes. In Bahrain itself several young men and women have been arrested under the Emergency Laws since the fall of 1972 on the charge of having either distributed PFLO literature in the country or of belonging to the Bahraini branch of PFLO.[ee] For obvious reasons, Bahraini authorities have deplored the activities of PFLO; as a sister revolution, the Palestine Resistance Movement has not been warmly received by the ruling family.

3. Bahrain's limited financial resources, unlike Kuwait, Qatar, or Abu Dhabi, do not allow it to offer significant material contributions to the Palestine resistance movement. Bahrain does not vie for any leadership position in the Gulf, nor can she do so. However, Bahrain has spoken strongly on behalf of Palestine in the United Nations.[ff]

4. In addition to its conservative, essentially antirevolutionary ideology and perhaps because of its limited resources, Bahrain has in the last five years actively worked for the establishment of an open, entrepôt, services-oriented economy. It has been the conscious policy of the government to provide international businesses and their local agents with all the enticements of an open society. These include favorable capital investment conditions, tax credits, inexpensive or free natural gas, environmental accomodations for personnel, and a rather efficient communications network with the outside world. In this attempt to become the Lebanon of the Gulf, the Bahraini government finds the revolution phenomenon a threat to the business-oriented image that the country has been trying to project.

One Western power more and more evident on the Gulf scene is the United States. Because of the increasing American concern with energy sources, the Gulf region will figure very highly in American long-range foreign policy in the coming years. Bahrain, like the rest of the Gulf states, will be affected by this increased concern; a country like Bahrain, because of its limited capabilities, cannot be an independent actor in the international arena. Whether Bahrain wills it or not, by its very location it will be caught in the squeeze of international politics.

[ee] Following the wave of arrests in March-April 1973, several elected members of the Constitutional Assembly met with the amir and the prime minister on 9 April 1973 and protested these arrests. The prime minister stated that the information which Bahrain's Special Branch had received from Oman's security department indicated that certain clandestine activities were taking place in the country.

[ff] Speaking before the United Nations General Assembly on 29 September 1972, Bahrain's foreign minister said that the United Nations must condemn Israeli terrorism and not the Palestinians, who were the victims of this terrorism. He asked the major powers, Israel's suppliers of offensive weapons, to reexamine their policy and halt delivery of these arms (*Akhbar al-Bahrain*, 2 October 1972, p. 2).

American-Bahraini relations in their present form began shortly after Bahrain declared itself an independent state on 14 August 1971. On August 15 Bahrain and the United Kingdom mutually agreed to terminate the special treaties that had been in effect since 1880 and all other treaties that contravened Bahrain's new status as a sovereign state. On the same day, the two countries signed a new treaty of continued friendship, understanding, mutual respect, and cultural, educational, and economic cooperation.[14] Although the British ambassador to Bahrain enjoys a special position among the diplomatic corps and although over 25 percent of Bahrain's total imports in the last three years have come from the United Kindom, the British political influence in the Gulf as an international force is, for all intents and purposes, declining.[gg]

In December 1971 the Bahraini government agreed to lease to the United States Navy a section of the formerly British-held Jufair naval base south of Manama. On the United States' side this was an executive agreement rather than a treaty.[hh] The onshore facilities, known by the navy as the Naval Control of Shipping Office (NCSO), are used to support the one navy flagship under COMIDEASTFOR. This minifleet is commanded by a rear admiral, who has his office on board ship when the flagship is in port and at Jufair when the ship is out. The agreement also provides for hanger space at the Muharraq airport for the admiral's plane; all in all, about 500 Americans use the Jufair facilities. The story of the Jufair agreement between December 1971 and October 1973, the date the agreement was terminated by the Bahraini government, is an interesting reflection of the United States' position in the Gulf, especially in regard to the Arab littoral states. Since COMIDEASTFOR has not yet dismantled its facility, the agreement remains in actual effect. The following discussion is based on the agreement as it presently exists.

Although Bahrain receives an annual rent from the United States Navy for the use of these facilities, which is probably much smaller than generally thought or officially indicated, the Bahrain-United States Executive Agreement has undeniable political implications. It has also caused Bahrain political embarrassment at home and abroad. The agreement was primarily negotiated by and put into effect under Rear Admiral Marmaduke

---

[gg] Individual Gulf countries still rely on a significant number of high-level British civil servants on secondment to these countries. Also, as was stated above, several British officers still head the internal security departments in these countries. For an examination of American relations with the Arab states of the Gulf see Emile A. Nakhleh, *Arab-American Relations in the Persian Gulf* (Washington, D.C.: American Enterprise Institute for Public Policy Research, 1975).

[hh] For a journalistic report on the Bahrain-United States agreement concerning Jufair see al-Rayyis, *Sira' al-Wahat wa al-Naft* [*Struggle of Oases and Oil*], pp. 315-326. See also *The New York Times*, 7 January 1972, and *Department of State Bulletin*, 28 February 1972, pp. 282-283.

Gresham Bayne, former Commander of COMIDEASTFOR, and John Gatch, the first American chargé d'affaires to Bahrain.[14] In commenting on the American presence in Bahrain, Rear Admiral Bayne stated that the primary mission of the America navy in Bahrain was to carry out friendly visits to the countries of the region, which would contribute to understanding and cooperation among the peoples of the area. He also stated that the activities of the navy in the Gulf fall within the broad United States-Gulf policy, namely, the establishment and maintenance of harmonious, friendly, and cooperative relations among the governments and peoples of the Gulf.[15] Rear Admiral Robert Hanks, who replaced Rear Admiral Bayne, expressed similar views.[16] Another point that should be made is that these visits cover a vast area extending from Pakistan to the eastern coast of Africa and including the Indian Ocean, the Arabian Sea, the Gulf of Oman, the Arabian-Persian Gulf, and the Red Sea.

Although the Jufair agreement was signed on 23 December 1971, it was not made public until 7 January 1972. At least two factors contributed to this delay: Bahrain's sensitivity to the question of an American presence on the island, and a desire on the part of the United States government to deemphasize the agreement, hoping that such a low profile would avoid a confrontation with the Senate over the use of executive agreements—a tactic that failed.[JJ] The announcement of the agreement on 7 January 1972 aroused the ire of the Senate Foreign Relations Committee, chaired by the redoubtable Senator J. William Fulbright.

In the Arab world the agreement was blown completely out of proportion, so much so that Bahrain's foreign minister, Shaikh Muhammad bin Mubarak al-Khalifa, held a press conference on 10 January 1972 to deemphasize the political implications of the agreement. He argued that the agreement was purely commercial and that Bahrain's independence and sovereignty would not be violated. He pointed out that the agreement does not require any military of political commitment, and that Bahrain retained the power to terminate the arrangement at any time without repercussions. He mentioned that there was a definite benefit to the national economy and that only one American flagship was in port at any one time.[17]

The Foreign Ministry announced at the same press conference that the state of Bahrain regretted the way in which the press has greatly exaggerated American-Bahraini relations. It was emphasized that American-Bahraini relations go back to a quarter of a century ago when an American ship used to call at Bahraini ports for fuel and supplies. Following the termination of the Anglo-Bahraini treaty, the United States asked the

---

[14]*United States and Other International Agreements*, vol. 22, pp. 2184-2189. TIAS 7263.

[JJ]Concerning Bahrain's sensitivity on this issue see al-Rayyis, *Sira' al-Wahat wa al-Naft* [*Struggle of Oases and Oil*], p. 325.

Bahraini government to continue offering those facilities and services that have no military or defense aspects. The government stressed that this agreement did not endanger the sovereignty and independence of Bahrain nor did it establish an American military base or military presence. The Foreign Ministry emphasized that no secret agreements or treaties had been signed.[18]

In the spring of 1973 the United States' seemingly sudden interest in the Gulf due to the energy crisis inadvertently created a new concern within the Bahraini government over the American presence at Jufair. This unease was accelerated by a succession of editorials in the Arab press and radio throughout April-May 1973 revealing alleged American attempts to establish a foothold in the Gulf. [kk] Whether these accusations are true or not is not terribly relevant to the average newspaper reader in the Arab world. What is important is the image that these press articles have formed in the mind of the reader. The attachment to the image renders the real insignificant, regardless of the irrationality of the former and the rationality of the latter.

This burgeoning anti-American emphasis has placed certain pressures on the government of Bahrain to reassess the Jufair agreement. Several factors would influence Bahrain's possible decision to review the Jufair agreement. First, the rent that Bahrain receives from the navy for the use of the Jufair facilities is relatively small; therefore, the financial benefits do not outweigh the political disadvantages. Also, when the agreement was concluded in December 1971, the government of Bahrain expressed an interest in receiving badly needed American technical assistance as a fringe benefit that would counterbalance the annual rent. The only technical assistance that Bahrain has received to date has been of a kind termed reimbursable, that is, Bahrain has had to pay for it. Third, under the new constitution all international agreements and treaties to which Bahrain is a party will have to pass under the scrutiny of the new National Assembly (Constitution, article 37). This means that the executive branch of the government will have to present the National Assembly with more convincing evidence than ever before of the tangible benefits that would accrue from such a treaty. Finally, the increasingly close economic and political relations between Bahrain and other Gulf countries, such as Kuwait, will more and more influence Bahrain's outlook on the establishment of such facilities as Jufair.

[kk] For a sample of these editorials see *al-'Usbu' al-'Arabi* (Beirut), 2 April 1973, pp. 23-29. The article was basically a commentary on the appointment of Richard Helms, the former head of the CIA, as the United States ambassador to Iran. The article was entitled "The Newcomers from the Bay of Pigs to the Gulf of Black Gold." On the cover the word CIA was sprawled across a picture of Helms and the map of Saudi Arabia. The I of CIA was a dagger stabbing Saudi Arabia, and the A was an oil derrick. See also *Sada al-'Usbu'* (Bahrain), 10 April 1973, pp. 16-18 ("Iran Attempts to Control the Waters of the Gulf"); *al-Hadaf* (Kuwait), 12 April 1973, pp. 10-11 ("Washington's Conspiracy to Transform the Gulf into Palestine No. 2"); and *Sada al-'Usbu'*, 24 April 1973, pp. 3 and 26-27.

In the light of the above, it would not be surprising if Bahrain would take a harder position on this agreement. The practical options available to Bahrain include the following:

1. Demand a higher rent
2. Demand certain technical assistance on a nonreimbursable basis
3. Continue to provide American ships with needed services for a specific sum without the availability of the onshore facilities. In other words, demand that the home port be established somewhere else.

Although the two extreme possibilities, that is, to keep the present agreement as it stood or to ask the United States Navy to dismantle its presence immediately and completely, seemed improbable, increasing Arab criticism of America's support of Israel during the October war compelled the government of Bahrain to react. Bahrain is too small and powerless to ride out such a storm of criticism. However, Bahrain's request that the United States dismantle its facilities in Jufair has not been vigorously enforced, and it is expected that a new understanding concerning this agreement will be reached. A possible course of action would be for the United States to reassess the need for and benefit from the Jufair agreement. Based on this reassessment, the American government would probably have to pay a price commensurate with the benefits—that is if Bahrain would be willing to conclude such a settlement.

On a two day visit to Bahrain, 2-3 July 1972, Secretary of State William Rogers stated at a press conference that the United States was interested in the peace and stability of the region and that the establishment of strong relations among the peoples of the region would be a primary contributor to this peace and stability. Secretary Rogers also indicated that the United States wished to cooperate with the countries of the region so that stable and successful governments would be formed. The secretary again emphasized that the United States did not have a naval base in Bahrain—only certain facilities.[18]

Accompanying Secretary Rogers on his visit to Bahrain was Joseph Sisco, the assistant secretary for Near Eastern and South Asian affairs. In restating the United States' interest in the Gulf, Assistant Secretary Sisco declared that the United States was interested in offering friendship and cooperation as a guarantee of the security of the Gulf.[19] The reaction to these statements in both Bahrain and Kuwait was critical. In a statement following Rogers' visit, the Kuwaiti government expressed the belief that the Gulf region should remain outside the major powers' spheres of interest and that the region's future should be determined by the peoples of the region.[20]

---

[18]*Sada al-'Usbu'*, 4 July 1972, p. 3, and *al-Adwa'*, 6 July 1972, pp. 2-3. The Rogers statements were strongly criticized in both newspapers.

It is obvious that the United States has definite views on Gulf regional security. To American policy planners the Gulf contains two critical factors: it is the world's largest reservoir of oil, and it is an extension of the Indian Ocean. Moreover, the United States is not the only major power with easy access to the region. Two other powers are directly involved: the Soviet Union and, to a much lesser extent, China. Hence, the possibility of American-Soviet rivalry in the region becomes increasingly relevant.[mm]

The Soviet Union's concept of regional security has been implemented along two parallel lines of action. It has established a friendly relationship with Iran, the most potent Gulf force, and the Soviet Union has also cultivated close relations with Iraq and India. Soviet-Indian policy culminated in the establishment of Bangladesh. Such a policy has a two-fold purpose: to weaken American influence in the area and to discredit the China-Pakistan alliance. Through Iraq, the Soviet Union has supported most of the revolutionary movements in the region, including the newly formed Baluchi national liberation movement, which promotes the liberation of Baluchistan from both Iran and Pakistan. Any fragmentation of Iran will indirectly serve Iraq, which has been in constant conflict with Iran, and any fragmentation of Pakistan will indirectly serve India.[nn]

The above discussion indicates that several possible troubles loom on the Gulf's horizon. And what gives these possible sources of conflict a larger-than-life size is the energy crisis and America's evident determination to secure its needed oil supplies.

[mm] For an excellent analysis of future trends in the Gulf see *al-Hawadith* (Beirut), 15 December 1972, pp. 28 and 31. The author of the article, a regular contributor to the magazine, is the former director of information in Bahrain. See also Emile A. Nakhleh, *The United States and Saudi Arabia: A Policy Analysis* (Washington, D.C.: American Enterprise Institute for Public Policy Research, 1975), and R.D. McLaurin, *The Middle East in Soviet Policy* (Lexington, Mass.: Lexington Books, D.C. Heath and Company, 1975).

[nn] On 10 February 1973 Pakistani authorities confiscated large quantities of weapons inside the Iraqi Embassy in Islamabad, which were believed to have been en route to the Baluchi tribes in Southwest Pakistan (*Gulf Weekly Mirror*, 11 February 1973, p. 1). Six days later, on 16 February 1973, the Pakistani president dissolved the regional parliament in the Baluchi region and introduced direct presidential rule.

6
Toward a Democratic Structure: The Constitutional Assembly

The Rhetoric of Democracy: Government and Citizens

In his 1971 National Day speech, the first since Bahrain's independence, the ruler, Shaikh 'Isa bin Sulman al-Khalifa, clearly referred to the immediate necessity of a constitution. He emphasized that a modern constitution was to be a prerequisite for the political organization of the state. Such a constitution would protect the society's unity and cohesion and guarantee to citizens their basic individual freedoms of education, work, social welfare, health, and free expression of opinion. It would also provide the people with the right to participate in the management of their country's affairs in a context of legitimacy and constitutionalism.[1]

The ruler stated in the same speech that he had authorized the Council of Ministers to prepare a modern constitution for the country, which would guarantee these rights and freedoms. Although several government officials subsequently made references to a constitution, the ruler's statement was the first explicit commitment by the government to a written constitution. This commitment signaled a move by the Khalifa family to urbanize and modernize its tribal rule, thereby attempting to establish a legitimate basis of government other than the traditional, autocratic tribal system of government. Bahrain's geographic proximity to Kuwait and the close relationship between the Khalifas of Bahrain and the Sabah's of Kuwait made it logical for Bahrain to emulate Kuwait's constitutional experiment, which has been in existence since 1962. Kuwait's constitutional prescripts were, with some modifications, to be the guideline for Bahrain's venture into constitutional government.

The articulation of particularistic interests concerning the constitution to which the ruler referred in his official addresses can best be monitored through a series of newspaper interviews, which appeared in *al-Adwa'*, a Bahraini weekly newspaper, early in 1972. The interviews were conducted and written by Muhammad Qasim al-Shirawi, an accomplished Bahraini journalist. He was assisted by Nuhad Qasab, a former reporter for *al-Adwa'*.[2]

In that series of interviews, entitled "What do the People Want in the Constitution?", al-Shirawi interviewed representatives of the wealthy and prominent from among the merchandizing class, middle-class merchants and businessmen, college graduates (who view themselves as the country's intelligentsia), and women. The author had planned to interview labor representatives as well, but labor troubles in March of 1972 and the sensitive political climate that ensued kept him from following through on his original plan.[a]

The views expressed understandably reflect the age, social status, and sex of the interviewees; it is worthwhile to note that a substantial number of those interviewed later became members of the Constitutional Assembly, either through election, appointment, or by virtue of ministerial rank.[b] In a society such as Bahrain, where the population is primarily divided into two classes, merchants and workers, the method of interest articulation and interest aggregation assumes a special significance, especially when these interests pertain to the preparation of a constitution, the first legal, binding, and authoritative document to govern the functional divisions of the polity.

The views expressed in these newspaper articles cut across the entire political spectrum of Bahrain, and the corresponding interests range from support from the Khalifa-maintained status quo to a democratic constitution written by popularly elected representatives. Yet, what is particularly significant about these interviews is the fact that in spite of the socioeconomic and ideological cleavages among the interviewees and in spite of their divergent particular interests, a common agreement was expressed on several issues, which formed the core of a common denominator. These issues included: (1) the need for a constitution; (2) a recognition, often overt and sometimes covert, of the need for popular participation; (3) an admission of the existence of a wide gap between the Khalifa government and the people; (4) a corresponding realization that a wall of mistrust and suspicion separates the government from the people.

Ahmad Fakhro, one of the five leading merchants and the first one to be interviewed, made several points. He stated that the country did not lack a constitution so much as it lacked cooperation between government and the people. He felt that government should not be restricted to the views of only one class of society; all the people should participate in the governing process. Fakhro refused to express his views on whether illegal police methods against the citizens should stop or whether the constitution should ban such methods as deportation or exile of citizens. Fakhro hastened to add that the merchants have always received excellent cooperation from the government, especially under the leadership of Shaikh Khalifa bin Sulman al-Khalifa.[3]

Ibrahim Khalil Kanoo, another leading merchant, maintained that any-

---

[a] The interviews were published in seven articles: two reflecting the merchants' views; two for the intelligentsia; one from the people as a whole; one interview with the minister of justice; and one on women.

[b] Some of those who later ran for election to the Constitutional Assembly were again interviewed by the same journalist in October and November of 1972 concerning their election program. See *al-'Adwa'*, October-November, 1972. See below.

one who violates the law should be punished but that *no one* should be exiled from his country, regardless of the offense. He also believed that Bahrain is not yet ready for political parties.[4] Ahmad Zayani took a more forceful position on the constitution. He averred that it was imperative to have a constitution, and he believed that a constitution is the basic support of national independence. However, he was confident that the wise and enlightened government would promulgate a constitution and that whatever the government decided would undoubtedly be for the good of the country. He also expressed the very strong and common conviction that Bahraini citizens should never be deported or exiled for any reason whatsoever.[5]

In common with the other prosperous merchants interviewed in these articles, Yusuf al-Mu'ayyad expressed strong support for the status quo. He emphasized that no Bahraini wished to substitute anything for their rulers, but at the same time he criticized the placement of all authority and decision-making power in the hands of one man. He believed that, no matter how wise and qualified, one man is just not able to attend to and do justice to every problem, large and small. He also contended that it would be necessary for the people to share in the writing of their constitution because then they would feel obligated to obey it.[6]

Below a small number of prosperous merchants and businessmen, Bahrain has a sizable group of successful middle-class businessmen, that is, furniture dealers, grocers, accounting firms, appliance agents, and pharmacists. Ideologically, this class espouses political pragmatism, bourgeoisie nationalism, and an at least rhetorical version of social and economic liberalism. The interviews also revealed a genuine consciousness of and support for the socioeconomic problems of the common man. Those interviewed unanimously advocated a state-supported program of social justice and general welfare.

Jasim Murad, the first interviewee of this group (later elected to the Constitutional Assembly), is the best representative of this class, and he is also one of the most liberally oriented merchants on social issues. To him, independence meant that the Bahraini citizen had finally freed himself from foreign domination and was about to participate in the governing of his country. He also believed that political parties should be allowed to function, otherwise there was a danger that secret and destructive movements would develop. Also the constitution should include the basic freedoms, an independent judiciary and the right of labor to unionize.[7]

Rasul al-Jishshi, a graduate in pharmacy from the American University of Beirut who later fulfilled an important role as a liberal Shi'a member of the Constitutional Assembly, expressed views similar to those of Jasim Murad. Addressing himself to the constitutional experiment, al-Jishshi stated that the basic change required was the establishment of a new relationship between the ruler and the people. If the nature of the new rule was to be democratic, then the atmosphere would be prepared for political groupings within the Assembly to perform the role of loyal opposition. The constitution should also guarantee basic democratic rights. On foreign policy he stated that the economic and geographic position of Bahrain dictated a moderate position in international politics but that this should not prevent her from taking definite positions, especially on Arab issues.[8]

A similar note was struck by 'Ali Rashid al-Amin, an urbane grocer in Manama who later ran for but failed to win election to the Constitutional Assembly. Concerning the political future of Bahrain, al-Amin expressed hope that the new constitution would produce a democratic parliamentary system, which would guarantee the people active participation in the governing of the country, and that the authorities would be responsive to the aspirations of their people. On the method of elections and the reaction to their recently achieved independence, he stated that direct, free elections would be the only way to insure true popular participation in the governing process. Also, he visualized loyal opposition as necessary and inevitable. Unfortunately, he believed that, in spite of some administrative changes in the government, the average citizen had not experienced any alteration in his daily life since independence. On foreign policy he advocated peaceful coexistence, with close cooperation between Bahrain and other Gulf states. Also, he realized that Bahrain should industrialize and that encouragement should be given to local industries.[c]

Concurring views on the necessity of guaranteeing individual freedoms and of allowing the people a larger role in the governing of the country were given by other businessmen as well. Ibrahim Ishaq, owner of the Middle East Trade Center, believed that the constitution should guarantee individual freedom.[9] 'Abd al-Rahman Taqi, co-owner of Asia Company, insisted that the constitution should include all of the freedoms, rights, and social guarantees found in other constitutions.[10]

Unlike the businessmen or workers, the college graduates of Bahrain find themselves in a somewhat unique position. They consider themselves to be the elite, policy-oriented public of Bahrain, and, by definition, they constitute the center of liberal thought in the country. Yet, a significant number of these college-educated Bahrainis are also civil servants, which means that they therefore occupy the decision-making positions within the governmental bureaucracy. Hence the dilemma of the intelligentsia: a liberal posture during social gatherings at the Alumni Club, and a status quo-supportive posture for the bureaucracy of which they are the guardians and which must above all reflect the traditional tribal nature of rule as conceived by the Khalifa family.

---

[c] *'al-'Adwa'*, 10 February 1972, pp. 3-5. On 8 May 1973 al-Amin was elected president of the Youth Federation Club in Muharraq.

In spite of these conflicting interests, the interviews, which al-Shirawi conducted with the graduates, evoked a forceful liberal image, with strong support for such issues as popular participation in government, individual freedoms, and constitutional guarantees. A random selection of these interviews is instructive. Hasan Zayn al-'Abidin (B.A., 1967, economics) insisted that the constitution should be written by a committee composed of bureaucrats, legal experts, and representatives of national clubs and societies. The constitution should then be put to a popular referendum. As did most people, he emphasized the constitution should guarantee basic individual freedoms, the separation of powers, and a free and independent judiciary.[11]

'Abd al-'Aziz Muhammad al-Khalifa (B.A., 1956, literature), the minister of education and formerly the president of the Alumni Club, maintained that independence meant the Bahrainis themselves had to create an atmosphere conducive to the development of freedom and democracy. He hoped that the constitution would be written cooperatively by both a committee representing the people and by legal experts from other Arab countries. He also strongly supported the inclusion of written guarantees of individual freedoms.[12]

The most eloquent spokesman for the intellectuals was Muhammad Jabir al-Ansari (M.A., 1965, literature, and a Ph.D candidate at American University of Beirut), the former director of information. In an interview published in *al-Adwa'*,[13] al-Ansari offered a thoughtful analysis of the future of constitutional life in Bahrain and of the responsibilities, duties, and guarantees that should be developed. He was mainly concerned with the necessity for a constitution that would allow all classes of people the opportunity for social justice and economic advancement. He emphasized that social justice and economic opportunity were the basic supports of political life and that the constitution should protect the common man from exploitation by the merchant class.[14] His second point was that the constitution should guarantee true democratic participation in the governing process by a majority of the people, and that the large merchant class should not be allowed to dominate the Constitutional Assembly because this would destroy the necessary democratic equilibrium. His third point was that the construction of a democracy required the active involvement of the entire society in a rational, gradual, and calm manner. He envisioned the constitution as being prepared in two stages: (1) it should be written by a committee of constitutional experts; (2) it should then be submitted to the people, especially the opinion makers, for their views. He hoped that loyal opposition would be allowed, and he appealed to the people's sense of national unity and dedication to insure the success of Bahrain's democratic experiment.

Many of the graduates emphasized this need to feel free from exploitation by the commercial class. Ghazi Rida al-Musawi (B.A., 1967, commerce) agreed that the constitution should express the people's aspirations and hopes and that it should be written by a constitutional assembly or committee freely elected by the people, albeit with the aid of constitutional experts. He felt that the constitution should guarantee freedom of thought and expression and that labor should be guaranteed the right to organize and unionize. In his view the constitution should also promote social justice by protecting the common man from exploitation by the powerful business and commercial class, and the constitution should provide for some separation of powers. He felt that loyal opposition would be inevitable and should be tolerated.[15]

One of the most interesting interviews with the people at large was with Hasan al-Sitrawi, a former bank employee. al-Sitrawi gave an interesting comparison between the Kuwaiti and Bahraini constitutional experiments, saying that the Kuwaiti constitutional experiment was not necessarily an ideal model for Bahrain. He indicated that many Bahrainis do not speak frankly because they are afraid of possible government retaliation; therefore, it was important to establish a modern democratic constitutional government based on legitimacy and on popularly elected legislative bodies. The executive branch should be accountable to the legislative branch, and there should also be an independent judicial system and political parties.[d]

'Ali Sayyar, editor and owner of the weekly *Sada al-'Usbu'* and later a member of the Constitutional Assembly, and Mahmud al-Mardi, editor and owner of the only other weekly newspaper, *al-Adwa'*, are two people in Bahrain who occupy a leading and often enviable position among the elite public. By their profession they stand at the heart of the ongoing process of political socialization. Concerning Bahrain's political life, 'Ali Sayyar advocated direct free elections and some form of democratic government. He implied that a frightened citizen would be an ineffective one and would in the end be nothing but a burden on the state.[16]

Mahmud al-Mardi, who later ran for the Constitutional Assembly but lost, viewed popular participation in government as having only two alternatives: either absolute trust and openness, which would accept the most modern methods of elections, or a retreat to "arranged" elections, as in many Arab countries. He hoped for a simple constitution, which could be understood by everyone, intellectual, worker, student, or farmer. Also, he stressed that in any constitutional committee or assembly the majority of the members should be elected by the people.[17]

---

[d] 'al-Sitrawi was arrested shortly after the publication of this article and questioned concerning his political views, in particular those expressed in the interview. However, during a meeting soon thereafter between Shaikh Muhammad bin Mubarak al-Khalifa, former minister of information, and both the writer of the article and the editor of the newspaper, the minister stated that the arrest was not a result of the views expressed in the article. al-Sitrawi was later released.

Women's views on the constitution understandably expressed their primary concern—women's equality and suffrage. However, those interviewed, three journalists, a government secretary, and a professional educator, also addressed themselves to the life of the Bahraini family under the constitution. Safiyya Dwayghir, director of higher education, called on Bahraini women to fight for their rights and not to wait for men to fight for them.[18]

The other women interviewed were equally emphatic in their statements. Layla Khalaf, one of two women appointed to the foreign service section of Bahrain's Foreign Ministry would like to see a constitution that would do justice to Bahraini women.[19] Bahiyya al-Jishshi, a journalist and radio broadcaster believed that the constitution should guarantee women equal opportunities and thereby restore their lost humanity.[20] Tifla Muhammad al-Khalifa, a journalist, hoped that the constitution would guarantee women all basic rights and work opportunities, protect women's rights in the home, forbid the father to deprive his daughter of an education, define the laws of marriage and divorce; forbid the use of religion to excuse women's servitude in the family, limit the number of wives, and prohibit physical or verbal insult of women. She also insisted that women should also have full political rights.[21]

It should be pointed out that, in spite of the well-articulated appeal of the educated women for political equality, the Constitutional Assembly law deprived women of the right to vote or to participate in the political life of the country. More on this point follows in chapter 7.

Four separate positions may be distinguished in these interviews. First, the older and wealthier merchants agreed on five major points:

1. They all saw the need for a constitution.
2. All felt the need for some sort of vague popular participation in the governing of the country, although they readily confessed that the constitution should be promulgated by the state.
3. The merchants enjoyed very favorable relations with the government.
4. They all believed that the country was not yet ready for political parties and/or loyal opposition; yet, all of those interviewed praised the high level of political awareness of the Bahraini people.
5. All emphatically agreed that no Bahraini citizen should be exiled or deported for any reason whatsoever.

The middle-aged and middle-class merchants interviewed also held common opinions on several main points:

1. They were generally more tolerant of the concept of loyal opposition, although not necessarily political parties.
2. They all advocated some degree of popular participation in the drafting of the constitution.

3. A constitution should clearly guarantee individual freedoms and a democratic form of government.
4. They generally approved of giving women the right to vote.
5. They envisioned a judicial body to settle constitutional questions.
6. On foreign policy, they all espoused moderation, peaceful coexistence, and closer relations with other Gulf states.
7. Economically, they supported the free enterprise system, and they encouraged the luring of foreign capital investments to Bahrain, with restrictions protecting local capital and industries.

The third group, the university graduates, endorsed more specific political issues:
1. They sensed a general demand for a democratic form of government, which be definition would include active popular participation.
2. There was a general demand for a constitution that would guarantee basic individual freedoms in accordance with the United Nations Charter and the Human Rights Charter.
3. They generally called for social justice, trust between government and people, and a more open government.
4. They generally criticized the Alumni Club for its failure to play a more positive role in the formative years of the country's history.
5. They hoped for an elective political life in which there would be room for loyal opposition.
6. The constitution should grant women equal rights with men, politically, socially, and economically.

The women interviewed, the fourth and final group, dealt almost exclusively with the problems of women in a modernizing society:
1. The constitution should clearly provide suffrage for women.
2. The constitution should guarantee women equal opportunities—socially, economically, and psychologically.
3. The constitution should give women a new sense of dignity.

In the last two weeks of May 1972, the ruler invited several leading citizens and representatives of national clubs and organizations to the palace and solicited their views as to the best method of writing a constitution for Bahrain. The Khalifa family had already decided to follow the route charted by Kuwait, that is, to establish a *majlis ta'sisi* (hereafter known as constitutional assembly) whose sole task would be to prepare the constitution. Therefore, the consultations with these community leaders focused on the structure of such an assembly. Three main views crystallized during these consultations: that the assembly would consist of government appointed members; that it would be completely elective; that a 50-50 principle would be applied whereby half of the members would be nationally elected and the other half appointed by the government. The third recommendation was adopted, and the government set out to write a law governing the proposed Constitutional Assembly.[22]

During these consultations, several underlying principles of the constitutional experiment were articulated by the ruling family, and these fundamental assumptions have so far been accepted by a majority of the population. First, the constitution would be granted by the Khalifa family to their subjects, primarily in accordance with the Qur'anic principle and the tribal tradition of *shura* (consultation).[e] Second, the constitution was not a governmental response to a specific popular demand for participation. In a tribal system of government, both traditional and urban, the basic source of authority and legitimacy resided in the tribe and/or the family. During the palace consultations the principle of popular sovereignty was not even raised; the ruling family as a symbol of sovereignty was never questioned. It is not the intention here to probe the value or functionality of the *shura* system of government, which is based on the principle that the ruler may solicit the advice of respected members of the system although he is not bound to follow it. It is simply one of the underlying assumptions for legitimacy of rule in an urban tribalism system of government. In its search for a new identity, the state of Bahrain is essentially an extension of the Khalifa ruler.[f]

The new political community is not the individual at large, as Aristotle would have it, nor is it a synthesis of a preceding revolutionary struggle between colonizers and the colonized (Fanon). Rather, Bahrain's new political society is an outgrowth of a political process that began while Bahrain was still bound by a special relationship to Britain. These processes did not occur within a broad popular base; they began at the apex of the pyramid of power—the inner councils of the Khalifa family. It is in this context that the move toward constitutionalism began to ferment.

The Legal Prescription

On 20 June 1972 the ruler promulgated Law No. 12 (1972) concerning the establishment of a Constitutional Assembly for the purpose of preparing a

---

[e]This principle was reiterated by the ruler when convening the Constitutional Assembly on 16 December 1972 (from a live radio broadcast of the opening ceremonies of the Constitutional Assembly in the Manama Municipality Hall). See this plus other speeches in *Akhbar al-Bahrain*, 18 December 1972, pp. 1-3.

[f]The phrase "my people" is frequently used by the ruler in his official addresses. The implication here is that the constitution is being given to the people by the ruler as an expression of royal benevolence.

constitution for the country.[23] According to this law, the Constitutional Assembly would be composed of 22 members popularly elected by secret ballot, a maximum of 10 members appointed by decree, and the ministers as members ex officio (article 1).[g]

As may be seen in table 6-1, article 3 divided the country into 8 election districts, which were later subdivided by Law No. 13, 19 July 1972 into 19 wards.

In the light of the country's political climate, especially the activities of the Special Branch as regards detention, interrogation, and exile of dissenters, article 5 of the Constitutional Assembly Law was considered by several leading citizens as being highly significant. It stated that members of the Assembly would be free to express their views and opinions during the sessions of the Assembly or of its committees without harassment. The article stated further that while the Assembly is in session no member shall be investigated, searched, arrested, or detained, unless caught in the act, without prior permission of the Assembly.

The process of preparing the constitution is described in article 6, which directs the Council of Ministers to prepare a draft constitution within four months from the date of the law's enactment (20 June 1972) and to present it to the Constitutional Assembly at its first meeting. The Assembly would then prepare the final draft of the constitution within six months of its first meeting, held on 16 December 1972. This draft would then be submitted to the ruler for approval and issuance.

Article 7 provided for the election of Assembly officers at the first meeting, at which time the Assembly would also adopt its procedural by-laws.[h] Article 8 defines the time and method of the Assembly meetings: The Assembly is to meet twice a week, a majority of the membership constitutes a quorum, and the decisions of the Assembly on constitutional questions require a two-thirds majority.[i]

Voting eligibility and eligibility for candidacy were spelled out in Decree/Law No. 13 (1972), which was promulgated by the ruler on 16 July 1972.[24] According to article 1 of this law, those eligible to vote in the elections to the Constitutional Assembly had to be male Bahraini citizens

---

[g] It should be noted here that this law is almost an exact replica of the Kuwaiti Law No. 35 for 1962 which detailed the electoral process for the Kuwaiti National Assembly. As a matter of fact, Kuwait's constitutional expert was summoned to Bahrain to help write this law and the draft constitution. The final figure was a total of 42 members: 22 elected; 8 appointed; and 12 ministers.

[h] On 16 December 1972 the Assembly elected an appointee, Ibrahim al-'Urayyid, as speaker, and two elected members, 'Abd al-'Aziz Shamlan and Qasim Fakhro, as deputy-speaker and secretary respectively. However, the Assembly took four meetings before adopting its by-laws.

[i] In its by-laws, the Constitutional Assembly changed the two-thirds majority requirement into a simple majority.

Table 6-1
Constitutional Assembly Election Districts

District	District Seat	Wards	Representatives
1st	Manama	1-6	8 (1st & 2nd have 2 representatives each)
2nd	Muharraq Island	7-11	6 (9th has 2 representatives)
3rd (North)	Jidhafs	12-13	2 (1 each)
4th (Western)	Budaya'	14	1
5th (Southern)	Jasra	15	1
6th (Central)	'Isa Town	16-17	2 (1 each)
7th	Sitra Island	18	1
8th	Rifa'	19	1
8 districts		19 wards	22 representatives

who had attained the age of 20 on election day. Naturalized citizens could vote only if they have been citizens for a minimum of ten years since the enactment of the 1963 Citizenship Law, which had the effect of denying suffrage to every naturalized citizen in Bahrain. Also, members of the armed forces and the police were forbidden to vote.[25] Finally, article 2 states that convicted criminals could not vote.

Candidates for the Constitutional Assembly, in addition to being qualified as voters, must have been at least 30 years of age on election day and must have been able to read and write the Arabic language well (article 9).[j] To become an official candidate, the person in question had to submit a written application to the Ministry of Municipalities and Agriculture carrying 15 signatures from his ward. He also had to pay a nonrefundable deposit of 25 Bahraini dinars. No election could be held in a ward where the number of candidates equalled the number of future representatives from that ward. In these cases the candidate(s) would win by acclamation (article 11, section C).[k]

The Constitutional Assembly Law obviously raised several serious questions with which prospective candidates were concerned in the months preceding the election. Government spokesmen found themselves engaged in a continuous dialogue attempting to underline what they saw as positive aspects of the law. For example, government officials generally presented such issues as the disenfranchisement of women, naturalized citizens, and the 18- to 20-year-old youth group as a reflection of the

---
[j] The literacy requirement for candidacy created an interesting case following the election to the Constitutional Assembly; one of the members who won his seat by acclamation was semiliterate.

[k] Five candidates actually won by this method in Wards 5, 6, 13, 15, and 19.

realities of Bahrain, not as a policy of restriction. The immediate reactions to this law are discussed in the following section.

The Constitutional Assembly Law and Popular Response

The Constitutional Assembly Law and the draft constitution were closely modeled on the Kuwaiti Constitution, promulgated on 11 November 1962, and the Kuwaiti Election Law, promulgated on 12 November 1962.[26] As a comparative sampling, consider the following articles, chosen for their importance, from Bahrain's Law No. 13 (1972) (Concerning the Election to the Constitutional Assembly) and Kuwait's Law No. 35 (1962) (Concerning the Elections to the National Assembly).

Article 1 in both laws restricts the voting eligibility to males and disfranchises females. The Bahraini law, however, merely restricts the minimum age to 20 years and the minimum period of naturalized citizenship to 10 years. In the Kuwaiti law the minimum age is 21 years of age and the minimum period of naturalized citizenship is 15 years. Both laws withhold the right to vote from members of the armed forces and the police.

Concerning eligibility for candidacy, the Bahraini law states that the candidate must be at least 30 years old and, if a naturalized citizen, he must have been naturalized for a minimum of 15 years since the enactment of the 1963 Citizenship Law (article 9). The Kuwaiti law simply states that the candidate for election must be an eligible voter and that his name should be on the voter registration lists (article 19).[1]

The fact that the Constitutional Assembly Law was modeled on the ten-year old Kuwaiti Elections Law occasioned the first objections to the law. Those who raised this issue pointed out the social, political, demographic, and economic differences between Bahrain and Kuwait. Three specific differences were cited: First, Bahrain's wealth is very limited as compared to Kuwait's national income, and the need for revenue carries over into the political sphere—a problem that does not exist in Kuwait. Second, due to the long tradition of education in Bahrain, Bahraini policy-oriented elites are more educated and therefore more politically conscious than were their Kuwaiti counterparts in 1962. Most importantly, Bahrain has known an active and relatively organized labor movement. In the last two decades, political disturbances in the country, especially in 1954, 1956, 1965, and 1972, could all be traced to the discontent of the working man. Prior to 1962 no national labor tradition of any stature had existed in Kuwait.

Other issues raised soon after the promulgation of the Constitutional

---

[1]There is a close similarity between the Kuwaiti Constitution and the draft constitution submitted to the Bahraini Constitutional Assembly on 16 December 1972.

Assembly Law included the tense political relationship between the Khalifa government and the people, the absence of individual freedoms (speech, press, association), and the disenfranchisement of women. The popular opinion as to the success of the constitutional experiment or as to the ability of the Constitutional Assembly to alter the government-sponsored draft constitution was determined by ideological orientation and socioeconomic status.

It must be pointed out, however, that these issues did not really crystallize until just prior to the election. Two factors were responsible for this delayed reaction. More time was needed for the issues to ferment in the public mind, and, more importantly, due to the absence of political parties and organized interest groups, no effective public medium existed through which particular interests could be articulated. Yet, the personal interviews conducted by the author in September and October, two months before the elections, indicated serious doubts in the minds of many concerning the establishment, structure, and effectiveness of the Constitutional Assembly. The most immediate critical response came from labor and the young intellectuals. The common man appeared to be lethargic toward the whole process,[m] but the press took a more optimistic stand on the future viability of the Assembly. As shown in the following chapter, the genuine fear of government reprisal, which permeated Bahrain's political atmosphere at the time, kept several dissenters from expressing their views openly or forcefully.

The position of the "new left" intellectuals, for lack of a better term, is best described in the statements of one young journalist who openly believed that the elections and the Constitutional Assembly could not really alter the country's political life, especially the suppression of political dissent and political imprisonment. He feared that the constitutional experiment would only accentuate the contradictions in class structure and thus precipitate a power struggle, since the ruling family would naturally resent losing some of its authority and the people would demand more participation. He asked how could one expect the executive branch of government (which has also acted as the legislative branch) to write a good constitution, which would inevitably diminish the powers of the executive, that is, the ruling family?[27]

Similar, albeit more ideological views, were expressed by a young political activist who was thought to have been speaking for certain factions within the labor force. He viewed the Constitutional Assembly in the context of the political and economic conditions of Bahrain at the time; he

---

[m] One day in the *suq* (marketplace) an old man was told to go and register to vote in the elections to the Constitutional Assembly. He looked around and asked, "Who owns this building?" "A Kanoo," he was told. "And this one?" "A Mu'ayyad." "And this third one?" "Shaikh Khalifa." Then the old man asked, "Will the elections change any of this?"

saw the society as being basically divided into two groups, workers and merchants. In his mind, the merchants were generally governed by greed, or *jasha'*, and the workers were oppressed. He maintained that, to be effective, the new constitution should contain a bill of rights and should guarantee labor the right to unionize. It should also uphold the principle of innocent until proven guilty. The authorities should immediately stop their harrassment and night arrests of political dissidents, and political prisoners on Jidda Island should be released. He confirmed that many people were suspicious of everything concerning the Constitutional Assembly; they believed that there could be no real debate on a constitution, since half of the Assembly were either ministers or government-appointed representatives.[28]

The reaction of the middle-class merchants and already established, self-employed college graduates was mainly pragmatic. They invariably expressed guarded optimism concerning the democratization of the governing process; they called for reform but showed willingness to give the new political move the benefit of the doubt. Others adopted a wait-and-see attitude. Still others, though not totally satisfied, felt that the Constitutional Assembly Law was a step in the right direction. One young college-educated merchant expressed a typical view of middle Bahrain. He indicated that the people must take a pragmatic view of the constitutional experiment. He stated that Bahrain was governed by a family that would continue to maintain a semitribal system, and yet the economy was based on free enterprise. He felt that the country needed reform in many areas, but that any improvements or changes should be gradual and moderate. He asserted that the constitution should grant labor the right to unionize; however, laws must be written to define further the responsibilities of labor unions. He also hoped that the constitution would clearly define the authorities of the three branches of government. He emphasized that the people of Bahrain must realize that the constitution was being granted by the ruler; it was not being forced on the ruler as a result of a popular uprising or a revolution.[29]

Several members of the upper middle class, merchants and otherwise, in spite of their own success, expressed the opinion that the country needed reform and that the authority of the ruling family should be checked. A successful, middle-aged merchant who was once exiled from Bahrain for political activities, said openly that the country needed a democratic government to curb the authority of the ruling family. He pointed out that the ruling family would try to influence the Assembly as much as possible and that although they would grant a constitution to the people, they would attempt to subvert the constitution to serve their own purposes. However, he believed that most of the opposition was reformist by nature and therefore would be seriously interested in compromising with the ruling family.

He considered it unfair that the ruling family received one-third of the national income while the poor were suffering from unemployment and high prices.[30]

The senior editors of the two Arabic language weeklies both supported the Constitutional Assembly Law and expressed hope that the democratic experiment would succeed. The editor of *al-Adwa'* strongly supported the inclusion of the basic freedoms in the constitution, including the rights of the press and free assembly. He was optimistic that the Assembly could produce a decent constitution, in spite of the membership of government appointees and the ministers. He felt that the government was forced into the Assembly and a constitution by its own rhetoric, that is, promises made to striking workers in March 1972. He suspected that some of the ruling family were still not convinced a constitution was really needed; however, he thought a constitution would work in Bahrain, since it was modeled on the Kuwaiti constitution, which has worked well for the past ten years.[31] A similar position was taken by the editor of *Sada al-'Usbu'*.[32]

On the other end of the political spectrum, the Khalifas found themselves in a position of trying to interpret the Constitutional Assembly Law positively. On several occasions the Ministry of Information, the Ministry of Municipalities (which was charged with conducting the election), and the Legal Department attempted to underscore the democratic nature of the Khalifa decision to establish a Constitutional Assembly, thereby expanding the base of popular participation in government. Dr. Husayn Baharna, minister of state for legal affairs, offered several explanatory comments on the Constitutional Assembly Law.[n] In his comments Dr. Baharna explained that a candidate should of course be able to campaign freely, within the law, in his district. He maintained that the decision to have half of the Assembly members elected and half appointed was based on the social, political, and cultural experience of the region. He explained that the voting age cutoff at 20 was chosen in the belief that a 20-year-old man was more mature than an 18-year old; also, this rule coincided with election laws in many democratic countries. He stated that women were not allowed to vote because of practical difficulties, such as the identification of veiled women. He emphasized that the Constitutional Assembly's explicit responsibility was not to write a new constitution; it rather would be limited to debating the draft constitution submitted to the Assembly by the Council of Ministers during the period specified in the law. Following this debate, the Assembly would resubmit this draft to the Council of Ministers for approval and issuance.

Shaikh' Abdalla bin Khalid al-Khalifa, minister of municipalities and agriculture, went a step further than Dr. Baharna in pointing out the

---
[n]These comments were made by Dr. Baharna in an interview published in *al-Adwa'*, 10 August 1972, and in a personal interview with the author on 31 August 1972.

democratic nature of the Constitutional Assembly. He maintained that the basic principle of the Assembly was that elected government is better than one-man rule, which can be despotic. Also, he reminded the author that much thought went into forming the Assembly and that several meetings were held with prominent citizens. He hoped that those not given the right to vote in the Assembly elections, that is, women, police, and armed forces, might be granted such rights by the new constitution. Also, he thought that the rights of other groups, such as naturalized citizens, 18- to 20-year olds, etc., might also be reviewed. He gave two major reasons for the exclusion of women: most are veiled and therefore difficult to identify; most are uneducated and cannot therefore vote intelligently. Also, he frankly admitted that Bahrain was still a male-oriented society.[33]

Shaikh Muhammad bin Mubarak, al-Kahlifa, minister of foreign affairs and information, shed more light on the attitude of the Khalifa family concerning the establishment of a constitutional form of government. He is by far the most eloquent spokesman for the ruling family. He believed that Bahrain's democratic experiment stemmed from her own realities—a small, Muslim Arab country of the Gulf. He supported collective decision making, and he hoped that popular participation in government would develop gradually. He repeated the government stand that the disenfranchisement of women in the Constitutional Assembly elections was due to very practical problems and not to an a priori decision to deprive women of their right to vote. He stated firmly that the government would proceed with its democratic experiment in spite of some criticisms, but that they would not surrender to demagoguery. He held out the hope that labor would be allowed to unionize, but he warned that this right would be viewed from the perspective of what would be best for the whole society.[34]

In spite of government assurances to the contrary, what developed in the last few weeks prior to the elections was a sharp polarization of views, and the country was gripped by tension and apprehension. Political dissent was subjected to extralegal governmental reprisal, and the candidates for the Constitutional Assembly began to direct their attention to the government's credibility gap. The elections and their surprising results are discussed in the next chapter.

7

The First National Election and the Formation of the Constitutional Assembly

In order to analyze meaningfully Bahrain's national election to the Constitutional Assembly, held on 1 December 1972, one must treat at least three major aspects of the polity prior to the election: the political environment; the campaign and the candidates; the election itself. To complete this analysis, a statistical overview of the campaign is in order. To develop as true a picture as possible of the social and political fabric of Bahraini society on the eve of the election and to ascertain correctly the average citizen's own perception of his country's first step toward democracy, it was necessary to conduct many formal and informal interviews with representatives from the polity at large. Representatives of special interests, especially the powerful merchants, generally took a positive attitude toward this new process. They apparently did not feel threatened by the prospect of an elected Assembly, nor were they active during the campaign.[a]

The Political Atmosphere on the Eve of the Election

The elections to the Constitutional Assembly and the campaigns for these seats were held in an atmosphere of concern for government reprisal against those who openly expressed their views. Many candidates firmly believed that there would be reprisals, and this fear was based on the fact that the State of Emergency imposed on the country in 1956 and reasserted in 1965 continued to prevail even until after the election. A political person felt the crunch of this State of Emergency directly through sudden arrest and interrogation without specific charges. Such a detainee was often held without trial, and both his arrest and interrogation were neither reported nor explained to the detainee himself or to the public. The press did not report such news lest the authorities invoke article 14 of the 1965 Press Law, which would mean a stoppage of publication.

In interviewing the candidates, especially as the election approached, one definitely sensed that they preferred not to talk in the open, nor did they like to use the telephone. Most of them felt more at ease talking in private meetings in some not-so-suspicious place. It must be borne in mind that

---
[a] All of those representing the country's major businesses in the Constitutional Assembly were appointed by government. None of them had actually run for election.

most of these candidates were, by Western standards, moderate middle-class merchants and professionals. They were by no means revolutionary, nor were they desirous of any radical change in the system of authority in the country. Pragmatism permeated the attitude of these candidates toward the sociopolitical fabric of the country. However, they all, in one way or the other, expressed an almost visceral belief that the government was not truly sincere in its public view of the election nor much interested in its success. One received the impression that the real sources of power within the Khalifa family were still not completely convinced of the wisdom of decentralizing the decision-making powers.

Critics frequently cited five incidents, which seemed to them to indicate the government's lack of goodwill.

1. A labor strike at the airport in September 1972 was immediately suppressed by the government. Four alleged strike leaders were arrested and interrogated. One was freed, two were sent to the Jidda Island prison without trial, and the fourth man was deported to Dubai.

2. Early in October 1972 three persons were arrested and questioned concerning the distribution of a stenciled statement issued by the Popular Front for the Liberation of Oman; the three were later released.

3. The publication of *Sada al-'Usbu'* was stopped by an administrative order from the minister of information in mid-September 1972 for alleged violation of the 1965 Press Law. The newspaper was brought to trial on 21 October 1972, over a month since publication was halted. The trial was postponed to 1 November 1972, and on 5 November 1972, the court found both 'Ali Sayyar and 'Aqil Swar guilty as charged and fined them each BD50.[b]

4. 'Ali Rabi'a, a prospective candidate for the Constitutional Assembly, was arrested and interrogated concerning an alleged connection with the Popular Front for the Liberation of Oman. He was also accused of undermining the election by withdrawing his name from the race. Although 'Ali Rabi'a was released a day later, it should be pointed out that he was arrested on 17 October 1972—two weeks before nominations to the Constitutional Assembly were officially opened.

5. Ya'qub Yusuf al-Muharraqi, president of the Society of Writers, was arrested on 22 October 1972, interrogated and released two days later. He was questioned concerning some alleged Communist tendencies; the substantiating evidence presented to him by his interrogators was that he did not fast during Ramadan and that he admittedly did not pray too much![1]

There was a common belief among many people that the Assembly would not be able to bring about any significant changes in the draft constitution submitted to the Assembly by the government. To support this

---

[b] See above, chapter 3.

view, people cited the 50-50 composition of the Assembly. Within the Khalifa family itself, three different positions developed concerning the Constitutional Assembly: The first position evolved around the realization that the Khalifa family would ultimately have to give up part of its power to popularly elected bodies; therefore, it was more advisable that the family promulgated a constitution voluntarily before it was forced to do so. This position was taken by the minister of foreign affairs and by several other ministers.

The second position represented a pessimistic attitude toward democracy, decentralization of authority, and popular participation in the governing process. This position appeared to be preponderant within the higher councils of the ruling family; it was believed that the prime minister was its main proponent.[c] This attitude emphasized the form of democracy rather than its content and sought to insure that, regardless of elections and popular representation, the real power would remain in the hands of the executive branch, that is, in the Council of Ministers.[d]

The third position was taken by several people who belonged to the second-level echelon of decision makers in the hierarchy. Some of these would have sincerely liked to see the democratic experiment succeed. Others were letting the whole process take its course, and they did not view the outcome with any particular anxiety. This was the closest one could come to being apolitical within a ruling family. However, most of those within this group were college educated, occupied respectable civil service positions, and received the annual royal allowance. They were by and large reasonable men who were, at least academically, familiar with the history of the modern world, including the popular struggle for justice and equality. Within the family they lacked the experience and the tradition of power; hence, they did not equate their real survival with the amount of power they would ultimately possess. Also, they were not influential enough within the inner councils of the family to oppose effectively the dominant view of social order or to change the outcome.

It is in the context of this reality-image dichotomy that the election for the Constitutional Assembly took shape. It was felt on the eve of the election that the government's move toward a constitutional form of rule had not closed the gap separating the people from the Khalifa government. This gap, argued the critics, had rendered these historic steps toward democracy, in the eyes of the policy- and issue-oriented Bahraini, just another ploy by the rulers to disarm the opposition and to bestow upon the

---

[c] This position was believed to have also been supported by Shaikh 'Abdalla bin Khalid al-Khalifa, minister of municipalities and agriculture, and Shaikh Khalid bin Muhammad al-Khalifa, former minister of justice.

[d] A similar view was expressed in a statement issued by the Popular Front for the Liberation of Oman in November of 1972.

existing system of urban tribalism a form of popular sovereignty without actual popular participation in government or without popular control of policy makers—the cornerstone of the democratic theory of government.

The core of the State of Emergency to which many candidates referred in their preelection statements was the 1965 Law of Public Security, decreed by Shaikh 'Isa bin Sulman al-Khalifa while Bahrain was still not an independent state.[2] Proclamation No. 1/1965 and Public Security Order No. 1/1965, both of which were based on the Security Law of that year, defined the method of implementing the Public Security Law itself. These three documents created a rigid political climate in the country, which in turn led to the development of what came to be known as the State of Emergency.

Law of Public Security—1965[3]

1. This law shall be known as the Law of Public Security—1965 and shall go into effect on 22 April 1965.

2. If, in the opinion of the Ruler and at any time, a crime is committed or is about to be committed by a person or group of persons which is sufficiently grave and dangerous to threaten the national security, the Ruler may put Article 3 of this Law into effect until further notice.

3 (1). If a proclamation is made concerning the previous article, the Ruler may, as long as this article is operative, issue any orders which he deems essential for the public good, safety and security.

3 (2). Whatever orders are established under Section (1) of this Article will supercede any contravening laws.

17 April 1965   Ruler of Bahrain and Its Dependencies

Proclamation According to the Law of Public Security—1965[4]

We, 'Isa bin Sulman al-Khalifa, Ruler of Bahrain and its Dependencies, proclaim on this date, 22 April 1965, the following:

Since we believe that a crime has been committed or is about to be committed which falls under Article 2 of the Law of Public Security—1965, We therefore proclaim that by the authority given to Us under said Law, We hereby put Article 3 of said Law into effect. It shall remain in effect until We shall withdraw it.

Public Security Order No. 1 According to Article 3 of the Law of Public Security—1965[5]

Considering Our proclamation of 22 April 1965 and in accordance with the Law of Public Security—1965, We, 'Isa bin Sulman al-Khalifa, order the following:

    1. This Order shall be called Public Security Order No. 1/1965 and shall go into effect beginning 22 April 1965.

    2. If in the opinion of the Ruler the detention of any person is in the interest of public security, then the Ruler may issue an order for the detention of said person.

    3. The detention of any person under this Order shall be considered legal, and said person shall be detained at a place designated by the Ruler and according to the Regulation issued by him.

22 April 1965   Ruler of Bahrain

The Campaign and the Candidates

Several would-be candidates met in July of 1972 to discuss the possibility of selecting a slate of 22 qualified people interested in running for the Constitutional Assembly.[6] The meeting, which was held at Mahmud al-Mardi's home, included the following, among others:

Mahmud al-Mardi	later a candidate from	Manama/1[e]
'Abd al-'Aziz Shamlan	"	Muharraq/8
Jasim Muhammad Murad	"	Muharraq/7
Yusuf Zubari	"	Manama/4
'Ali Rashid al-Amin	"	Muharraq/9
Muhammad Qasim al-Shirawi	not a candidate	
Rasul al-Jishshi	later a candidate from	Manama/1
Hasan al-Khayyat	"	Manama/2
Muhammad Khalifat	"	Jidhafs/12
Hamid Sanqur	"	Manama/2
Khalifa Ghanim	"	Manama/1
Khalifa al-Bin'ali	"	Hidd/10
Muhammad al-Zamil	"	Manama/1
Makki Husayn	not a candidate	

[e] The number indicates the ward.

It was decided at that time that another meeting would be held at Khalifa Ghanim's, which would include more people. It was also agreed that the proposed meeting would be held that same month and that a slate of 22 candidates would be chosen to run as a bloc. Such a bloc, it was thought, would exert more influence in the Assembly, especially since the other 22 members would be government appointees. The meeting never took place. Two developments contributed to the disintegration of this proposed slate. First, 'Abd al-'Aziz Shamlan had a change of heart about the whole concept and decided to form his own group, who would revolve in his orbit. This group came later to be known as the Bloc of Fourteen.[f] Second, a new group of eight appeared under the leadership of Hisham al-Shahabi, who at the time seemed to enjoy a warm relationship with labor.[g] This meant that Mahmud al-Mardi was left with his own small group of candidates.[h] It should be noted here that nominations did not officially open until 1 November 1972.

In addition to these three unofficial slates, several individuals entered the race as independent candidates. Late in October the Shahabi group approached Mahmud al-Mardi and suggested that the three groups meet to discuss the political atmosphere of the country, in particular the State of Emergency under which the Constitutional Assembly elections were to take place. A meeting was held during the last week in October at 'Abd al-'Aziz Shalman's, which was attended by over 20 persons, both would-be candidates and their supporters. The discussion focused on three parallel courses of action:

1. The minister of municipalities and agriculture should be contacted requesting that the distribution of voter registration cards be facilitated to enable a large number of registered voters to receive their cards. The delegation for this task included 'Abd al-'Aziz Shamlan, Mahmud al-Mardi, Rasul al-Jishshi, and Jasim Muhammad Murad.

2. A committee from among those present should be selected to write a petition to be presented to the ruler, asking him to lift the State of Emergency Law. The committee chosen included Mahmud al-Mardi, Kamal al-Shahabi, Hasan Zayn al-'Abidin, and Muhammad Qasim al-Shirawi.

3. The third and most important item on the agenda was a suggestion

---

[f] The 14 were: Rasul al-Jishshi, Hamid Sanqur, Hasan Khayyat, Muhammad Hasan Kamal al-Din, 'Ali Salih al-Salih, Saqir Zayani, 'Abd al-'Aziz Shamlan, Khalifa al-Manna'i, Khalifa al-Bin'ali, Muhammad Khalifat, Ja'far al-Dirazi, 'Abd al-'Aziz al-Rashid, Nasir Muhammad al-Mubarak, and Muhammad Hasan al-Fadil.

[g] The eight were: Hisham al-Shahabi, 'Ali Rabi'a, Muhammad Salman Ahmad, Jawad Habib Jawad, Makki Husayn, Sayyid Ibrahim Sayyid Makki, Hamad 'Ubul, Muhammad Jabir al-Subah.

[h] Mahmud al-Mardi, Jasim Murad, Yusuf Zubari, 'Ali Rashid al-Amin, Yusuf Kamal.

that the group take a clear position on the "responsibility of this democratic experiment and its dimensions."[7]

Because of the sensitivity of the subject and the dangers to which some of the would-be candidates felt this might expose them, it was decided to hold a wider meeting on the whole question of the Constitutional Assembly at al-Ahli Club on 30 October 1972. A meeting was held at the club as scheduled, and the discussion centered around the petition, the delegation which would present this petition and the position of the group in the event the government responded negatively to the petition. Those present, upon agreeing on the language of the petition as written by the committee, signed it—32 signatures in all.

The delegation chosen to present the petition to the ruler included 'Abd al-'Aziz Shamlan, Mahmud al-Mardi, Rasul al-Jishshi, and Hamid Sanqur. A majority of the candidates at the meeting said they would continue with their candidacy regardless of the nature of the ruler's answer to the petition. They felt that they had already accepted participation in the Assembly experiment, knowing well the political climate of the country. Following is a translation of the petition:

A Petition Presented to His Highness by the Delegation Representing the Candidates to the Constitutional Assembly[1]

In the Name of God the Most Merciful and Beneficient. His Highness Shaikh 'Isa bin Sulman al-Khalifa, Ruler of Bahrain, may God keep him.

Greetings of Allegiance.

We the undersigned citizens would like to express to our beloved Ruler our sincere gratitude for the pioneering positive steps which you have taken in the development of the country's rule toward popular participation. There is no doubt that this development emanates from your strong belief in the sincerity of your generous people and in their awareness and ability to rise with you to the high level of historic responsibility dictated by the importance of this stage during which the country embarks on the promulgation of a constitution, thereby laying the cornerstone of a democratic rule which you have advocated and whose fulfillment you have always desired.

Your Highness,

No doubt Your Highness is the first to recognize the extent of openness, cooperation and mutual confidence between the government and the people which this stage requires. You have previously, and on more than one occasion, expressed your strong desire to provide these conditions during the period of election to the Constitutional Assembly and during its sessions. Based on this point, and extending

---

[1] The copy of the petition from which this translation was made is one of the three original copies.

from the desire of Your Highness to create a climate of mutual trust between the State and its citizens and to cement the relations between the two sides, we submit this petition kindly requesting that Your Highness order null and void the laws and decrees by which a State of Emergency had been maintained, the actions taken based on this state and the return to regular civil laws which can no doubt guarantee all of the requirements for security and justice to the State and the citizens.

The positive action of your Highness on this petition will leave a great impression in the hearts of the citizens who look to Your Highness as the leader of this blessed democratic step, for which history will emblazon your name in the brightest of colors. We are confident that this petition will meet with a positive reception from Your Highness, as it does coincide with a royal desire which you have always promoted and expanded: the establishment of mutual trust between the State and its citizens.

May God keep you a symbol and a leader of honor and democracy in this country.

Respectfully yours,
(32 signatures)[j]

The delegation presented the petition to the ruler on Tuesday, October 31. Present at the meeting were the heir apparent, Shaikh Hamad bin 'Isa al-Kahlifa, and Shaikh Muhammad bin Mubarak al-Khalifa, the minister of foreign affairs.[k] Both the ruler and Shaikh Hamad, stated members of the delegation, were very sympathetic to their request. Although Shaikh Muhammad bin Mubarak tried to point out to the delegation that legally there was no State of Emergency, the delegation brought forward several actual cases of search, arrest, and investigation, which had occurred in the preceding weeks. The delegation indicated that such activities were primarily conducted by the Special Branch of the Security Department. His Highness promised to look into the situation, and together with Shaikh Hamad and Shaikh Muhammad bin Mubarak he confirmed that the Bahraini government was sincerely interested in the success of the democratic experiment at hand. They promised that the government's action on the petition would be conveyed to the delegation in two weeks.

The Council of Ministers discussed the petition at its regular meeting on Sunday, November 12, and a resolution was adopted, which was to be conveyed to the four-member delegation on Tuesday, November 14. However, no answer came, and the delegation spokesman was informed that the

---

[j] Jawad Habib, Jasim Murad,* Muhammad 'Abdalla 'Ubul, Hasan 'Isa al-Khayyat, 'Abd al-Karim al-'Alaywat,* 'Abd al-'Aziz Sa'd Shamlan,* Muhammad Hasan al-Fadil,* 'Ali Rashid al-Amin, Hasan Muhammad Zayn al-'Abidin, Rasul al-Jishshi,* Mahmud al-Mardi, Muhammad Qasim al-Shirawi, Hisham al-Shahabi, Qasim Ahmad Fakhro, Muhammad 'Abdalla al-Zamil, Muhammad Yusuf Mahmud, 'Ali 'Abdalla Sayyar,* Saqir al-Zayani, Muhammad bu Mahfur, Muhammad Jabir al-Subah, Khalifa 'Abdalla al-Mana'i,* Salman Ahmad Matar, Hamid Sanqur, Muhammad Kasan Kamal al-Din,* Hamad Salman al-Zayani, Yusuf Zubari, Yusuf Salman Kamal, Hasan 'Ali al-Mutawwaj,* Muhammad Salman Ahmad, Makki 'Ali Husayn Jum'a. (The asterisk indicates election to the Assembly.)

[k] The prime minister, who was directly in charge of the State of Emergency regulations, was not present at the meeting.

entire delegation would be called upon to meet the prime minister on Saturday, November 18. It should be noted, however, that several candidates were anxious to hear the government's response to the petition before November 15—the deadline for registration for candidacy. In fact, the November 18 meeting never did materialize, and no response to the petition was ever given by the government.[1]

As the last deadline for registration (1:00 P.M. of 15 November 1972) drew near and as the government had thus far failed to respond to the petition, the Shahabi group held several meetings to plan a course of action. By Tuesday, November 14 it became obvious that a governmental response was not forthcoming, and it was rumored that the Shahabi group would not register for candidacy. By 1:00 P.M. of November 15 it was known everywhere that the group had failed to register.

During the two interviews the author conducted with 'Ali Rabi'a on November 12 and Hisham al-Shahabi on November 15, they emphasized that the Shahabi group had originally had every intention of participating in the elections and that they withdrew only after becoming convinced of the government's lack of sincerity, citing the lack of response to the petition as proof. They also confirmed that the decision against participation was a result of long deliberation and was by no means a spontaneous reaction. They further stated that this decision came from the group itself; it was not dictated by any outside influences.[m] Hisham al-Shahabi[n] stated that by boycotting the elections, the people would deprive the entire Constitutional Assembly of any popular legitimacy.[o]

Most of the other candidates openly criticized the decision of al-Shahabi's group to withdraw. Their criticism centered around four main points and obviously reflected the desire of most candidates to justify remaining in the race. First, by withdrawing, the Constitutional Assembly would be deprived of some intelligent, educated, and nationalistic voices,

---

[1] In a personal interview on 16 November 1972, the public prosecutor stated that all nonpolitical cases were handled in the courts under the 1966 Code of Criminal Procedure. However, the State of Emergency 1965 Public Security Law was applied to those few cases that threatened national security. Those cases were primarily political, and few government officials were fully apprised of the activities of the Special Branch. The author was unable to secure an interview with Ian Henderson, the head of the Special Branch.

[m] Reference here was to the November statement of the Popular Front for the Liberation of Oman urging an election boycott.

[n] Both Hisham al-Shahabi and 'Ali Rabi'a were members of *al-Hay'a al-Ta'sisiyya* [*The Founding Committee*], which in August of 1971 had petitioned the government, through the minister of labor, for permission to form a labor union according to part 3 of the 1957 Labor Law. No permission was given, and several members of the group were arrested.

[o] al-Shahabi reiterated these views in an interview published in *al-Siyasa* (Kuwait), 25 November 1972, pp. 1 and 11. 'Ali Rabi'a discussed the general political atmosphere in Bahrain on the eve of the elections in an interview published in *al-Siyasa*, 28 November 1972, pp. 5 and 11. The Shahabi-Rabi'a group later participated in the December 1973 election of the National Assembly and sent eight members to the Assembly.

especially since some of the group had been expected to win in their districts. Second, the demand to lift the State of Emergency was only one of the several critical issues. The failure to win this point did not justify such a drastic step. [p] By withdrawing the al-Shahabi group had played directly into the hands of those elements of the ruling family who had not supported the entire move toward a constitutional government. Finally, the petition submitted to the ruler did not mention a specific date for reply, upon which would be contingent the decision of the candidates to run or withdraw. In any event, the al-Shahabi slate, which had made their participation contingent upon the removal of this State of Emergency, had prior knowledge of the existence of these laws and yet had originally agreed to participate in the elections. They had even been very influential in the fight against public apathy toward voter registration.[8]

Another issue that contributed to political tension on the eve of the election was the active protest staged by representatives of the women's societies over the disfranchisement of women. The government had not foreseen that article 1 of the Constitutional Assembly Law No. 13/1972, which restricted voting eligibility to males only, would create such a furor among the women's elite groups. In September 1972 representatives from the women's societies, in particular the Bahrain Young Ladies' Association, the Awal Women's Society, and the Rifa' Women's Society, held several meetings and organized a concerted effort on behalf of the Bahraini women. These meetings had a three-fold purpose: to deplore the disfranchisement of women; to rally the support of other societies and clubs; and to petition the government to reopen the question of women's suffrage.

The first effort toward this goal was a joint panel on women's rights at al-Bahrain Club on 28 August 1972. The panel was composed of a representative of the Awal Women's Society, another representative of the Rifa' Women's Society, a lawyer, and a young journalist.[9] During the following week, women's societies issued a statement asking for popular support for their right to vote[10] in which they argued against the government's position on this issue.[11] The country's two Arabic-language weeklies came out in support of granting women the right to vote. One columnist wrote that women should be treated on an equal footing with men and not as commodities to be exploited.

In a letter dated 23 September 1972, women's representatives asked the Ministry of Labor and Social Affairs for a permit to collect signatures on a

---

[p] Actually, some of the critics told the author that the whole question of the State of Emergency did not surface until the al-Shahabi group pushed it to the forefront. However, most of the candidates were aware of the activities of the Special Branch, especially the detention and interrogation of 'Ali Rabi'a and Ya'qub al-Muharraqi. These activities were also cited in two stenciled statements issued by the Popular Front for the Liberation of Oman in August and October of 1972, and most of the candidates had received copies of these statements.

petition to be presented at a later date to the government. On 9 October 1972 the Ministry responded by refusing the request to collect individual signatures; however, women's societies were granted permission to collect signatures representing groups, that is, clubs, associations, and societies, not individuals.[12]

On 20 November 1972, ten days prior to the Constitutional Assembly elections, women's representatives presented the following petition to the ruler at his office in Government House in Manama. Shaikh Khalifa bin Sulman al-Khalifa, the prime minister, was present at the meeting. The ruler expressed sympathy for their cause, but nothing positive was done.[13]

Petition Presented by the Women's Societies in Bahrain Concerning Women's Political Rights[q]

We, the undersigned, the popular societies which represent women in Bahrain, in order to underline the democratic laws and principles which should have been included in the election laws of the Constitutional Assembly, whose task will be to produce a constitution for the country, submit to the Council of Ministers our protest to the decision to deny women the right to participate in the nomination and election process. Bahrain has always been the cultural, social and civilizational leader in the Gulf; why does it today remove an active segment of its population from participation in the march toward progress?

The decision to keep the woman away from the formation of the Constitutional Assembly and the discussion of the constitution is the most severe insult which can be given to women, who have raised generations and who have exerted every effort over the centuries in the service of their country. Today for little reason she is removed from the political scene.

The two reasons given for depriving women of their political rights, which are not at all valid, may be summarized as follows:

1) The woman is veiled, and therefore it is difficult to ascertain her identity.
2) The woman is uneducated, and therefore she has no independent opinion, so that a man can influence her vote.

We believe both reasons are unconvincing. As to the first, procedures may be taken to ascertain the identity of the veiled woman, and secondly a large percentage of ignorant men also exist—men who have no independent opinions. The election laws do not require that men must be aware and knowledgeable before they are given the right to vote. Legally the United Nations Charter clearly prohibits discrimination on the grounds of sex in the area of human public rights. The Universal Declaration of Human Rights, adopted by the United Nations General Assembly in 1952, also grants men and women equal political rights.

In this region, Arab societies who face similar difficulties have recognized women's suffrage, as do many African constitutions. Today, when we demand in the name of

---
[q] The Arabic copy of this petition was obtained from a member of the Awal Women's Society.

the Bahraini women that you review this decision, we are acting in accordance with a long tradition of participation of Bahrain's women in the cultural, social and political affairs of the country. As an example, we met the United Nations Special Representative, and to him we insisted on the Arabism of Bahrain.

In the name of the women of Bahrain, who have had a tradition of education for over fifty years, we present this petition, hoping it will produce positive results. Woman's humanity is inseparable from the whole of humankind, and we believe that on the day when injustice against women is eradicated, Bahrain will reassert its belief in freedom, democracy and equality in human rights and responsibilities.[r]

External Stresses During the Campaign

As a recently independent small island country, Bahrain especially in its first formative years, had been subject to varied regional influences, which have acted as inputs to its developing political system. In the context of Bahrain's Gulf setting, these external inputs are organically connected, often to the disliking of some Bahraini leaders, to political development on the island. These external pressures have placed new strains and stresses on the political system, thereby bringing into play contradictions whose roots lie outside Bahrain and therefore concerning which Bahrain's political system could make no binding and authoritative decisions. These influences may be classified into two general categories: conservative and change oriented.

The *conservative* influences flow into Bahrain's body politic from neighboring tribal and family-ruled states, which are overtly interested in preserving a tribalist status quo not only in Bahrain but throughout the region. Although representatives of this traditionalist interest have closely observed Bahrain's constitutional experiment and first venture into democracy, they have been particularly interested in containing this experiment. Since the Khalifa ruling family had a similar goal in mind and had tailored the democratic experiment to perpetuate a modern version of tribalist government, the conservative external pressure did not necessarily place such a strain as would exhaust the elasticity of the new political system.

Change-oriented external inputs have been generated by revolutionary ideologies in the region, in particular the Popular Front for the Liberation of Oman (PFLO). In the months preceding the Constitutional Assembly elec-

---

[r] Signed by representatives of the various clubs and societies in Bahrain. Another letter was later presented to the Constitutional Assembly concerning what the letter described as the Assembly's lack of a clear commitment to women's political rights. The letter, which was signed by three women's societies (Bahraini Young Ladies' Association, Awal Women's Society, and Rifa' Women's Society), was entered into the record of the Constitutional Assembly on 20 February 1973.

tions, PFLO issued at least three statements[s] pertaining to Bahrain which were secretly distributed throughout the country.[t] Regardless of the very limited support that PFLO and its Bahrain branch have found within the country's political stratum, that is, both the powerful governing elite and the power-seeking, issue-oriented elites, PFLO's statements on the election created noticeable tension within the ruling family and contributed to the uneasy preelection atmosphere.

The election results, as shown below, indicated that PFLO's position on the Constitutional Assembly was based on limited popular support. However, what is of significance to this study, is the role that PFLO's statements played in the evolution of the campaign, especially between November 15 and election day, the period following the withdrawal of the al-Shahabi group when rumors of an impending voter boycott spread rapidly.

In the August 1972 statement on the Constitutional Assembly Law, PFLO called on the government of Bahrain to guarantee that the following demands would be met:

1. The basic public freedoms of opinion, press, and assembly would be allowed.
2. Workers would be allowed to form labor unions, through which workers' rights could be defended freely.
3. All political prisoners would be released, and all exiles returned.
4. All activities of the Special Branch, that is, harassments and arrests, would be terminated.
5. The State of Emergency, imposed on the country since 1956, would be eliminated.
6. Political and democratic rights for women would be guaranteed.
7. The 50-50 composition of the Constitutional Assembly would be eliminated.
8. The minimum age for candidacy would be lowered to 26, and the minimum age for voters would be lowered to 18.[14]

The last three points referred specifically to the Constitutional Assembly Law, which had just been promulgated. However, PFLO failed to rally any measurable support for these points. As to the other points, several politically active people furthered the argument that basic freedoms, labor

---

[s] One statement was issued in August, a second in October, and a third in November. A fourth statement was issued in January 1973, which called on the elected members of the Constitutional Assembly to withdraw from the Assembly.

[t] Some came by mail, others were hand delivered, and still others distributed on street corners. These statements often reached a large segment of the opinion makers in the country and the method of distribution has often intrigued and baffled Bahrain's security agents.

unions, and due process of the law (the crux of PFLO's position) were by nature constitutional issues and therefore would have to be reviewed in the context of the draft constitution after the Constitutional Assembly had been convened. The emergency regulations and the curtailment of the freedom of expression became, as was stated above, the issue par excellence for the prospective candidates in the last weeks of the campaign. It was precisely that issue which prompted the candidates to petition the ruler.

In October 1972 PFLO issued another statement on the Constitutional Assembly in which it called on the people to organize themselves and to work for the realization of the demands that PFLO had enumerated the preceding August. The ideological stand of PFLO at the time—equating the entire Constitutional Assembly with an imperialist plot—seemed to many Bahrainis to be just too farfetched.[u] Following are some excerpts from PFLO's October statement:

Through the observation of recent successive events in Bahrain and the feverish movement to implement the plots woven by imperialism in Washington and London, we have become convinced of the connection between the nature of the regime, which has expanded its tools of suppression, and the game of elections, i.e., the Constitutional Assembly. . . .

The elections to the Constitutional Assembly are a new cloak which imperialism is attempting to don in order to confuse and deceive the masses, thereby transferring the struggle from its popular context to such establishments as the Constitutional Assembly and a National Assembly. The intention of the authorities is to pre-empt the popular demand for a true popular participation in the preparation of the constitution. . . . At the same time that the authorities are speaking of democracy we find them still enforcing the State of Emergency imposed in 1956 which has included harrassment and savage confrontations with striking workers, who demanded their usurped rights. An example of this is the crushing of the airport strike in September. . . .

In the face of this, our masses must take the initiative of organizing collective action and exercising their democratic political rights, which they then can impose by force on the authorities. The structures which the regime creates will, in the end, serve only the ruling class, powerful merchants and landlords and all other elements which are connected to and benefit from the imperialist presence. . . . Based on this reality, the PFLO-Bahrain Branch will struggle on a daily basis to force popular demands on the authorities with the consideration that the political freedoms which the authorities will relinquish in favor of the people are not a gift from the regime or from the Constitutional Assembly; they are an inevitable result of the long popular struggle in which tens of martyrs have been sacrificed and hundreds arrested and exiled from their country. Therefore it is necessary that a broad national popular front be established which would include all of the nationalist forces and groups in Bahrain.

By November 1972 it had become apparent to PFLO that the Bahraini government was not in a hurry; manifestly it did not intend to comply with

---
[u]This theme was again reiterated in PFLO's November statement.

either PFLO's demands or any other demands, including those raised by the establishment candidates themselves. Moreover, PFLO became strongly convinced that no collective popular action was being contemplated. Whatever meager, albeit well-intended attempts as were made by such candidates as Mahmud al-Mardi and others to form a unified national slate came to nothing. Obviously, since nothing along the lines advocated by PFLO in its October statement ever materialized, PFLO's November 1972 statement assumed a harsher tone than in the previous statements.

Three parallel lines of polemic could be delineated in the November statement. The first was PFLO's attempt to identify its statements with popularly supported labor demands and issues in the country. The March 1972 labor strikes and the strikers' bread-and-butter demands at the time were still fresh in the people's minds; hence, the statement was entitled "5 March" to commemorate the anniversary date of the strike. The second definite line of thought was PFLO's attempt to present the democratization process as part of a general face-lifting that imperialist powers were giving the regimes of the Gulf amirates. Naturally the Constitutional Assembly was PFLO's first target. The third polemical thread running through the November statement emphasized the tribalist nature of the Khalifa regime. It pointed out what PFLO saw as the inner contradictions with the Khalifa tribe, leading to the conclusion that such a regime was incapable of supporting a true democratic rule.

Based on this reasoning, PFLO called on the people of Bahrain to boycott the election. The rationale offered for the boycott was that by not participating in the election, the Constitutional Assembly would be deprived of popular legitimacy. Following are some excerpts from this November statement:

It seems clear that the Constitutional Assembly was born deformed and will die so. . . . This project is not different from the other paper projects which colonialism has distributed throughout the Gulf in order to support the various medieval regimes since the 1930's while they struggle with the national desires of the peoples of the region. The Constitutional Assembly is not much different from the surface changes which colonialism has created in Muscat, Qatar and the Amirates. . . . Official information sources attempt to show that the Constitutional Assembly will guarantee the citizen freedom and democracy and will close the gap between regime and people. . . .

The undemocratic tenets of the Constitutional Assembly decree, which the regime seems unable to revise, gives the authorities complete control of the Assembly. These tenets include the following: nomination; the 50-50 ratio; the minimum voting age; and the disenfranchisement of women. . . . It is very clear that, by its very nature, the tribal regime, which is closely tied to Anglo-American imperialism is incapable of fulfilling the demands which the people continue to voice. . . .

PFLO emphasizes once again that any discussion of elections and the Constitutional Assembly separate from and prior to the fulfillment of our urgent popular demands is considered to be an organized dissemination of falsehoods and lies against our people which in the end will guarantee the success of world imperialism and the continued existence of tribal regimes completely unrelated to the spirit of our struggling poeple. Since the participation of the people in these projects is dependent on the existence of a democratic atmosphere, which is dictated by the demands of this period in our people's history, *a popular boycott of the elections is the only solution which will compel the authorities to respond to these demands* [author's emphasis]. The blood which was shed in March 1972 has not yet dried. . . .

A close look at the Ruling Family will indicate that the Ruler, 'Isa bin Sulman, is no more than a titular head without any real role in forming the country's public policy, save the traditional one of distributing lands, watches and routine appointments and the signing of already prepared documents. The tension is symbolized in the question 'Why is the Heir Apparent the third man in the country when he should be the second?' This is a somewhat abnormal situation here when we reflect that in Kuwait, Abu Dhabi, and Qatar the heir apparent is usually the prime minister, i.e. the second man in the country. . . .

The Khalifa family feels that the proposed parliamentary system might minimize the anger of the masses and win the confidence of the people. Also they feel that the regime must reconcile itself to the increasing popular consciousness through such reforms as the constitution in order to emasculate basic popular demands and to deprive these demands of their proper context. . . . True democracy is made by the masses and is not to be granted by the authorities or by a royal decree from above.

The influence of these statements on the election campaign, especially in its last weeks, was very noticeable. The nervous reaction of the regime to PFLO's statements was magnified particularly following the decision of the al-Shahabi group not to participate in the election. At many cabinet and subcabinet meetings held in the last two weeks prior to the elections several ministers had open reactions to the PFLO statements. Some intimated that the timing of PFLO's call for a boycott and the al-Shahabi slate's decision to withdraw from the race was no coincidence. Although the election itself disproved PFLO's preelection claims of popular support, the regime's perception of PFLO's influence significantly affected the process of decision making in that period.

The Final Days of the Campaign

As the elections drew near, the government's attitude became steadily more pessimistic: "Three disasters befell Bahrain in 1972—the cholera, the BAPCO fire, and the elections," lamented one government official.[v] This

---

[v] A cholera outbreak in October-November 1972 almost led to the closing of the airport, but the Ministry of Health was finally able to contain the disease. On November 24, 1972 a disastrous fire ravaged the Bahrain Petroleum Company refinery destroying eight storage tanks and causing a $10-15million loss. It was contained 48 hours later.

description of the elections illustrates the conflict and tension within the Khalifa family as regards the whole democratic experiment.

As the candidates' slogans grew louder the inner contradictions of the ruling family sharpened and polarized. Two main groups emerged clearly—the tribalists and the realists. The tribalists were those of the family who really saw no need at all for any of the forms of modern democracy. They felt that the Kahlifas had ruled for generations and had always provided their people with what they felt was needed. And they believed it was good. The realists, on the other hand, were said to hold that in order to perpetuate the Khalifa rule in the face of rising popular demands for participation, they should support the creation of some sort of popularly elected body that would give the populace some participation in the decision-making processes. However, the realists also wanted the real power to remain in the hands of the Khalifa family. The prime minister, who was said to represent the first group, acceded to the realists, said at the time to be headed by the minister of foreign affairs, Shaikh Muhammad bin Mubarak al-Khalifa, "the Machiavelli of the Gulf."[15]

The government had hoped that the electoral process could be conducted quietly without any serious demands or embarassing issues being raised. The decision makers within the Khalifa regime did not fully realize the dimensions of this process and the demands and pressures that any move toward democracy creates. The perfect consensus, which is the mark of autocratic rule, is usually the first casualty of the move toward democracy. Opposition and dissent are the price that any democratic people, nation, or government must pay for the luxury of a government by the people and for the people. In a democratic government constitutions are not royal decrees or government pronouncements that the regime can alter or ignore at will. The founding of a democratic system of government or writing a constitution for that system often brings forth painful reminders to the autocrat that a society and a people exist who intend to have a say in their own governing. The ruler's benevolence is put to a hard test because once a constitution is written, he and his family will henceforth govern under the scrutiny of their citizens.

What happened in Bahrain on the eve of the election was that the government's statements on the advantages of democracy created their own momentum, which moved events and issues at a much faster pace than originally expected. The issues raised by the candidates in public meetings and the questions asked at those meetings did nothing to bring the government and people into greater rapport; the apprehension of the Khalifa family were only intensified.

The primary concern of the campaign was speculation on the contents of the proposed constitution. It was in this context that discussion on major issues was conducted. In almost every public appearance the candidates were asked whether they supported basic human rights, labor unions, women's suffrage, and constitutionalism in government. They were also frequently asked whether they would speak out in the Assembly on such issues as illegal police activities, inflation, the ruling family's share of the national revenues, and deportation of Bahraini citizens.

Several prospective candidates expressed their views on major issues in a series of newspaper interviews conducted by Muhammad Qasim al-Shirawi in the two months preceding the election.[16] Although some of the persons in this series of articles had previously been interviewed by the same journalist earlier in 1972, their comments on the eve of the election were more specific concerning the function and effectiveness of the Constitutional Assembly and concerning their stand on issues that would be debated at the Assembly.[w]

Rasul al-Jishshi, a candidate from Manama's first ward, expected that members of the Constitutional Assembly would be subject to all kinds of pressures, but he did not think there was any room for compromise on the basic rights that the constitution should guarantee.[x]

Jasim Muhammad Murad, a candidate from Muharraq's seventh ward who later in the Assembly became the preeminent spokesman for extremely liberal positions on socioeconomic issues, dealt with the question of political immunity for Assembly members by urging that the constitution should guarantee certain basic rights and freedoms in accordance with those rights recognized by the United Nations.[17]

Qasim Ahmad Fakhro, a candidate from Manama's fourth ward and later the secretary of the Assembly and a voluble liberal, expected the debates in the Assembly to be free and open. He did not expect any pressures, and he believed that the constitution would be written by the Constitutional Assembly. He stated that the important thing was not who wrote the constitution as much as the spirit in which it was written. He maintained that citizenship was one and the same for men and women.[18]

'Abd al-'Aziz Shamlan, a candidate from Muharraq's eighth ward and later the deputy-speaker of the Assembly and one of its most respected members, reflected on the type of constitution he wished to see the Assembly approve. He hoped for a constitution that would guarantee individual freedom and insure a free legislative body. He advocated a completely independent judiciary, the separation of powers, and a guarantee of all the basic freedoms.[19]

'Ali 'Abdalla Sayyar, a candidate from Muharraq's ninth ward and the owner and editor of *Sada al-'Usbu'* took a stand on certain constitutional issues similar to that expressed in several of his editorials. He was a

---

[w]The author personally interviewed most of those appearing in al-Shirawi's articles, and they expressed views similar to those quoted in the newspaper.

[x]*al-Adwa'*, 18 October 1972, p. 4. al-Jishshi, a liberal Shi'a, later came to play a central role in the Assembly as a mediator and vote strategist between the liberal faction, which was mostly Sunni, and the rather considerable conservative Shi'a faction.

political liberal on such issues as basic freedoms, separation of powers, women's suffrage, education, finance, and due process of law. Later in the Assembly, Sayyar was to become a leading spokesman for the liberal faction. His position was that the constitution should insure the independence of the judiciary and the supervision of the executive legislative branch. The constitution should further guarantee the members of the legislative branch the right to question members of the cabinet, and members of the Assembly should have parliamentary immunity.[20]

Muhammad 'Abdalla Muhammad al-Samahiji, a candidate from Muharraq Island's eleventh ward, later became one of the few Assembly members representing Bahrain's meager agricultural sector. He obviously spoke for very particularistic interests in his district when he stated that the constitution should include some policies concerning the development of the agricultural sector. He expressed concern that the village dweller should have equal opportunities in education, housing, health care, and general economic development.[21]

Although he lost in the election, Mahmud al-Mardi, the owner and editor of *al-Adwa'*, perhaps more eloquently than any other candidate summed up the hopes that many people had optimistically placed in their country's first step toward modern democracy. In a "Meet-the-Candidate" panel at al-'Arabi Club held on 25 November 1972, al-Mardi felt that the people should participate in the democratic experiment because working with the Constitutional Assembly should help produce a good constitution. He argued that the constitution should guarantee a number of very essential principles on which the members of the Assembly should not compromise, such as the basic freedoms, the right to form labor unions, women's suffrage, social welfare, government by law, and "innocent until proven guilty." He also maintained that there should be an absolute right to citizenship and that assembly sessions should be open to the public.[y]

The above interviews point to at least five areas of agreement common to most of the candidates:

1. Basic individual freedoms should be guaranteed—some sort of bill of rights.
2. Labor unions are necessary and should be allowed.
3. Women's suffrage is inevitable and should be allowed.
4. A constitutional government would involve a separation of powers, which would include an independent judiciary and which would designate the elected National Assembly as the sole regulatory body.
5. Due process of the law would be an essential inclusion whereby the rights of the accused would be protected. This would insure no more arrests or long detention without specific charges or trial.

---
[y] The author was present at this panel.

On the negative side, several candidates felt that the election and the entire Constitutional Assembly would be hampered by a number of factors:

1. The newness of the democratic experiment in Bahrain and the lack of a well-established popular tradition of political socialization in the field of citizenship
2. The feeling that the government did not show an enthusiastic commitment to the success of the democratic experiment
3. The people's suspicion of any initiative by the government along the lines of popular participation
4. Labor unrest and the tense relationship between labor and large-scale employers such as Aluminum Bahrain and Gulf Aviation
5. The government's refusal to grant labor permission to organize, regardless of part 3 of the 1957 Labor Law
6. Governmental application of the 1965 State of Emergency Law to political cases without due process of law
7. Governmental refusal to end this State of Emergency, even after the Palace had been petitioned to do so by a majority of the Constitutional Assembly candidates[z]
8. PFLO's November 1972 statement urging Bahrainis to boycott the election
9. The withdrawal of the 'Ali Rabi'a-Hisham al-Shahabi group of nationalistic, leftist labor representatives from the campaign
10. The belief of many people that the Constitutional Assembly would not be able to change existing government policy

As a consequence of these influential factors, it was generally believed down to the last week before the election that a relatively small percentage of the population would actually participate in the election and that the political atmosphere in the country was simply not conducive to a true democratic experiment.[aa] The gap between the government and the people remained wide, prices continued to rise, and labor was angrily muttering about boycotts. In this atmosphere, the government became progressively more nervous, and its tendency toward secrecy increased. On 1 December 1972, voters finally went to the polls in 14 wards to elect 17 representatives.

---

[z] The State of Emergency Law was again invoked following the election, even after the government had viewed the election as being successful. Three persons from Manama's Hura district were detained in the first week of December for political reasons. At the same time, however, two others who had been political prisoners on Jidda Island since March 1972 were released.

[aa] These plus other views were expressed at a special private panel held on 27 November 1972 to discuss the campaign and the candidates during the last days of the campaign. The panelists included: Hasan al-Jishshi; Mahmud al-Mardi; 'Ali Sayyar; Ahmad Kamal (director of publications, Ministry of Information); Hafiz 'Imam (journalist); Jasim Murad; and Muhammad Qasim al-Shirawi (organizer of the panel).

Election Analysis and the Composition of the Constitutional Assembly

Much to everyone's surprise, Bahrain's first national election took place in a calm and civil manner. No disorderly incidents were reported.[bb] The election produced several surprises in the unexpectedly large voter turnout (88.5%), in the type of candidates elected and in the polarizing role of sectarianism (*Shi'a* vs. *Sunni*). The first and probably the most important hint of the future course of democracy in Bahrain was that the election completely disproved the authorities' preelection feelings of anxiety. The vote demolished the frightening image of democratic participation held by the traditional bulwarks of the Khalifas. The Assembly vote showed that the people were not necessarily revolutionary; on the contrary, the popular vote revealed tendencies that were as conservative and as status quo oriented as those held by the Khalifa leaders.

As previously mentioned, the large turnout came as a considerable surprise. The decision of the al-Shahabi group not to participate led many people, both right and left, to believe on the eve of the election that a significant number of eligible voters would boycott the elections. In retrospect, one may conclude that both the Kahlifa hierarchy and the left erred in their judgment and failed to really comprehend the forces at work. The Khalifa view of the entire electoral process was colored by their negative preconceptions of democracy and of popular participation. The closer the elections came, the more nervous they became. Their judgment and evaluations became more conservative and less realistic. On the other hand, the left, as represented by the al-Shahabi-Rabi'a group, showed an equally high level of misjudgment in their preelection optimism. Their hopes for a voter boycott of the election were based solely on wishful thinking and not on any firm assessment of the nature of Bahrain's real majority.[cc] In district after district, especially in Muharraq's eighth and ninth labor-oriented wards, voters thronged to the polls in large numbers (83% in the eighth ward and 90% in the ninth).

By the time the polls closed, the left was in shock and in dire need of reassessing its future program. However, one must quickly add that this voter turnout could not be considered a victory for the status quo forces. To say, as some government officials were saying following the election, that by their high turnout at the polls, the Bahraini people showed a high level of political sophistication is to fall into the same naivete that distorted the

---

[bb] Shakih Khalid bin Muhammad al-Khalifa, former minister of justice and one of the Khalifa old guard, stated following the closing of the polls that Bahrain's first experiment in democracy was a success. Reuter's news dispatch, 2 December 1972.

[cc] For a thoughtful analysis of the election see *al-Siyasa* (Kuwait), 18 December 1972, p. 8. Published in the form of a letter to the editor written by a Bahraini student at the American University of Beirut.

left's image of the average voter. For, like any other system of government, democracy can be destroyed by camplacency because in complacency there is a tendency to emphasize form at the expense of matter. To present a conspicuous democratic front, shiny as it may be, is never a long-term substitute for the actual democratic experience, with all of its hopes and frustrations, consensus and dissent, responsibility and openness.

The third point, which the election brought out clearly, was the deeply entrenched sectarian alignment in Bahrain, primarily Shi'a vs. Sunni. The vote analysis in every major district in the country, particularly in Manama's most populated and cosmopolitan first and second wards (91% and 90% voter turnout respectively), indicated a distinct cleavage along religious lines. It is clear that the Shi'as cast a bloc vote and worked hard to bring out the vote, regardless of the competence and qualifications of the candidates. This unity is perhaps understandable in the light of the Shi'as historical experiences in a Sunni-ruled country. [dd]

An analysis of the vote in Manama's first ward and the two Shi'a candidates elected reveals that the first of the two, Rasul al-Jishshi, received, in addition to the Shi'a vote in that ward, at least 250 Sunni votes. Evidently both Sunnis and Shi'as thought he was well qualified for the Constitutional Assembly. [ee] The second candidate was carried to victory by a straight Shi'a vote. Obviously the numerous Sunni candidates in that ward split the vote, thereby bringing down to defeat such qualified candidates as Mahmud al-Mardi and Hasan Zayn al-'Abidin. [ff] The Shi'a bloc vote was extremely effective—it sent 14 out of a total of 22 elected members to the Constitutional Assembly, a much larger percentage than the proportion of Shi'as in the population. [gg]

In those wards, especially in the rural areas, where the competition was primarily among Shi'a or Sunni candidates, the vote split on religious grounds as well, but in these cases, the candidate was judged as to whether he was a practicing Muslim. The twelfth ward (90% voter turnout) illustrated this point well. The most obviously qualified candidate, Muhammad Khalifat (a graduate of the American University of Beirut), was a Shi'a but a religious liberal. He was soundly defeated by a mulla (a Shi'a priest). [hh]

[dd] It must be pointed out that the Shi'as have fared very well under the Khalifa regime. Shi'as occupy four ministerial positions in the Cabinet and are well represented in Bahrain's wealthy merchant class.

[ee] Someone quipped that the Jishshi Sunni vote reminded him of Senator Edward Brooke's victory in Massachusetts.

[ff] Fearful of just such a phenomenon, Mahmud al-Mardi and others met prior to the election and attempted to persuade some lesser-known Sunni candidates in the first ward to withdraw, but they failed.

[gg] The Shi'a candidates frequently used their mosques (ma'tams) for campaigning.

[hh] It was enough for the mulla to remind the electorate that the front-runner, Khalifat, did not fast during Ramadan nor did he appear to pray frequently.

Another parameter, which the election brought out, was racism based on national origin, primarily Arab (Muslim Sunni) vs. Persian (Muslim Shi'a). The third ward (83% turnout) was a case in point. Arab voters solidly supported the winner, Muhammad 'Ali Kamal al-Din, against Husayn Muhammad Baqir Aryan, a Bahraini of Persian stock. Aryan went down to defeat with Kamal al-Din at 986 votes to Aryan's 219 votes. The second and ninth wards revealed a somewhat similar trend, where two candidates of Persian origin, who might have otherwise had some chance of winning, were badly defeated.[11]

As for the preelection political groupings, three points must be emphasized. Those blocs consisted primarily of a group of people who were bound together by loose ties of friendship and camaraderie. The candidates did not officially run as members of blocs, but the opinion-making public knew what candidate belonged to which group. The Shamlan bloc, known as the National Democratic Slate, did very well; 8 out of 14 were elected.[JJ] Aside from personal-image factors, the primary reason behind the success of the Shamlan bloc was that it contained both Shi'as and Sunnis. As was stated earlier, the third bloc, the al-Shahabi group, did not participate in the election, and the second bloc, the al-Mardi group, was badly defeated except for the success of Jasim Murad in the seventh.

In addition to the religious bloc vote and the racial vote, the high degree of voter participation was caused by at least five other factors:

1. Since this was the first democratic experiment in Bahrain, many people felt that it should be given every chance to succeed.
2. In spite of the 50-50 composition of the Constitutional Assembly, many felt that the loyal opposition should at least be heard within the Assembly.
3. The Constitutional Assembly candidates, regardless of qualification, were compatriots, which meant to many that this experiment might produce new and good elements on the political scene.[22]
4. Another factor contributing to the high percentage of voting was that the candidates themselves invariably spoke out during the campaign against the decision of the al-Shahabi group to withdraw. To a man, the candidates attacked this decision as being negative and unproductive.
5. Still another reason was the fear of government reprisal against nonvoters, so claimed by some voters, especially in that a special stamp was affixed to one's passport to indicate that the bearer had voted. Nonvot-

---

[11] All the Arabs had to do to insure election was to make a few remarks about the Arabic grammar of the Persian candidates.

[JJ] Rasul al-Jishshi (first ward), Muhammad Hasan Kamal al-Din (third), 'Ali Salih al-Salih (fifth—by acclamation), 'Abd al-'Aziz Shamlan (eighth), Khalifa 'Abdalla al-Manna'i (ninth), Khalifa al-Bin'ali (tenth), 'Abd al-'Aziz al-Rashid (sixteenth), and Muhammad Hasan al-Fadil (nineteenth—by acclamation).

ing, as indicated by the absence of such a stamp in the passport, might have caused some trouble later on.[kk]

The elected Constitutional Assembly members were mostly Shi'a, young[ll] and relatively educated.[mm] One can safely conclude that those elected represented, at least socially, a typical cross section of Bahrain. A close analysis of tables 7-1 and 7-2 indicates that a total of 59 candidates ran for election in the 19 wards, 33 percent of whom ran from Bahrain's most heavily populated and politically conscious districts—Manama's first and second wards and Muharraq's ninth ward. The multiplicity of candidates in these three wards and the sectarian undertones, particularly in the first and second wards, created a great deal of excitement, which in turn brought out the vote. These three wards recorded the heaviest voting in the country: 91 percent in the first; 90 percent in the second; and 90 percent in the ninth. The three wards also have the highest number of registered voters: 1,732 in the first; 1,531 in the second; and 1,640 in the ninth.

The eight candidates who ran from the first ward included a liberal Shi'a pharmacist (who also headed Shamlan's Slate of Fourteen), a conservative Shi'a (a retired school teacher), a college-educated young merchant, a realtor, a journalist, two other merchants, and an aged religious. The vote produced two surprises: the victory of the Shi'a retired educator (al-'Urayyid with 662 votes out of 1,585); and the clear-cut defeat of a rather well qualified and liberal journalist (al-Mardi with 171 votes). The victory of the front-runner (Jishshi with 885 votes) was expected. al-'Urayyid's victory indicated that the Sunni candidates split their vote and that sectarianism, especially as emphasized by some of the Shi'a candidates during the campaign, was much more invidious than the candidates cared to admit.[nn]

Various reasons contributed to the defeat of Mahmud al-Mardi. Among them were the following:

1. He ran in a ward in which he did not live.[oo]
2. He did not appeal to sectarianism but concentrated on the issues.
3. Although ideologically al-Mardi may have been in a good position as a

---

[kk] In retrospect, such a claim might have been plausible had the elections failed due to a small turnout. The heavy voting seemed to have rendered this possibility invalid.

[ll] Eleven members are under 39 years old—over 80 percent of the population are also in this category.

[mm] Eight were college graduates, and two had concluded two or more years of college education.

[nn] Even such liberal Shi'a candidates as Rasul al-Jishshi openly courted the Shi'a vote and used the *ma'tams* for campaigning, and it was a Shi'a bloc vote that carried al-'Urayyid to victory.

[oo] He lived in the third ward—Sulmaniyya.

Table 7-1
Official List of Constitutional Assembly Candidates

District/Ward	Number and Name of Candidates	Total Votes	Votes Won
Manama/1		1,585[a]	
	1. Rasul al-Jishshi		885
	2. 'Abd al-Hamid al-'Urayyid		662
	3. Hasan Muhammed Zayn al-'Abidin		336
	4. Muhammad Yusuf Mahmud		315
	5. Muhammad 'Abdalla Zamil		211
	6. Mahmud Muhammad al-Mardi		171
	7. Khalifa Ghanim al-Rumayhi		165
	8. Muhammad Salih al-'Abbassi		134
Manama/2		1,378[a]	
	1. Abd al-Karim 'Ali al-'Alaywat		841
	2. Muhammad Sa'id Ja'far al-Mahuzi		451
	3. Hamid 'Ali Sanqur		347
	4. Hasan 'Isa Khayyat		343
	5. 'Abd al-Rasul al-Halawaji		268
	6. 'Abd al-Husayn Mirza Jawahiri		207
	7. 'Abd al-Min'im 'Ali Kathim		182
Manama/3		986	
	1. Muhammad Hasan Kamal al-Din		869
	2. Husayn Muhammad Aryan		117
Manama/4		619	
	1. Qasim Ahmad Fakhro		243
	2. Muhammad 'Abdalla Hirmis		173
	3. Hamad Salman Zayani		134
	4. Yusuf Zubari		69
Manama/5			
	1. 'Ali Salih al-Salih[b]		
Manama/6			
	1. 'Ali Ibrahim 'Abd al-'Al[b]		
Muharraq/7		1,069	
	1. Jasim Muhammad Murad		648
	2. Saqir Muhammad Zayani		260
	3. Ahmad Sanad Muhammad Sanad		142
	4. Khalil Ibrahim al-Duy		119
Muharraq/8		1,041	
	1. 'Abd al-'Aziz Shamlan		716
	2. Jasim Mansur Nayim		149
	3. 'Ali 'Abdalla Karime		136
	4. Muhammad Hasan al-Hasan		40
Muharraq/9		1,472[a]	
	1. 'Ali 'Abdall Sayyar		841
	2. Khalifa 'Abdalla al-Manna'i		452
	3. Hajji Ibrahim Hajji		408
	4. 'Ali Rashid al-Amin		377
	5. Sabt Salim Sabt Fazi'		105

Table 7-1 (cont.)

District/Ward	Number and Name of Candidates	Total Votes	Votes Won
Muharraq/10		692	
	1. Khalifa Ahmad al-Bin'ali		353
	2. Mahmud Ibrahim al-Mahmud		339
Muharraq/11		806	
	1. Muhammad 'Abdalla Muhammad al-Samahiji		420
	2. 'Ali Hasan Ibrahim		386
Jidhafs/12		1,458	
	1. Mulla Hasan Ahmad Zayn al-Din		596
	2. Muhammad 'Ali Salim Khalifat		323
	3. Muhammad 'Ali al-'Ikri		273
	4. 'Abdalla 'Isa al-Zira		266
Jidhafs/13			
	1. 'Abdalla Muhammad 'Ali al-Madani[b]		
Budaya'/14		1,260	
	1. 'Isa Ahmad Qasim		984
	2. Ja'far 'Ali Ahmad al-Dirazi		215
	3. Muhammad Ja'far Muhsin al-'Arab		61
Dumistan/15			
	1. Muhammad 'Ali al-Dayf[b]		
'Isa Town/16		834	
	1. 'Abd al-'Aziz al-Rashid		469
	2. Yusuf Salman Kamal		197
	3. Faysal 'Abd 'Ali al-'Alaywat		168
'Aali/17		1,194	
	1. 'Abd al-'Aziz Mansur al-'Ali		468
	2. Yusuf al-Shaykh Muhammad al-Mubarak		359
	3. Nasir Muhammad Nasir		165
Sitra/18		1,194	
	1. Hasan 'Ali al-Mutawwaj		1,025
	2. Hasan Ahmad 'Ali		135
	3. Shaykh 'Ali Yusuf al-Sitri		34
Rifa'/19			
	1. Muhammad Hasan al-Fadil[b]		

[a]Sends two representatives.
[b]No contest.

bourgeois nationalist, ideological alignment could not withstand the tide of sectarianism.

As to the defeat of the college-educated businessman (Hasan Zayn al-'Abidin with 336 votes), two explanations could be given:

Table 7-2
Elected Constitutional Assembly Members and Their Districts

Ward	Registered Voters	Votes Cast	%	Candidate	Age[a]	Sect	Education	Profession	Votes Received
1	1,732	1,585	91%	al-Jishshi	38	Shi'a	B.S.	Pharmacist	885
				al-'Urayyid	50	Shi'a	Elementary	Teacher	662
2	1,531	1,378	90	'Alaywat	43	Shi'a	High school	Merchant	841
				al-Mahuzi	32	Shi'a	High school	Druggist	451
3	1,211	986	83	Kamal al-Din	31	Shi'a	B.A.	Teacher	869
4	768	619	88	Fakhro	46	Sunni	B.A.	Accountant	243
5	No contest[b]			al-Salih	30	Shi'a	B.A.	Merchant	—
6	No contest[b]			al-'Al	49	Shi'a	High school	Contractor	—
7	1,235	1,069	87	Murad	41	Sunni	High school	Merchant	648
8	1,255	1,041	83	Shamlan	61	Sunni	2 years college[c]		
9	1,640	1,472	90	Sayyar	44	Sunni	High school	Merchant	716
				al-Manna'i	36	Sunni	High school	Journalist	841
10	799	692	86	al-Bin'ali	33	Sunni	B.A.	Merchant	452
11	900	806	89	al-Samahiji	31	Shi'a	3 years college	Lawyer	353
12	1,566	1,458	90	Zayn al-Din	42	Shi'a	Religious training	Teacher	420
13	No contest[b]			al-Madani	39	Shi'a	B.A.	Mulla	596
14	1,449	1,260	86	Qasim	32	Shi'a	B.A.	Teacher	—
15	No contest[b]			al-Dayf	53	Shi'a	Religious training	Mulla	984
16	942	834	87	al-Rashid	35	Sunni	B.A., LL.B	Businessman	—
17	1,024	992	97	al-'Ali	40	Shi'a	Elementary	Lawyer	469
18	1,316	1,194	90%	al-Mutawwaj	38	Shi'a	High school	Contractor	468
19	No contest[b]			al-Fadil	47	Sunni	High school	Merchant	1,025
								Merchant	—

[a] Minimum age requirement for candidacy is 30.
[b] No election held in these wards. The number of registered voters in these five wards totals 4,995.
[c] The first Bahraini scholarship student to the American University of Beirut (1928-30).

1. He was known among, and his votes came from, only a specific segment of the first ward.[pp]
2. His campaign posters called on the voters to support "your *college-educated* candidate" (emphasis added), which had the unintended effect of projecting an elitist image. The devastating effect of this type of advertising can only be gauged when one realizes that between 1950 (when the first Bahraini graduated from a university) and 1970, barely 300 Bahrainis had graduated from a university.

In the second ward, the defeat of the qualified Hamid Sanqur (347 votes out of 1,378 cast) was a major surprise. The victory of al-'Alaywat with 841 votes and al-Mahuzi with 451 again underscored the extent of the sectarian alignment and the conservative tendencies of voters on the intrasect level. This intrasect preference for conservatism also contributed to the defeat of Muhammad Khalifat in the twelfth ward (323 out of 1,458 votes cast). Four Shi'a candidates ran in the twelfth, and Khalifat's liberal views on basic freedoms, women's suffrage, and governmental structure[qq] were overpowered by the appeal of his opponent Mulla Hasan Zayn al-Din, to the Shi'a faithful to support him at the polls. The conservative religious leader was swept to victory with 596 votes.

The definitive victory of Jasim Murad, a prosperous businessman, in the seventh ward by 648 out of 1,069 votes primarily reflected the popularity of the man himself. The Murad family had lived in that part of Muharraq for a long time, and he had always been active in community affairs. He had always been generous in almsgiving, and he showed concern for the problems of the common man. His only viable opponent, Saqir Zayani, was badly defeated, drawing only 260 votes. Zayani was a government-appointed judge until he resigned prior to entering the campaign.[rr]

The victory of 'Abd al-'Aziz Shamlan in the eighth ward, with 716 out of 1,041 votes case, was almost a foregone conclusion, especially when 'Ali Rabi'a, the leftist labor-supported candidate, stepped out of the race. Rabi'a was a member of the al-Shahabi group, which had decided to withdraw from the race altogether. Shamlan's name and history of nationalist activities, together with his personal sacrifices in being exiled to St. Helena in 1956, had built for him an unshakeable base of popular support. He was also elected vice-speaker of the Constitutional Assembly.

[pp] Many of his votes came from a group that consider themselves *al-Hawala*, Arabs who originally had settled on the western coast of Persia during the seventh century and who later emigrated back to the Arab coast of the Gulf.

[qq] See his statements in *al-Adwa'*, 26 October 1972, pp. 2-3 and 16.

[rr] For example, al-Jazira Club in Muharraq's seventh ward has received regular financial support from Murad. Zayani was reappointed to the judgeship of the Lower Court on 31 December 1972. State of Bahrain, *Official Gazette*, 4 January 1973, p. 3.

In the ninth ward, 'Ali Sayyar, was also expected to win, and his victory was insured when Hisham al-Shahabi withdrew from the race. Sayyar's victory (841 votes out of the 1,472 votes cast) was significant in that it reflected an obvious sympathy vote. His weekly magazine suspended publication by government order for almost two months between September and November 1972. Another candidate who had a reasonable expectation of winning but who lost was 'Ali Rashid al-Amin (377 votes). Two reasons contributed to his defeat: he was a newcomer to the ninth ward (most of his family still reside in other parts of Muharraq); and he did not campaign vigorously, thereby failing to sustain a strong beginning drive.

In order to complete the statistical profile of the election to the Constitutional Assembly and to place the high voter participation in a proper demographic perspective, examine table 7-3. The first point to be made here is that the Constitutional Assembly Election Law restricted the right to vote to Bahraini males who were at least 20 years of age on election day (article 1). This requirement had the immediate effect of excluding women, naturalized citizens, and members of the police and defense forces. Table 7-3 reveals a number of interesting facts. Most significant is the indication that the move toward democracy through an elected Constitutional Assembly was restricted to less than 10 percent of the entire population of the state. The democratization process was therefore carried out by a small segment of the population, which rendered legitimate an elitist system of government in which the Khalifa family continues to maintain the controlling interest.

One final comment should be made on the delicate balance of Shi'a and Sunni, which the government has always tried to maintain. In view of the large number of Shi'as elected, the prime minister stated following the election that the government would correct this imbalance through appointments. To be sure, of the eight appointed members three were Shi'a (Ibrahim al-'Urayyid, Sadiq Baharna, Muhammad Hasan Dawani). These appointments gave a balance of 17 Shi'as compared with 13 Sunnis. However, when one considers the ministers (4 Shi'as and 8 Sunnis), who by law were members ex officio of the Constitutional Assembly, the balance becomes perfect—21 Sunnis and 21 Shi'as for a total of 42 members (see table 7-4).

These are the "founding fathers" of modern constitutional Bahrain.[55]

---

[55] It is instructive that in its opening session, the Assembly elected Ibrahim al-'Urayyid as speaker and 'Abd al-'Aziz Shamlan as deputy-speaker. al-'Urayyid is a poet, writer, literary critic, and a man of letters known throughout the Arab world. Shamlan is a nationally known political figure in Bahrain. He was one of the leaders of the Committee of National Union in the mid-fifties. For the complete story of this movement see 'Abd al-Rahman al-Bakir, *Min al-Bahrain 'ila al-Manfa* [From Bahrain to Exile](Beirut: Dar Maktabat al-Haya, 1965).

Table 7-3
Demographic Analysis of the Electorate

Total population (1971)		216,078[a]
Total Bahraini population	178,193	
Total number of Bahraini females	88,421	
Total number of Bahraini males	89,772	
Total number of Bahraini males under 19	53,248[b]	
Total number of Bahraini males of voting age	36,524	
Approximate number of males excluded (armed forces and police)	2,000[c]	
Approximate number of naturalized citizens excluded from voting	4,000[c]	
Total number of Bahraini males eligible to vote	30,524	
Total number of registered voters	22,363	
Percent registered/eligible voters		73.2%
Total number of registered voters in the 5 no-contest wards	4,995	
Total number of registered voters in the remaining 14 wards	17,368	
Total number of actual voters		15,385
Percent actual-registered voters		88.5%
Percent voters-total Bahraini population		8.6%
Percent voters-total population of Bahrain (Bahrainis and non-Bahrainis)		7.1%

[a]State of Bahrain, Ministry of Finance and National Economy, *Statistics of the Population Census,* 1971.
[b]Over 50 percent of the entire population of Bahrain are under 19 years of age; when only the Bahaini population is considered, the figure rises to 60 percent.
[c]Based on estimates obtained from the Ministry of Information.

These men and the factions they formed represented a cross section of the sociocultural fabric of Bahrain. Consequently, the daily problems and worries of the Bahraini, rather than an abstract theory of democracy, formed the mold that shaped Bahrain's new constitution.

Qasim Ahmad Fakhro, who was elected secretary of the Assembly, is a college graduate and a successful businessman. In his acceptance speech on the opening day, Secretary Fakhro stated that by electing these three people to positions of leadership, the Assembly gave recognition to Bahrain's literary and cultural tradition, to the long political struggle of its people and to the new generation of education and technology (from a live radio broadcast of the opening ceremonies of the Constitutional Assembly). It is interesting to note that the three officers of the Constitutional Assembly ran for election to the National Assembly; the three lost.

Table 7-4
Membership of the Constitutional Assembly

Members	Sect
I. *Elected members*	
1. Rasul al-Jishshi	Shi'a
2. 'Abd al-Hamid al-'Urayyid	Shi'a
3. 'Abd al-Karim 'Ali 'Alaywat	Shi'a
4. Muhammad Sa'id Ja'far al-Mahuzi	Shi'a
5. Muhammad Hasan Kamal al-Din	Shi'a
6. Qasim Ahmad Fakhro (secretary of the Assembly)	Sunni
7. 'Ali Salih al-Salih	Shi'a
8. 'Ali Ibrahim 'Abd al-'Al	Shi'a
9. Jasim Muhammad Murad	Sunni
10. 'Abd al-'Aziz Shamlan (vice-speaker of the Assembly)	Sunni
11. 'Ali 'Abdalla Sayyar	Sunni
12. Khalifa 'Abdalla al-Manna'i	Sunni
13. Khalifa Ahmad al-Bin'ali	Sunni
14. Muhammad 'Abdalla Muhammad al-Samahiji	Shi'a
15. Mulla Hasan Ahmad Zayn al-Din	Shi'a
16. 'Abdalla Muhammad 'Ali al-Madani	Shi'a
17. 'Isa Ahmad Qasim	Shi'a
18. Muhammad 'Ali al-Dayf	Shi'a
19. 'Abd al-'Aziz al-Rashid	Sunni
20. 'Abd al-'Aziz Mansur al-'Ali	Shi'a
21. Hasan 'Ali al-Mutawwaj	Shi'a
22. Muhammad Hasan al-Fadil	Sunni
II. *Appointed Members*	
1. Ibrahim Hasan Kamal	Sunni
2. Ibrahim al-'Urayyid (speaker of the Assembly)	Shi'a
3. Ahmad 'Ali Kanoo	Sunni
4. Muhammad Hasan Khalil Dawani	Shi'a
5. Muhammad Yusuf Jalal	Sunni
6. Tariq 'Abd al-Rahman al-Mu'ayyad	Sunni
7. Sadiq Muhammad Baharna	Shi'a
8. Rashid 'Abd al-Rahman Zayani	Sunni
III. *Members Ex Officio* (Council of Ministers)	
1. Shaikh Khalifa bin Sulman al-Khalifa (prime minister)	Sunni
2. Shaikh Hamad bin 'Isa al-Khalifa (heir apparent & minister of defense)	Sunni
3. Shaikh Muhammad bin Mubarak al-Khalifa (minister of foreign affairs & information)	Sunni
4. Shaikh Khalid bin Muhammad al-Khalifa (minister of justice)	Sunni
5. Shaikh 'Abdalla bin Khalid al-Khalifa (minister of municipalities & agriculture)	Sunni
6. Shaikh 'Abd al-'Aziz bin Muhammad al-Khalifa (minister of education)	Sunni

Table 7-4 (cont.)
Membership of the Constitutional Assembly

Members	Sect
7. Dr. 'Ali Fakhro (minister of health)	Sunni
8. Mahmud Ahmad al-'Alawi (minister of finance & national economy)	Shi'a
9. Yusuf Ahmad al-Shirawi (minister of development & engineering services)	Sunni
10. Ibrahim Hmidan (minister of labor & social affairs)	Shi'a
11. Dr. Husayn Baharna (minister of state-legal affairs)	Shi'a
12. Jawad Salim al-'Urayyid (minister of state-cabinet affairs)	Shi'a

8 Conclusion: Toward a Functional Model of Urban Tribalism

Any attempt to develop a model in social science should take into consideration at least three elements: the components of the reality represented by the model; the components of the model itself; and the degree of correlation between the reality and the representation. Unless these elements are internalized and placed in proper perspective relative to each other and to the system that the theoretical construct is designed to represent and upon which future changes within the system are predicated, any attempts at model building will not bear fruitful results. If this is the case, the social scientist will have but compounded the confusion of both the system under study and the process of theoretical extrapolation, which the model approach was expected to set in motion.

The fundamental consideration in constructing a model is the linguistic definition of the word model; lack of a precise definition of this concept has oftentimes led astray those social scientists using this approach. Specifically, the sociologist should define his model in terms of the community he is concerned with, the economist in terms of production, and the political scientist in terms of the political unit—tribe, city, megapolis, and state.[a] Therefore, anyone attempting to construct a model as a representation of a certain reality should clearly define his concept of a model and what he expects it to accomplish.

Another element must be considered in model building. Generally, models in social science are either normative or descriptive. *Normative* models tend to be value-charged representations of the good society, not just any society. This means that the predictive capability of these models is enmeshed in the model builder's own vision of a particular utopia, not in the functionalism of the model itself. In this context, Plato's Philosopher King is not simply the head of a certain political unit; he is the only qualified agent through whom the best society assumes shape.

The *descriptive* model, on the other hand, describes a particular reality that lends itself to analysis. Furthermore, when predicting future changes within this reality, the model is value neutral. The model's descriptive-anticipatory function is geared toward the humanly possible rather than the unattainable. The value of the model's futurism simply lies in its ability to

---
[a] For an excellent discussion of models and their use in social sciences see Irving Louis Horowitz, *Three Worlds of Development, The Theory and Practice of International Stratification*, 2nd ed. (New York: Oxford University Press, 1972), pp. 271-283.

minimize the shock of surprise. Since both the normative and the descriptive models are designed to transcend the reality they are built to represent and to apply to other similar realities, the social scientist must at the outset define the philosophical underpinnings of his model.[b]

Upon the examination of the general characteristics of the developing countries and all of the factors that set them apart as a group, and although the newly independent tribal states of the Gulf are technically a part of this Third World, it is possible to consider the new Gulf states as an identifiable subgroup with its own characteristics. The Islamic culture and history of these states, the tribal system of government, which they have evolved through the centuries, the philosophical-theocratic supports of their tribal rule, their demographic makeup, and their oil-based developing economies—all of these factors have contributed to the uniqueness of this group of small states. This group is comprised of Kuwait, Qatar, the United Arab Emirates (Abu Dhabi, Dubai, al-Shariqa, Umm al-Qaywayn, Ra's al-Khayma, al-Fujayra, and 'Ajman), and Bahrain.

Some of the distinguishing characteristics of the Gulf's small states include the following:

1. They are all ruled by powerful families, which are a modern extension of an old tribal tradition.

2. The reins of government are tightly held in the hands of the ruling family, which usually makes decisions on every major issue, with minimal popular input into the decision-making process.

3. In most of these tribal states, the ruling families have set afoot a cautious process of inviting some form of popular participation in government. However, the ruling families have generally made it known to their peoples that this form of popular participation is basically an extension of the Islamic concept of *shura* (consultation). Translated into reality, the consultative basis of popular participation means that the ruler is not bound by any decisions of or resolutions passed by the consultative bodies.

4. The moves, which the ruling families in these states have initiated, toward popular participation have focused on the preparation of a constitutional document, first approved by the ruling family and then submitted to some type of representative body, generally known as a constitutional assembly.

5. Territorially, demographically, and administratively, the new states of the Gulf are closer in form and political structure to classical city-states than to the modern version of the nation-state, especially as it is defined by the law of nations. However, in almost each one of these states, the ruling

---
[b] Professor Horowitz has identified three types of social science models: the model as a society, as a strategy, and as a theory. As a *society*, the model would indicate "how the world is carved up." As a *strategy*, the model describes "how one goes about carving a world up," and as a *theory*, the model states "how the explanation of changes in the world can best be made." Ibid., p. 271.

family has displayed a certain flexibility and a desire to transform the Gulf's littoral city-states into modern entities aspiring to the title of nation-states.

6. Economically, the new Gulf states are engaged in a vigorous process of development. Though they have generally lacked a scientific long-range development plan, the governments of these states have for the most part intuited a relatively modern image of the new society they are building. The new wealth from oil has helped these states to forge ahead with the physical transformation of their tribal societies, thereby preparing the ground for the sociological, psychological, and organizational modernity to follow.

At least two observations can be made in view of the preceding characteristics. First, the uniqueness of the Gulf subregion in the international political system and particularly in the Third World makes especially alluring the prospect of a scholarly study of the new Gulf littoral states. The promise that such scholarship will open up the horizons is sufficient grounds for separate scholarly endeavors.

The second observation to be made is that the models, approaches, and other attempts at theorizing, which social scientists have devised during the past two decades to describe present and future developmental processes in the Third World, are of limited use when applied to the new Gulf ministates. In logic, rationale, and purpose these models do not fit the Gulf region; herein lies the need for a fresh theoretical attempt at model building in the Gulf.

It has been possible to discover a new model that corresponds to the new Gulf reality. The new model should probably be called the urban tribalism model. *Model* is defined in this context as a description of a set of interconnected functions that has a predictive capability. Philosophically, this model is, for the most part, descriptive, not normative. It is designed to represent a new reality and to anticipate future changes in this reality. It is also designed as a functional tool, which would make it possible to test the probability of various propositions in political theory against empirical data.[1]

Admittedly still in the nascent stage and in need of further research, the urban tribalism model is nonetheless a logical synthesis of traditional tribalism and modernity. Urbanization in the new Gulf states has proven to be a long process, consisting essentially of one major component—the psychological transformation of a tribal culture into a twentieth century organization within which the Islamic principles of *shari'a* and *shura* find expression in the modern political techniques of political democracy.

This book, as was stated in its introduction, is a case study of Bahrain—a new society in the making. The case study has, through the analysis of the different function of Bahrain's political system, suggested the urban tribalism model. The promise that this model can apply to other tribal political formations in the Gulf is indeed exciting, and this excitement is added to by the mounting evidence that it might be possible to synthesize traditional tribalism and modernization. The urban tribalism model is a description of the emerging results of this synthesis—the new Gulf community.

Epilogue

The political developments, which have occurred in Bahrain since the writing of this book, have underscored the theme that runs throughout this study—the tension between traditional tribalism based on family rule and popular participation based on representation, accountability, and openness in government. The National Assembly, which was first elected and convened in December 1973, served for less than two years. As a result of continuing disputes between the National Assembly and the government, the amir of Bahrain, upon the recommendation of his brother the prime minister, decreed on 26 August 1975 that the National Assembly be dissolved immediately. In defense of its action the ruling family has maintained that certain elements in the National Assembly, presumably the leftist bloc, had thwarted any possibility of mutual cooperation between the Assembly and the government. In his statements to the press the prime minister has consistently claimed that the National Assembly had hindered progress in the country by sheer inaction.

The constitutional crisis, which culminated in the dissolution of the Assembly, obviously runs much deeper than any specific conflict between the prime minister and members of the leftist bloc over specific legislation. The crisis, as was shown throughout this book, is fundamentally linked to the democratization of the regime. The National Assembly had afforded the first public forum in the country's history for popularly elected representatives to criticize economic, political, and social policies. Although these criticisms were protected by the new constitution, individual rights outside the Assembly, as regards the freedoms of press, speech, organization, and assembly, were still governed by restrictive preconstitution laws. Indeed, it was the government's proposed public security law that eventually polarized the conflict. When the Khalifa government realized that it could not muster enough votes to pass the proposed bill in the Assembly, the government bloc boycotted the sessions, thereby depriving the Assembly of a quorum and leading to its ultimate dissolution. Since the spring of 1975 the Assembly has been dissolved, and a quasi state of emergency has been imposed in the country.[a]

---

[a] For a detailed exposition of the conflict and the dissolution of the National Assembly see *al-Adwa'* (Bahrain), May-August 1975; *Sada al-'Usbu'* (Bahrain), May-July 1975; *al-Tali'a* (Kuwait), May-August 1975; *al-Bahrain al-Yom* (Bahrain), May-August 1975; *al-Maqawif* (Bahrain), May-August 1975; and the official minutes of the National Assembly (Bahrain), May-June 1975.

Notes

Chapter 1
Introduction

1. Lucian W. Pye, "Transitional Asia and the Dynamics of Nation Building," in Marian D. Irish, ed., *World Pressures on American Foreign Policy* (Englewood Cliffs, N.J.: Prentice-Hall, 1964), pp. 154-171.
2. Gabriel A. Almond and James S. Coleman, eds., *The Politics of the Developing Areas* (Princeton, N.J.: Princeton University Press, 1960). Page reference herein is made to the 1970 paperback edition.
3. Ibid., pp. 3-64.
4. Lucian W. Pye, ed., *Communication and Political Development* (Princeton, N.J.: Princeton University Press, 1963), p. vii.
5. Leonard Binder et al., eds., *Crises and Sequences in Political Development* (Princeton, N.J.: Princeton University Press, 1971), p. vii.
6. Ibid., p. 75.
7. Ibid., p. 77.
8. See State of Bahrain, Ministry of Finance and National Economy, *Statistical Abstract*, 1972, pp. 1 and 9. See also *Geology of the Arabian Peninsula: Bahrain* (Washington, D.C.: U.S. Government Printing Office, 1967), p. E1.
9. Memorandum No. 1, from the British Political Resident to the Ruler of Bahrain. *Memoranda Exchanged Between the United Kingdom of Great Britain and Northern Ireland and the State of Bahrain Concerning the Termination of Special Treaty Relations Between Them*. Copy obtained from Bahrain's Ministry of Foreign Affairs.
10. Memorandum No. 2. Ibid.
11. United Nations Security Council, *Resolution 287*, 1970.
12. Article 33, section a.
13. Ibid., section e.
14. Ibid., section h.
15. Article 43.

Chapter 2
Education and Bahrain's Political Development

1. James S. Coleman, ed., *Education and Political Development* (Princeton, N. J.: Princeton University Press, 1965), pp. vi, vii. Foreword

by Lucian W. Pye. Page reference herein is made to the 1968 paperback edition.

2. Ministry of Education, State of Bahrain, *al-Ta'lim fi al-Bahrain: Waqi'uhu wa Mustaqbaluhu* [Education in Bahrain: Its Present and Future], 1972.

3. Ibid., pp. 2-4.

4. State of Bahrain, Ministry of Education, *Educational Statistics, 1971-1972*, 1973, p. 41.

5. Ibid., pp. 10-12.

6. State of Bahrain, Ministry of Finance and National Economy, *Statistical Abstract*, 1972, p. 31.

7. *al-Adwa'*, 28 September 1972, pp. 2-4.

8. Government of Bahrain, Department of Education, *Primary School Curricula*, 1969, p. 5.

9. Ibid., p. 21.

10. Ibid., pp. 23-24.

11. Ibid., pp. 75-76.

12. Muhammad Ahmad Jad al-Mawla et al., *al-Bidaya fi al-Tahajji wa al-Mutala'a* [Elementary Spelling and Reading] vol. I, (Cairo, Egypt: Dar al-Ma'arif, 1972).

13. Ibid.

14. Muhammad Ahmad Jad al-Mawla et al., *al Bidaya fi al-Tahajji wa al-Mutala'a* [Elementary Spelling and Reading] vol. II, (Cairo, Egypt: Dar al-Ma'arif, 1972).

15. Rida al-Musawi et al., *al-Qira'a al-'Arabiyya al-Haditha* [Modern Arabic Reader], Third Grade (Manama, Bahrain: Ministry of Education, 1967), p. 8.

16. Rida al-Musawi et al., *al-Qira'a al-'Arabiyya al-Haditha* [Modern Arabic Reader], Fourth Grade (Manama, Bahrain: Ministry of Education, 1966), p. 9.

17. Ibid., p. 38.

18. La'ali' A. Zayani, "English Supplementary Reading for the First Intermediate Class of Bahrain," unpublished M.A. thesis (Beirut, Lebanon: American University, 1971), pp. 29-37.

19. Ibid., p. 30.

Chapter 3
Communication and Political Socialization: The Role of the Clubs and the Press

1. Lucian W. Pye, ed., *Communication and Political Development*

(Princeton, N.J.: Princeton University Press, 1963), pp. 38-42.

2. Personal interview, 19 October 1972.

3. United Nations Security Council, *Resolution 287* 1970; especially *Report of the Personal Representative of the Secretary-General in Charge of the Good Offices Mission, Bahrain* (S/9772).

4. Charles Belgrave, *Personal Column*, 2nd ed. (Beirut, Lebanon: Librairie du Liban, 1972), p. 144.

5. *Basic Law*, article 5.

6. Ibid., articles 3 and 4.

7. See interview by Mohammad Qasim al-Shirawi with members of Alumni Club in *al-Adwa'*, 2 March 1972, pp. 6-9 and 14.

8. *Constitution*, article 4.

9. Ibid., article 2.

10. Ibid., part II.

11. Ibid., part I.

12. *Basic Law*, article 3.

13. Ibid., article 2.

14. Ibid., article 7.

15. Ibid., articles 2-6.

16. *Constitution*, articles 8-14.

17. Ibid., article 2.

18. Ibid., article 7.

19. Ibid., article 2.

20. Pye, *Communications and Political Development*, pp. 3-11.

21. Ibid., pp. 7-8.

22. Constitutional Assembly, *Minutes*, 16th session, 17 February 1973.

23. Ibid.

24. Ibid.

25. Personal interview, 23 October 1972.

26. Personal interview, 25 September 1972.

Chapter 4
Labor and Political Development

1. Irving Louis Horowitz, *Three Worlds of Development: The Theory and Practice of International Stratification*, 2nd ed. (New York: Oxford University Press, 1972), pp. 190-191.

2. Ibid., p. 191.

3. Charles Belgrave, *Personal Column*, 2nd ed. (Beirut, Lebanon: Librairie du Liban, 1972), pp. 84-85.

4. 'Abd al-Rahman al-Bakir, *Min al-Bahrain ila al-Manfa* [From Bahrain to Exile] (Beirut, Lebanon: Maktabat al-Haya, 1965), pp. 75-80.

5. Ibid., pp. 80-305. See also, Belgrave, *Personal Column*, pp. 207-233.

6. Government of Bahrain, *The Bahrain Labor Ordinance*, 1957, 3rd ed. (Manama, Bahrain: Oriental Printing Press, n.d.).

7. *al-Tali'a*, 29 April 1972, pp. 22-23.

8. Ibid.

9. Section 43.

10. Section 44.

11. Section 45.

12. *Sada al-'Usbu'*, 14 March 1973, p. 5.

13. Ibid.

14. Ibid.

15. *al-Tali'a*, 3 June 1972, p. 16.

16. State of Bahrain, Ministry of Labor and Social Affairs, *Manpower Requirements and Employment in Bahrain* (31 January 1972), p. 11, known hereafter as the *Manpower Memorandum*.

17. Ibid., pp. 1-2.

18. *Manpower Memorandum*, p. 9.

19. State of Bahrain, *Official Gazette*, 18 January 1968, p. 3.

20. State of Bahrain, Ministry of Labor and Social Affairs, *Manpower Memorandum*, p. 13.

21. Ibid., p. 14.

22. *Sada al-'Usbu'*, 11 January 1972, p. 6.

23. I. William Zartman et al., "An Economic Indicator of Socio-Political Unrest," *International Journal of Middle East Studies*, October 1971, pp. 293-310.

Chapter 5
Foreign Policy and Political Development

1. See Saudi Arabia, *Statistical Abstract*, 1972 and The Bahrain Petroleum Company, *Annual Report*, 1971.

2. The Bahrain Petroleum Company (BAPCO), *Annual Report*, 1971, pp. 4-7.

3. David Easton, *A Framework for Political Analysis* (Englewood Cliffs, N.J.: Prentice-Hall, Inc., 1965), pp. 103-117.

4. State of Bahrain, *Official Gazette*, 19 August 1971, pp. 3-5.

5. State of Bahrain, Ministry of Information, *Huna al-Bahrain*, December 1971, p. 3.

6. State of Bahrain, Ministry of Information, *Akhbar al-Bahrain*, 18 December 1972, pp. 2-3.

7. State of Bahrain, *Official Gazette* 16 January 1969, p. 3.

8. Ibid.

9. State of Bahrain, *Official Gazette*, 2 September 1971, p. 3.

10. United Nations Security Council, *Resolution 287*, 1970; especially *Report of the Personal Representative of the Secretary-General in Charge of the Good Offices Mission, Bahrain* (S/9772).

11. *Akhbar al-Bahrain*, 19 March 1973, pp. 1-2.

12. *Al-Tali'a* (Kuwait), 26 June 1971, p. 7.

13. *Sada al-'Usbu'*, 7 December 1971, pp. 12-14.

14. *A Treaty of Friendship Between Bahrain and the United Kingdom of Great Britain and Northern Ireland*, signed in Bahrain on 15 August 1971. (Copy obtained from the government of Bahrain.)

15. Personal interview, 28 October 1972.

16. Personal interview, 27 January 1973.

17. *Sada al-'Usbu'*, 11 January 1972, p. 7.

18. Ibid.

19. *Sada al-'Usbu'*, 22 August 1973, p. 15.

20. Ibid.

Chapter 6
Toward a Democratic Structure: The Constitutional Assembly

1. State of Bahrain, Ministry of Information, *Huna al-Bahrain*, December 1971, p. 3.

2. See *al-Adwa'*, February-April 1972.

3. *al-Adwa'*, 3 February 1972, pp. 3-5.

4. Ibid.

5. Ibid.

6. Ibid.

7. *al-Adwa'*, 10 February 1972, pp. 3-5.

8. Ibid.
9. Ibid.
10. *al-Adwa'*, 17 February 1972, pp. 3-5.
11. Ibid.
12. Ibid.
13. 2 March 1972, pp. 6-9 and 14.
14. *al-Adwa'*, 2 March 1972, pp. 6-9.
15. Ibid.
16. *al-Adwa'*, 9 March 1972, pp. 4-6.
17. Ibid.
18. *al-Adwa'*, 22 April 1972, pp. 4-5.
19. Ibid.
20. Ibid.
21. Ibid.
22. *Sada al-'Usbu'*, 23 May 1972, pp. 4-5. See also 30 May 1972, p. 5.
23. State of Bahrain, *Official Gazette*, 20 June 1972, pp. 3-8.
24. State of Bahrain, *Official Gazette*, 19 July 1972, pp. 11-15.
25. Ibid., article 1, section 6.
26. State of Kuwait, *Dastur Dawlat al-Kuwayt wa Qanun al-'Intikhab* [Constitution of Kuwait and the Election Law] (Kuwait: Kuwait Government Press, 1962).
27. Personal interview, 23 September 1972.
28. Personal interview, 9 October 1972.
29. Personal interview, 10 October 1972.
30. Two personal interviews, 27 September and 5 October 1972.
31. Personal interview, 23 September 1972.
32. Personal interview, 21 September 1972.
33. Personal interview, 18 September 1972.
34. Personal interview, 19 October 1972.

Chapter 7
The First National Election and the Formation of the Constitutional Assembly

1. Personal interview, 29 October 1972.
2. State of Bahrain, *Official Gazette*, 22 April 1965, pp. 3-4.
3. Ibid., p. 3.

4. Ibid., p. 4.
5. Ibid.
6. *al-Adwa'*, 23 November 1972, pp. 4-5.
7. Ibid., p. 5.
8. See comments by Mahmud al-Mardi, prominent candidate and journalist, in *al-Siyasa*, 29 November 1972, pp. 1, 5, and 11.
9. *al-Adwa'*, 7 September 1972, p. 8.
10. *Sada al-'Usbu'*, 5 September 1972, pp. 18-19.
11. *al-Adwa'*, 21 September 1972, p. 13.
12. *al-Adwa'*, 18 October 1972, p. 12.
13. *al-Adwa'*, 23 November 1972, p. 3.
14. PFLO-Bahrain branch, statement issued in August 1972.
15. Salim al-Lozi, *Rasasatan fi al-Khalij* [Two Bullets in the Gulf] (Beirut: Mu'assasat al-Hawadith, 1971), p. 80.
16. *al-Adwa'*, October and November 1972.
17. *al-Adwa'*, 18 October 1972, pp. 4-5.
18. Ibid., p. 5.
19. *al-Adwa'*, 26 October 1972, pp. 2-3.
20. *al-Adwa'*, 2 November 1972, p. 22.
21. *al-Adwa'*, 23 November 1972, p. 19.
22. *Sada al-'Usbu'*, 5 December 1972.

Chapter 8
Conclusion: Toward a Functional Model of Urban Tribalism

1. Gabriel A. Almond and James S. Coleman, eds., *The Politics of the Developing Areas* (Princeton, N.J.: Princeton University Press, 1960), p. 59.

Bibliography

General Works on Bahrain and the Gulf

'Abd al-Karim, Ibrahim. *al-Bahrain wa Ahhammiyyatuha Bayna al-'Imarat al-'Arabiyya* [Bahrain and Its Importance Among the Arab Amirates]. Beirut, Lebanon: Matabi' Dar al-'Ilm li al-Malayin, 1970.

al-Ansari, Muhammad Jabir. *Lamahat min al-Khalij al-'Arabi* [Glimpses from the Arabian Gulf]. Manama, Bahrain: al-Sharika al-'Arabiyya li al-Wikalat wa al-Tawzi', 1970.

Anthony, John Duke. *Arab States of the Lower Gulf: People, Politics, Petroleum.* Washington, D.C.: The Middle East Institute, 1975.

al-Baharna, Husayn M. *The Legal Status of the Arabian Gulf States: A Study of Their Treaty Relations and Their International Problems.* Manchester, England: Manchester University Press, 1968.

al-Bakir, 'Abd al-Rahman. *Min al-Bahrain ila al-Manfa* [From Bahrain to Exile]. Beirut: Dar Maktabat al-Haya, 1965.

Belgrave, Charles. *Personal Column.* 2nd ed. Beirut, Lebanon: Librairie du Liban, 1972.

Belgrave, James H.D. *Welcome to Bahrain.* 8th ed. Manama, Bahrain: The Augustan Press, 1973.

Busch Briton Cooper. *Britain and the Persian Gulf, 1894-1914.* Berkeley, California: University of California Press, 1967.

_____. *Britain, India and the Arabs, 1914-1921.* Berkeley, California: University of California Press, 1971.

al-Falaki, Yusuf (pseudonym). *Qadiyyat al-Bahrain* [The Case of Bahrain]. Bahrain: no publisher, no date.

Hawley, Donald. *The Trucial States.* New York: Twayne Publishers, Inc., 1971.

Kelly, J.B. *Britain and the Persian Gulf, 1795-1880.* London: Oxford University Press, 1968.

Koury, Enver M. *Oil and Geopolitics in the Persian Gulf Area: A Center of Power.* Beirut, Lebanon: Catholic Press, 1973.

al-Lawzi, Salim. *Rasasatan fi al-Khalij* [Two Bullets in the Gulf]. Beirut, Lebanon: Manshurat al-Hawadith, 1971.

al-Madani, Salah, and Karim 'Ali al-'Urayyid. *Min Turath al-Bahrain al-Sha'bi* [Bahrain's Folklore Heritage]. Beirut, Lebanon: Matba'at Samya, 1972.

Nakhleh, Emile A. *Arab-American Relations in the Persian Gulf.* Washington, D.C.: American Enterprise Institute for Public Policy Research, 1975.

———. *The United States and Saudi Arabia: A Policy Analysis.* Washington, D.C.: American Enterprise Institute for Public Policy Research, 1975.

Nanu, John. *Ittihad al-'Imarat al-'Arabiyya* [Federation of Arab Emirates]. Beirut: Dar al-'I'lam al-'Arabi, 1971.

Popular Front for the Liberation of Oman and the Arabian Gulf. Statements on the Elections and al-Majlis al-Ta'sisi in Bahrain, August, October, November 1972, and January 1973.

Rafi', Abd al-Rahman. *Aghani al-Bihar al-Arba'a* [Songs of the Four Seas]. Beirut, Lebanon: Dar al-'Awda, 1970 (Poetry).

———. *Qasa'id Sha'biyya* [Popular Poems]. 2nd ed. Manama, Bahrain: al-Sharika al-'Arabiyya, 1972.

Ramazani, Rouhallah K. *The Persian Gulf: Iran's Role*. Charlottesville, Virginia: University Press of Virginia, 1972.

al-Rayyis, Riyad Najib. *Sira' al-Wahat wa al-Naft: Humum al-Khalij al-'Arabi Bayna 1968-1971* [Struggle of Oases and Oil: Troubles of the Arabian Gulf, 1968-1971]. Beirut, Lebanon: al-Nahar Press, 1973.

Rida, 'Adil. *'Uman wa al-Khalij: Qadaya wa Munaqashat* [Oman and the Gulf: Issues and Debates]. Cairo, Egypt: Dar al-Kitab al-'Arabi, 1969.

Sadik, M.T., and W.P. Snavely. *Bahrain, Qatar, and the United Arab Emirates*. Lexington, Massachusetts: Lexington Books, D.C. Heath and Company, 1972.

al-Ta'rif bi al-Haraka al-Adabiyya al-Jadida fi al-Bahrain [The Contemporary Literary Movement in Bahrain]. Manama, Bahrain: Society of Writers, 1973.

United Nations, *Bahrain*. Beirut, Lebanon: UNESOB, July 1972. Prepared by a United Nations Inter-Disciplinary Reconnaissance Mission of the United Nations Economic and Social Office in Beirut.

Wilson, Arnold T. *The Persian Gulf*. London: Allen and Unwin, Ltd., 1954.

World Energy Demands and the Middle East. Washington, D.C.: The Middle East Institute, 1972. Record of the 26th Annual Conference, 24-30 September 1972.

Zayani, Amal Ibrahim. "al-Bahrain min al-Himaya ila al-Istiqlal," [Bahrain from Protection to Independence]. M.A. thesis, University of Cairo, 1972.

Periodicals and Newspapers

al-Adwa' [Lights]. Bahrain weekly. 1965-75.

al-Anwar [Lights]. Beirut, June 1970. A special issue on Bahrain.

al-Ayyam [The Times]. Kuwait, 15 December 1971. A special issue on Bahrain.

"Bahrain," *The Arab Directory*. 23rd ed. Beirut, Lebanon, 1970-71, pp. 1-64.

Bahrain Chamber of Commerce and Industry. *al-Hayat al-Tijariyya* [Commercial Life] Bahrain monthly. 1971 and 1972. The December issue is a special annual issue.

The Guardian. London, 15 December 1972. A special report on Bahrain.

Middle East Sketch. Beirut weekly. 15 December 1972. A special issue on Bahrain. Also the 2 February 1973 and 16 March 1973 issues have featured articles on oil and the Gulf.

al-Mawaqif [Positions]. Bahrain Weekly. 1974-75.

al-Nahar [Today]. Beirut, June 1970. A special issue on Bahrain.

"Patterns and Progress in the Middle East," *'Alam al-Tijara* [Commerce World]. Beirut, August-September 1972. A special supplement.

Sada al-'Usbu' [Echo of the Week]. Bahrain weekly. 1969-1975. Publication interrupted between 19 September 1972 and 5 November 1972 under an official order by the government of Bahrain and between 14 July and 25 October 1975.

Sawt al-Bahrain [Voice of Bahrain]. Bahrain weekly. 1952-55.

State of Bahrain, Ministry of Information. *Akhbar al-Bahrain* [Bahrain News]. Weekly. 1972-73.

_____. *al-Bahrain al-Yom* [Bahrain Today]. Weekly. 1972-73. Formerly known as *Huna al-Bahrain*. December 1972 was a special issue.

_____. *Huna al-Bahrain* [Bahrain Calling]. December 1971. A special issue.

al-'Usbu' al-'Arabi [Arab Week]. Beirut weekly. 2 April 1973. A special issue on oil and the Gulf.

Adelman, M.A. "Is the Oil Shortage Real? Oil Companies as OPEC Tax Collectors," *Foreign Policy*, Winter 1972-73, pp. 69-107.

Akins, James E. "The Oil Crisis: This Time the Wolf is Here," *Foreign Affairs*, April 1973, pp. 462-490.

Berry, John A. "Oil and Soviet Policy in the Middle East," *The Middle East Journal*, Spring 1972, pp. 149-160.

Brewer, William D. "Yesterday and Tomorrow in the Persian Gulf," *The Middle East Journal*, Spring 1969, pp. 149-158.

Holden, David. "The Persian Gulf: After the British Raj," *Foreign Affairs*, July 1971, pp. 721-735.

Hurewitz, J.C. "The Persian Gulf: British Withdrawal and Western Security," *The Annals*, May 1972, pp. 106-115.

"The Gulf States," *The Middle East and North Africa, 1971-1972.* 18th ed. London: Europa Publications, 1972.

Sayigh, Yusif A. "Problems and Prospects of Development in the Arabian Peninsula," *International Journal of Middle East Studies*, January 1971, pp. 40-53.

Thoman, Roy E. "The Persian Gulf Region"' *Current History*, January 1971, pp. 38-50.

Specific Sources on Bahrain

Annuals

Government of Bahrain. *Annual Report for Years 1966-1969.*

_____. *Official Gazette.* 1955-75.

_____. Finance Department. *Statistical Abstract.*1967-69.

_____. _____. *Budget.* 1970.

_____. *The Fourth Population Census of Bahrain.* 1969.

State of Bahrain. *Official Gazette.* 1972, 1973.

State of Bahrain, Ministry of Finance and National Economy. *State Budget.* 1971-74.

_____. *Statistical Abstract.* 1971-74.

_____. *Statistics of the Population Census.* 1971.

Clubs

Alumni Club. *By-Laws as Amended.* No date.

Bahrain Club. *Basic Law.* 2nd ed. 1949.

_____. *Revised Basic Law*. No date.

Government of Bahrain. *The Bahrain Licensing of Societies and Clubs Ordinance–1959*.

_____. *The Exhibition of Plays, Theatrical Shows and Musical Performances Ordinances–1960*.

Jam'iyyat Awal al-Nisa'iyya. *Constitution*. 1969.

Jam'iyyat Nahdat Fatat al-Bahrain. *Basic Law*. No date.

Jam'iyyat Ri'ayat al-Tifl wa al-'Umuma. *Basic Law*. 1961.

_____. *Bayan Mujaz* [Brief Report]. No date.

al-Jazira Club. *Basic Law*. No date.

al-'Uruba Club. *The Constitution*. 1960.

'Usrat al-'Udaba' wa al-Kuttab fi al-Bahrain. *Dustur* [Constitution]. 1969.

_____. *al-Nahj al-Fikri* [Intellectual Program]. 1970.

Decrees and Laws

Government of Bahrain. *Bahraini Citizenship Law–1963*.

_____. *Press Law–1965*.

_____. *The Code of Criminal Procedure*. 1966.

_____. *Administrative Organization of the State*. Decrees No. 1, 2, 3, 19. January 1970.

_____. *Decree No. 5 for 1970–Concerning the Establishment of a Legal Committee for the Council of State*. 4 March 1970.

_____. *Law No. 7 for 1970–Concerning the Temporary Law for Land Development*. 8 July 1970.

_____. *Law No. 16 for 1971–Extension of the Temporary Law for Land Development*.

_____. *Decree No. 7 for 1971–Bahrain Agrees to Adhere to the Geneva Agreements of 1949*. 14 April 1971.

_____. *Decree No. 13 for 1971–Concerning the Organization of the Judiciary*. 7 August 1971.

State of Bahrain. *Declaration of Independence by the Ruler of Bahrain*. 14 August 1971.

_____. *Decree No. 1–Concerning the Political Organization of the State of Bahrain*. 15 August 1971.

_____. *Decree No. 2–Concerning the Political Organization of the State of Bahrain*. 15 August 1971.

———. *Notices Exchanged Between the United Kingdom and the State of Bahrain Concerning the Termination of Special Treaty Relations Between Them.* 15 August 1971.

———. *A Treaty of Friendship Between Great Britain and the State of Bahrain.* 15 August 1971.

———. *Decree No. 11—Concerning the Establishment and Organization of a Legal Affairs Department.* 22 April 1972.

———. *Intikhabat al-Majlis al-Ta'sisi–al-Marasim wa al-Ahkam* [Elections to the Constitutional Assembly]. July 1972.

———. Legal Affairs Department. *A List of Laws, Decrees, Orders and Decisions, 1969-1972.* 1973.

State of Kuwait. *Constitution of the State of Kuwait and the Law of Election.* 1962.

United Nations Security Council. *Report of the Personal Representative of the Secretary General in Charge of the Good Offices Mission, Bahrain.* S/9772. 30 April 1970.

———. *Resolution 287 (1970).*

Education

al-Hamir, 'Abdal-Malik. *Development of Education in Bahrain, 1940-1965.* Manama, Bahrain: Oriental Press, 1969.

Mertz, Robert A. *Education and Manpower in the Arabian Gulf.* 1972. A study prepared for American Friends of the Middle East, Washington, D.C. Chapter I is on Bahrain.

Government of Bahrain, Department of Education. *Manahij al-Dirasa li al-Marhala al-Ibtida'iyya* [Grade School Curricula, Grades 1-6]. 1969.

———. *Manahij al-Dirasa fi al-Madaris al-'I'dadiyya* [Junior High School Curricula, Grades 7-8]. 1966-67.

———. *Manahij al-Dirasa fi al-Marhala al-Thanawiyya al-'Amma* [Public High School Curricula]. 1969.

———. *Manahij al-Dirasa li al-Marhala al-Thanawiyya al-Tijariyya* [Trade High School Curricula]. 1969.

———. *Manahij al-Ma'ahid al-'Ulya li al-Mu'allimin wa al-Mu'allimat* [Curricula for Male and Female Teachers Institutes]. 1969.

———. *Names of Bahraini Graduates of Foreign Universities and Institutes of Higher Learning, 1950-1970.* 1970 (est. date).

———. *Recommendations of the UNESCO Experts Concerning the Development of Education in Bahrain.* 1970 (est. date).

_____. *A Report on Public Education in Bahrain*. Presented to the Arab Organization for Education in Cairo. 1971.

al-Sa'di, Wafiq, et al. *Mabadi' al-'Ulum wa al-Tarbiya al-Sihhiyya* [Elementary Science and Hygiene]. Third-Sixth Grades. 1970.

_____. *al-'Ulum al-'Amma wa al-Sihha* [General Science and Hygiene]. First and Second Intermediate. 1969.

State of Bahrain, Ministry of Education. *al-Bidaya fi al-Tahajji wa al-Mutala'a* [Introduction to Spelling and Reading]. I, II. First and Second Grades. Cairo, Egypt: Dar al-Ma'arif, 1972.

_____. *al-Bilad wa al-Nas* [The Country and the People]. Fifth Grade. 1969.

_____. *Educational Statistics, 1961-1971*.

_____. *Educational Statistics, 1971-1972*.

_____. *al-Jughrafya al-Khalifiyya* [Geography]. Fourth Grade. 1970.

_____. *al-Jughrafya al-Khalifiyya* [Geography]. Sixth Grade. 1965.

_____. *al-Qira'a al-'Arabiyya al-Jadida* [New Arabic Reading]. I, II, III, IV. Third-Sixth Grades. 1970.

_____. *al-Qisas al-Tarikhiyya* [Stories from History]. Fourth Grade. 1970.

_____. *al-Ta'lim fi al-Bahrain: Waqi'uhu wa Mustaqbaluhu* [Education in Bahrain: Its Present and Future]. A report presented by the Bahraini delegation to the Conference of Arab Ministers of Education held in San'a, Yemen, 23-20 December 1972.

_____. *Tarikh al-'Arab fi al-Jahiliyya wa al-Islam* [History of the Arabs in the Age of Ignorance and Early Islam]. Fifth Grade. 1970.

_____. *al-Tarikh al-Islami* [Islamic History]. Sixth Grade. 1970.

Zayani, La'ali' A. "English Supplementary Reading for the First Intermediate Class of Bahrain." M.A. thesis, American University of Beirut, 1971.

Foreign Trade

State of Bahrain, Ministry of Finance and National Economy. *Foreign Trade, Bahrain Imports and Exports*. 1969-74.

Industry

The Bahrain Petroleum Company. *Annual Reports 1969-1972*.

Government of Bahrain, Department of Development and Engineering Services. *Draft Report on the Feasibility of Alternative Power and Water Production Plants.* November 1970. Prepared by Preece, Cardew & Rider, Consulting Engineers, Sussex, England.

_____. Ibid. Figures and Tables.

State of Bahrain, Ministry of Finance and National Economy. *Incentives for Industrial Investment.* 1972. A two-page mimeographed sheet.

Labor

Aluminum Bahrain (ALBA). *Minutes of the Meetings of Discussion Groups.* Monthly reports beginning in April 1972.

_____. *Some Facts and Figures.* 1972. A special mimeographed report.

Government of Bahrain. *The Bahrain Employed Persons Compensation Ordinance, 1957.* As amended.

_____. *The Bahrain Labor Ordinance, 1957.* As amended.

State of Bahrain, Ministry of Labor and Social Affairs. *Manpower Requirements and Employment in Bahrain.* 1972. A special mimeographed memorandum.

Selected Readings in Comparative Politics

Almond, Gabriel A., and James S. Coleman, ed. *The Politics of the Developing Areas.* Princeton, N.J.: Princeton University Press, 1960.

Apter, David E. *The Politics of Modernization.* Chicago: The University of Chicago Press, 1965.

Binder, Leonard et al. *Crises and Sequences in Political Development.* Princeton, N.J.: Princeton University Press, 1971.

Coleman, James A. ed. *Education and Political Development.* Princeton, N.J.: Princeton University Press, 1965.

Easton, David. *A Framework for Political Analysis.* Englewood Cliffs, N.J.: Prentice-Hall, Inc., 1965.

Horowitz, Irving Louis. *Three Worlds of Development.* 2nd ed. New York: Oxford University Press, 1972.

Jaleé, Pierre. *The Pillage of the Third World.* New York: Modern Reader, 1968.

_____. *The Third World in World Economy*. New York: Modern Reader. 1969.

LaPalombara, Joseph, ed. *Bureaucracy and Political Development*. Princeton, N.J.: Princeton University Press, 1963.

LaPalombara, Joseph, and Myron Weiner, eds. *Political Parties and Political Development*. Princeton, N.J.: Princeton University Press, 1966.

Macridis, Roy C., and Bernard E. Brown. *Comparative Politics: Notes and Readings*. 4th ed. Homewood, Illinois: The Dorsey Press, 1972.

Mayer, Lawrence C. *Comparative Political Inquiry: A Methodological Survey*. Homewood, Illinois: The Dorsey Press, 1972.

Pye, Lucian W. "Transitional Asia and the Dynamics of Nation Building" in Marian D. Irish, ed., *World Pressures on Foreign Policy*. Englewood Cliffs, N.J.: Prentice-Hall, Inc., 1964.

_____, ed. *Communication and Political Development*. Princeton, N.J.: Princeton University Press, 1963.

Pye, Lucian W., and Sidney Verba, Eds. *Political Culture and Political Development*. Princeton, N.J.: Princeton University Press, 1965.

Tachau, Frank, ed. *The Developing Nations: What Path to Modernization?* New York: Dodd, Mead and Company, 1972.

Ward, Robert E., and Dankwart A. Rustow, eds. *Political Modernization in Japan and Turkey*. Princeton, N.J.: Princeton University Press, 1964.

Index

al-'Abidin, Hasan Zayn, 121, 138, 154, 158
al-Adwa', 5, 62, 66, 70, 79, 117, 121, 122, 131
al-'Alawi, Mahmud Ahmad, 79
al-'Alaywat, 'Abd al-'Ali, 78
al-'Alaywat, 'Abd al-Karim 'Ali, 160
Aluminum Bahrain (ALBA), 80, 81, 82, 83
al-Amin, 'Ali Rashid, 120, 161
'Aniza tribe, 8
al-Ansari, Muhammad Jabir, 121
Aryan, Muhammad Baqir, 155

Bayne, R. Adm. M.G., 112-113
al-Baharna, Dr. Husayn, 131
al-Baharna, Sadiq, 161
Bahrainization of labor, 84. *See also* Labor; Manpower
Bahrain Petroleum Company (BAPCO), 77, 79, 83
al-Bakir, 'Abd al-Rahman, 78
Belgrave, Sir Charles, 57-64, 65-66

Candidates, eligibility requirements, 126-128
Clubs, 41-58; al-Ahli Club, 48' 139; Alumni Club, 48-49, 120, 121; 'Arabi Club, 48, 50-51; Awal Women's Society, 54-55, 142; Bahrain Club, 51, 142; Bahrain Young Ladies Society, 54, 142; Children and Mothers Welfare Society, 53-54; Intaj al-Rif Club, 51-52; laws regulating clubs, 43-47; mixed societies, 43, 55-56; political socialization function, 41-42, 56-58; Rifa' Women's Society, 142; Society of Writers, 55-56, 134; 'Uruba Club, 48, 49-50; women's societies, 43, 52-55, 142. *See also* Women
COMIDEASTFOR, 97, 112, 113
Committee of National Union, 78
Communications. *See* Press
Constitution, 83, 101, 117; interviews concerning, 117-124
Constitutional Assembly, 5-6, 124-125; composition, 135, 156, 161; laws concerning, 125-127, 131. *See also* Elections
Council of Ministers, 11, 72, 117, 126, 135, 140

Dawani, Muhammad Hasan, 161
al-Din, 'Ali Kamal, 155
al-Din, Mulla Hasan Zayn, 160
Dwayghir, Safiyya, 123

Economy, 4, 86-88
Education, 5, 13, 37; budget, 25; curricula, 32-37; enrollment in schools, 26-29; Gulf Technical College, 17, 25, 27; illiteracy, 17-21, 60-61; manpower planning and, 25-31; political socialization function, 31-37; private schools, 25; school-age population, 16-21 *passim*; statistics, 16-25; texts, 35-36; teacher training, 31, 35; teacher training institutes, 16, 17, 25; university graduates, 22-23, 29-30, 48-49; women, 17, 21, 28-29
Elections, 133-164; analysis, 153-164; Bloc of Fourteen, 138, 156; external stresses, 144-148; petition to lift State of Emergency, 138-141; political atmosphere, 133-144; role of sectarianism, 153, 154, 161; withdrawal of Shahabi group, 141-142. *See also* Voting; Women

Fakhro, Qasim Ahmad, 118, 150
Foreign policy, 95-116; background, 95-98; constitutional supports, 101; geopolitical subdivisions, 106; Iranian claims, 98, 102, 103, 104; Palestine, 99, 100, 105, 110-111; supports of, 98-102
Foreign workers, 77, 79, 84, 86-88. *See also* Labor
Founding Committee, 80

Gatch, John, 113
Ghanim, Khalifa, 138
Guicciardi, Vittorio Winspeare, 9, 103

Hanks, R. Adm. R., 113
History of Bahrain, 8-9
Husayn, 'Ali, 79

Illiteracy, 17-21; statistics, 60-61
Iran, 36; peace-keeping power, 107; relations with Bahrain, 109; territorial claims to Bahrain 9, 98, 102, 103, 104, 109-110
Ishaq, Ibrahim, 120

al-Jishshi, Bahiyya, 123
al-Jishshi, Hasan, 64
al-Jishshi, Rasul, 119, 138, 139, 150, 154
Jufair agreement, 112-115
Jufair facility, 97; rent of, 112-115. *See also* Naval Control of Shipping Office

189

Kanoo, Ibrahim Khalil, 118
Kanoo, Muhammad, 79
Khalaf, Layla, 123
al-Khalifa family, 8-11; attitude toward Constitutional Assembly, 135, 149
al-Khalifa, Shaikh 'Abd al-'Aziz, 121
al-Khalifa, Shaikh 'Abdalla bin Khalid, 131
al-Khalifa, Shaikh 'Ali bin Ahmad, 79
al-Khalifa, Shaikh 'Ali bin Muhammad, 79
al-Khalifa, Shaikh Hamad bin 'Isa, 99, 140
al-Khalifa, Shaikh 'Isa bin Muhammad, 72
al-Khalifa, Shaikh 'Isa bin Sulman, 7, 9, 11, 98, 99, 117, 139, 169
al-Khalifa, Shaikh Khalifa bin Sulman, 99, 118, 143, 169
al-Khalifa, Shaikh Muhammad bin Mubarak, 41, 72, 98, 101, 132, 140, 149
al-Khalifa, Shaikh Sulman bin Hamad, 57, 64
al-Khalifa, Tifla Muhammad, 123
Khalifat, Muhammad, 154, 160
Kuwait, 95, 106, 111, 115; relations with Bahrain, 109, 117

Labor, 75-93; expatriate workers, 77, 79, 84, 86-88; female workers, 86; history of, 76-82; necessity of unions, 83-84; right to unionize, 75-76, 97, 145; strikes, 76-82, 134. *See also* Bahrainization of labor; Manpower
Laws, Constitution, 83, 101; Constitutional Assembly Laws, 125-127, 131; Decrees, 101; Labor Ordinance, 78-79; Press Law, 79, 133, 134; State of Emergency Laws, 78, 79, 136-137. *See also* Constitution; Labor; Press; State of Emergency
Literacy. *See* Illiteracy

Magazines. *See* Press
al-Mahuzi, Muhammad Sa'id Ja'far, 160
Manpower planning, 25-31, 84-93; absorption of secondary school graduates, 88; profile of labor force, 85-88. *See also* Education
al-Mardi, Mahmud, 64, 121, 138, 139, 151, 154, 156
Marshall, C., 79
Ministry of Education, 13-37 *passim*
Ministry of Foreign Affairs, 101-103, 113
Ministry of Information, 66, 70
Ministry of Labor and Social Affairs, 45, 80, 82, 85
al-Mu'ayyad, Yusuf, 119
Muharraqi, Ya'qub Yusuf, 134
Murad, Jasim, 119, 138, 150, 155, 160
al-Musawi, Ghazi Rida, 121

National Assembly, 11, 114, 169
National Democratic Slate, 155. *See also* Elections
National Manpower Planning Council, 88-93; Technical Committee, 93. *See also* Manpower planning
Naval Control of Shipping Office, 112. *See also* Jufair facility
Newspapers. *See* Press

Oil, 95-97, 104; production, 95, 97, 116

Palestine, 99, 100, 105, 110-111
Pax Judaica, 107
Pax Persiana, 107
Pearl industry, 77
Political development, 1-7; education and, 13-16; labor and, 75-76, 93
Political parties, 119. *See also* Clubs
Political socialization, 1; clubs and, 41-42; communication and, 39-41; education and, 31-37; press and, 59-63, 74
Popular Front for the Liberation of Oman (PFLO), 111, 134; actions in Constitutional Assembly elections, 144-148; call for boycott, 147-148
Population, 96
Press, 5, 58-74; history of, 63-66; laws regulating, 68-70; non-Bahraini publications, 67-68; political socialization, 59-63, 74; suspension of publication, 71-73, 134. *See also al-Adwa'* and *Sada al-'Usbu'*

Qasab, Nuhad, 117

Rabi'a, 'Ali, 134, 141, 160
Rogers, William, 115

Sada al-'Usbu', 5, 62, 63, 66, 70, 122, 131; suspension of publication, 71-73, 134
al-Salih, 'Ali Salih, 138n
al-Samahiji, Muhammad 'Abdalla Muhammad, 151
Sanqur, Hamid, 139, 160
Sayyar, 'Ali 'Abdalla, 122, 134, 150, 161
al-Shahabi, Hisham, 138, 141
al-Shahabi, Kamal, 138
Shamlan, 'Abd al-'Aziz, 60, 78, 138, 139, 150
Shari'a, 167
Shi'a Muslims, 96, 153, 154, 161
al-Shirawi, Muhammad Qasim, 79, 117, 138; interviews on the Constitution, 117-124, 150
Shura, 4, 14, 125, 166, 167
Sisco, Joseph, 115

al-Sitrawi, Hasan, 122
Smith, L.A., 79
Societies. *See* Clubs
Special Branch, 56, 126, 140, 141n, 145
State of Emergency, 56, 78, 79, 133, 136, 138, 145, 169; petition against, 138-142
Strikes, 76-82, 134. *See also* Labor
Sunni Muslims, 96, 153, 154, 161
Swar, 'Aqil, 71, 134

Taqi, 'Abd al-Rahman, 120
Treaties, 9
Tribes, 8

Uchi, Sulman, 79
al-'Umran, Ahmad, 32
Unions. *See* Labor
United Arab Emirates, 103-104
United Kingdom, 9, 97, 103, 112
United Nations, 9, 99, 103, 111
United States, 97; American-Bahraini relations, 111-116
United States Navy, 112-115
al-'Urayyid, 'Abd al-Hamid, 156
al-'Urayyid, 'Ibrahim, 64
Urban tribalism, 11; model of, 165-168

Voting, eligibility, 126-128, 131, 132, 145. *See also* Elections; Women

Women, education, 17, 21, 28-29; petitions for women's rights, 143-144; rights, 123, 124, 145; societies, 52-55; suffrage, 123, 124, 127, 131, 132, 142

Zayani, Ahmad, 119
Zayani, La'ali, employment preference study, 36-37
Zayani, Saqir, 160
Zubara, 8

About the Author

Emile Nakhleh was a senior intelligence service officer and director of the Political Islam Strategic Analysis Program in the Directorate of Intelligence at the Central Intelligence Agency. He holds a PhD in international relations and is a member of the Council on Foreign Relations. He is the author of *A Necessary Engagement: Reinventing America's Relations with the Muslim World*.